Ali-Ogba:
A History of the Ogba People

By

Francis J. Ellah

Published 1995 by
Fourth Dimension Publishing Co., Ltd.
16 Fifth Avenue City Layout. PMB 01164, New Haven,
Enugu, Nigeria.

© 1995 F. J. Ellah

ISBN 978 156 400 8

CONDITIONS OF SALE

All rights reserved. No part of this publication may be reproduced, stored in a retrieval system, or transmitted in any form or by any means, electronic, mechanical, photocopying, recording, or otherwise without the prior permission of the Publisher.

*This Book Is Dedicated
To
My mother and the memory of my father.*

The historian can discover what has been completely forgotten, in the sense that no statement of it has reached him from eye-witnesses. He can even discover what until he discovered it, no one ever knew to have happened.-R.G.Collingwood.

BOOKS BY THE SAME AUTHOR

THE UNFINISHED MOTION

NIGERIA AND STATES CREATION
(Based on THE UNFINISHED MOTION)

NIGERIAN SOCIETY AND GOVERNANCE

RURAL DEVELOPMENT

Contents

	Page
Dedication...	iii
Foreword	ix
Preface	xi

Chapters

1. **Introducing Ogbas and Ali-Ogba**
   Existing Customs and Traditions tell the story of Ali-Ogba
   a *The Onuobdos*--Their Origin 1
   b The Three Ogba groups................................. 2
      Omoku the capital of Ali-Ogba 4
   c Ogba view of Cosmogony - *Oruligmo*............... 4
   d Geography of Ali-Ogba - Omoku - Obrikom Onita
      Creek -River Omoku - *Ogboru-Aliulo*............... 5
   e Economic and Social life of the Ogbas................ 7

2. **The Origin of Ogbas**
   Predecessors of Ogbas...................................... 13
   Ogba nwa Aklaka, Ekpeye nwa Aklaka 14
   Ogbas and Ekpeyes Claim Benin Origin............... 17
   Edos (Binis) Claim Origin from Elsewhere............ 20
   Settlement in Obiebe-The South-Northerly Route Taken
      by Ekpeye, Umuezeali, Obosi, Umuekedi etc 21
   The Mboaki Tragedy and the Flight into Obigwe
      (Haven of Peace); C. 1390 27
   The North-Southerly Route Taken by Umuenyike
      (Umudei), Umualinwa 30
   The West-Easterly Route (Umunkaru, Umuoyro)...... 33

The East-Westerly Route (Umuagbda) 35
Dispersal From Obigwe (Diaspora) and foundation of a
  capital at Omoku (Umuezeali, Umueke, Umuorodu,
  Ihiukwu, Umuogidi) 36
Dispersal of Uriems - the tragedy of Eyio's wife and
  the exploits of Umeri Nwube 46
Movements by Umuokrocha, Umuimegi, Umuohali,
  Umuossia 48
The Second Coming of Umuagbda (East-Westerly Route) 50
General Observation 53

3. **Political Organisation of Ali-Ogba**
Isiali 57
Schedule or Table of *Onuobdo* Titles 58
Landlords (Ezeali)- Umuezeali 60
"Kingship" Title (Eze-Ogba, Eze-Ohali) - Umuebe,
  Umuenyike (Umudei), Umuohali 61
Obi nwa Chukwuma versus Akwokwu Dike 66
Iyasra (Prime Minister) - Umuogidi and Umuagbda 78
Isoma and "*Igbazu-keze* " - Ihiukwu and Umuorodu 79
Owerre (Guard, Commander) - Umueke 81
Ojoka (Hawk) - (Obosi) 82
Ochioha (Leader of all) - Umuekedi, Umuodogwu 83
Ajie-Ike-Oha (Uriem, Umuimegi, (Alias Umuolota)
  and Umuokrocha, Umuokirie 84
Akogu (Loyal Leader) - Umunkaru, ... 84
Oyro - Umuoyro, ... 88
Ewo (Peace-maker) - Umualinwa, Umuohali 88
Omodi or *Onueze* (Mouth-piece of the king) - Umuossia 88
Probable Existence of an earlier Political Order 89
"Kingmakers" 89
Law and Custom 91
Judicial Hierarchy 92
The Executive 94
General Observation 95

4. Social and Economic Organisation

Ogba Houses and Towns 97
Food Drink and Health 98
Ogba Cultural Development 100
   Speech 100
   Ogba dress 100
Ogba Traditional Religion 101
   Transmigration 102
   Totems of Transmigration 103
   The "Skills" of transmigration 107
   Shrines 113
   The place of the Supreme Deity in Ogba
   Traditional Religion 117
   Re-incarnation 118
Economic Pursuits 120
   Yam and Cassava 121
   Maize, Tomatoes, Bananas, Cocoyams, Plantains 124
   Fishing, Hunting, Arts and Crafts 125
   Iron-Working (Agbda-Luzu) 127
   Markets 128
   Money 129
Social Organisation 131
   Marriages 131
   Births 132
   Age-grades 135
   Wrestling 136
   Dancing 138
   Death and Burial ceremonies 143
Observations 145

5. The Colonial Experience

Colonial Influence through Benin 147
   Deposition and Banishment of the Oba of Benin 148
Influences through Arochukwu 149
Influences from the Atlantic Coast 155
The Abohs And Ali-Ogba 161
Colonial Activities in Ali -Ogba 164

Agha-ka-Olowu nwa Amadi Nw' Ekiodu 161
The Burning of Ogu, Obloko and Obrikom 167
The Breaking of weapons at Omoku 168
Occupation of Ali-Ogba 170
"Pacification" of Ali-Ogba, Establishment of Native
   Courts, and appointment of Warrant Chiefs........... 171
Observations 189

Change And Continuity
Zig-Zag Movements... 190
Political System... 191
Language... 194
Dress... 195
Food.. 196
Housing... 197
Dancing... 197
Religion... 198
Education.. 200
Economics... 201
Political Development... 201

Appendix 211

Bibliography 220

Index 223

Foreword

Ali-Ogba: A History of the Ogba People

To understand a people well, any reader has to begin with a careful study of their way of life as portrayed by a competent authority. Sir Francis J. Ellah, the author of the present work, is one such recognised authority.

Not only is the author a distinguished son of the Ogba soil, he is also one who has devoted a lot of his time to a careful study of change and continuity in the life of his people. His book, therefore, has the additional merit of a well-researched and well-written work which has gained a great deal from the author's familiarity with the subject-matter of his study.

Through his properly-woven account, the author has given the reader an interesting picture of the origins of the Ogba people, their environment, their political, economic and social institutions, the impact of colonialism on them, among other items of value. Wherever possible, the author also provided useful illustrations. It is, therefore, obvious that whatever else the Ogba people lacked in their long history from Benin (Edo) origins, they possessed and utilised a fulsome culture which met their basic needs and aspirations from the cradle to the grave.

This book further helps the reader to understand the effects of colonialism on the Ogbas in the general context of the experience of the various Nigerian ethnic groups who rose or fell under the heavy weight of alien rule and related influences. The Ogba experience, on balance, provides a further example of the resilience and adaptability of Nigerian cultures in an era of change and challenges. Studies elsewhere have demonstrated that familiar phenomenon under colonialism in Nigeria.

Hence, the Ogbas, as a people, gained something and lost something under colonialism. Here, for example Warrant Chief 'Mallam Agu', of Hausa stock, functioned at the Omoku Native Court. The Ogbas witnessed other forms of what the author termed 'contradictions' of colonialism. One of these included the Ogba-Egbema experience under local government authority arrangements since the nationwide reforms of 1976. Under these arrangements, the Egbema, for example, have been split and placed under the jurisdictions of two states: Rivers and Imo.

Ogba cultural heritage and related institutions also had to contend with alien influences represented by the activities of Christian missions and organisations. Yet, the factors of resilience and adaptability were in evidence among the Ogbas in their hour of need. Thus, Ogba traditionalists represented by the *Okrosu* group of believers did steady combat with the several groups of evangelical bodies that invaded their homeland. Among these were the Garrick Movement (*Oso Churchi*), Salvation Army, Seventh Day Native Church of God, Roman Catholic Mission, African Church, Seventh Day Adventists, Jehovah's Witnesses, and others. Whatever the traditionalists lost in Ogba culture, modernists in their midst gained through schools and western education.

Understandably, this work provides another useful contribution to the growing body of micro-histories of the various groups which together constitute the Nigerian multi-nation state. If we regard Nigerian history as one form of macro-history, it is possible to argue that here, as elsewhere in life, little streams flow into the big river.

For the doubting Thomases in this regard, the author provides a soothing balm. He aptly observes in Chapter 2:

> Foreign scholars have made much fuss about the multitude of ethnic groups in Nigeria. Impartial investigation indicates that these multitudinous (P) (*sic*) groups have in fact very much in common - common origins, common cultural traits, common ancestors. It may be that Nigeria is, after all, not a mere "geographical expression", but an association of peoples whose ancestors had a common history and a common experience - a people with a common destiny.

In that pertinent observation lies another demonstration of the value and significance of this work. More of its kind will certainly expand and improve our understanding of Nigeria, our common motherland or fatherland, a land with its familiar problems as well as promises.

Tekena N. Tamuno
(Former Vice-Chancellor University of Ibadan.)
Now Research Professor in History,
Institute of African Studies of the same University.

Preface

This work is based on oral tradition, archival materials, published works, and archaeological evidence. All the archaeological materials are with the Archaeological Department of the University of Port-Harcourt. Tapes and manuscripts containing oral evidence are to be deposited in a Public Library.

The overriding aim is to tell the story of the Ogba people as faithfully as possible, using the available data. This "case-study" may also be of help in clarifying or correcting some popular assumptions in Nigerian and African history. For instance, the ancient migrations from place to place by the different communities and the various contacts among them appear to have enhanced national homogeneity to a greater extent than is usually recognised by contemporary historians. In regard to the attitude of our ancestors to colonialism, the Ogba story of initial resistance and subsequent acceptance is in conformity with the classical pattern.

After the first chapter which introduces the Ogbas and Ali-Ogba, the next chapter deals with the origin of Ogbas based mainly on oral evidence obtained from the fourteen major extended families or *onuobdos* in Ogba. The source materials obtained were collected during the course of extended field-work in Ali-Ogba over a period of more than three years. The text of these source materials, will be made available for reference in due course. With the narrators' approval, some of the stories were recorded on tape so as to preserve the originality and vivacity of each narrative.

Materials obtained from the archives have been listed in the bibliography and include three "Intelligence Reports" prepared by government administrative officers - two by Mr. W.F.H. Newington in 1930 and 1931, and one by Mr. D.O. Standfield in 1935. Each of these officers visited Ogba villages and held discussions with the people. Although they were somewhat handicapped by the fact that they had to speak through career "interpreters", their informants were simple village folk who were yet unspoilt by political sophistication and manipulation. From the point of view of impartiality and attention to detail, these reports are among the best available written evidence on the history of various groups in Southern Nigeria today.

The archaeological material is based on the results of excavations kindly carried out on my behalf by Dr. Nwanna Nzewunwah (of blessed memory) of the Faculty of Humanities, Department of History and Archaeology, University of Port Harcourt, during the period July to September 1984. I owe Dr. Nzewunwah and the University of Port Harcourt a debt of gratitude for this assistance and cooperation.

I must express sincere gratitude to others who have helped me greatly in the production of this work: To *Eze Ogba Nwadei Ogbuehi,* Eze John Wokocha Ellah, my late father, who first aroused my interest in Ogba history; to the late Rev. Dickson Ewo and Chief Victor Onyecha Obowu whose earlier publications provided a regular source of guidance and inspiration to me; to Professors Rowland Oliver, Ikénna Nzimiro, S.J.S. Cookey, E.J. Alagoa, Kay Williamson and Chinua Achebe, for their professional advice and encouragement; to Mrs. Patricia Ellah and our sons, Francis (Junior), Patrick and Michael (alias Chux), for their usual encouragement, unflinching support and optimistic expectations.

I will not fail to thank my uncle, Ambrose Ellah, who helped me with some sketches and designs and whose first-hand knowledge of Ogba customs and institutions has proved most helpful to me; to John Item for friendly encouragement and advice at the earliest stages; to the oral historians of various *onuobdos* - the late Chief Mark Ogwe of Obigwe, the *Owerre of Umueke,* Osi nwa Orji of Umuohali, and Gilbert Nwajari of Umuohali; the late Chief Nwokogu Adah Osiah, Benedict Osiago (the Akogu), and Pius Adah of Umunkaru; Chief Godfrey Onwugbonu of Umuoyro; Chief David Ojadi of Ihiukwu; Albert Nwoko, Jeremiah Eleba (*Onuobdo* Head), Wilson Onyige and Bathwel Ibra all of Ihiukwu; the *Iyasra* of Umuogidi, Chief Ebenezer Osima, and Johnson Ake and Chief Lawyer Eluozo, the *Ajie* of Umuimegi; Chief Will Orike of

Umualinwa; the *Iyasra* of Umuagbda, Chief Sunday Onyeocha Amadike; *Okie Onuobdo* Chief Lazarus Ezi *Ossere* of Umuenyike; the *Emodi* of Edihuru, Chief Mark Obiohuru; Chief S. Okoroma, the *Okie Obudo* of Umuorodu, the *Eze Ohali* of Ogba, Eze Moses Igwe, Thompson Ezegbrika of Umuorodu, and many other helpers and supporters.

I have kept as close as possible to the text of the *onuobdo* legends as they were narrated by the various *onuobdo* oral historians whose accounts in Ogba were sometimes recorded (frequently on tape) by my field assistants. I have edited these records freely without departing from the salient features of the original text.

I also acknowledge help from all the authors whose works I have consulted as indicated in the relevant sections. Many thanks are due to Mrs Ogugua Achebe (nee Ndukwe) who helped me trace and copy the Intelligence Reports and other records from the National Archives. I am grateful to my research assistants, Uche Eluozo and Uche Osere, and to Mrs H. N. Okirie, our Publications Manager. I thank Messrs Ekinde Frimenjibo, Iyalla Igani, Jack A. Eduok, Abel Ngolu, Felicia Onwuka and Ishmael Anwuri for typing the illegible manuscripts and Miss Sylvia Ogbonna for producing the Index.

I owe special thanks to Prof. T.N. Tamuno for the exquisite foreword which this humble effort hardly deserves. I sincerely thank him for many useful suggestions and recommendations.

All mistakes or errors found in this work (printers' devil excepted) remain entirely my own responsibility.

F.J.E.
-Jan., 1995-

Map of Ali-Ogba

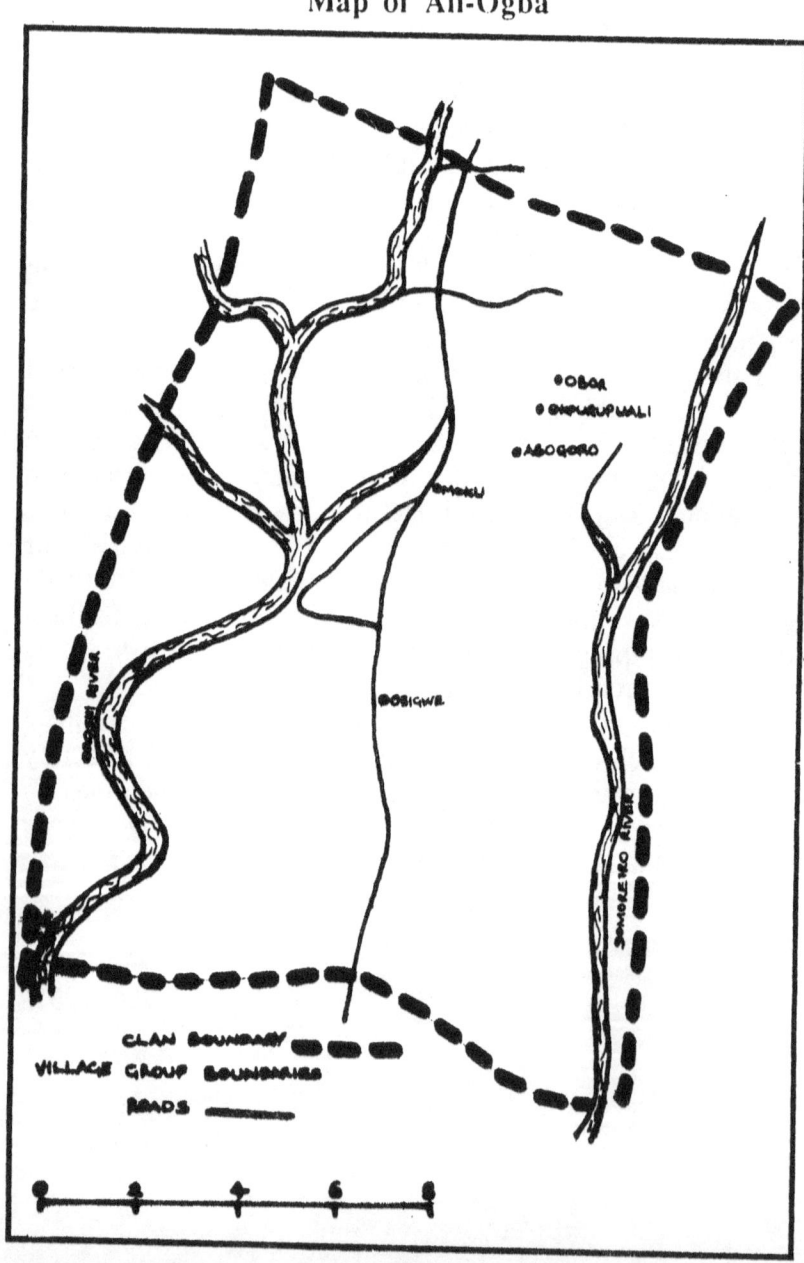

Chapter 1

Introducing Ogbas and Ali-Ogba

Ali-Ogba is the land of the Ogba[1] people. There are few communities in which the culture and tradition of the people, as exhibited in their daily lives and habits, provide so much evidence of their background and origin as in Ali-Ogba: The elaborate greeting ceremonies, the praise names and titles, the ancient sayings or proverbs and slogans, the peculiar traditional festivals, the obsequies, the stratified age grade organisations, the wedding customs, the speech, the folklore, the historic sites and ruins, the shrines, the cultural associations, the traditional religion, and the geographical terrain itself, all tell a vivid story, in clear unmistakable terms, if only we take the trouble to analyse and study them objectively.

The *Onuobdos*, Their Origin

Ogba people comprise about fourteen extended families or *onuobdos*[2] (literally mouths of the city i.e. quarters), each named after an eponymous ancestor, (e.g. the Umuenyike *Onuobdo* are the sons of Enyike, the "strong elephant"). An *onuobdo* is an agnatic, exogamous group, with its own history of origin, its own *ohuo* or family idol, its own totem. The average population of each *onuobdo* today is about 7,000; but all the members of an *onuobdo* do not occupy a restricted area on the ground. The members of the various *onuobdos* are to be found in all parts of Ogba. That every *onuobdo* today has its own centre of highest population, which is usually the original home of the founding ancestor, indicates that originally the

---

[1] For some unknown reason, Ogba is indicated as "Okogba" or "Okoba" in older maps and in publications by such authors as Amoury Talbot. Some "Intelligence Reports" use the version "Oba".
[2] See List of *Onuobdos* in the Appendix.

various *onuobdos* occupied exclusive geographical locations on the ground until they began to disperse and intermingle with their neighbours.

The Three Ogba Groups

The Ogbas fall into three major clans, groups or sections viz: Usomini, Igburu and Egi, which differ in customs, traditions and speech, notwithstanding the universal territorial spread of the *onuobdos*. Each of the three main Ogba groups contains some representatives of practically every *onuobdo* who retain and project their separate *onuobdo* identity. For example, Umuenyike and Umuebe exist in Usomini, Igburu and Egi. Counterparts of the various *onuobdos* exist even outside the boundaries of Ali-Ogba, such as in Ekpeye, Uguta and elsewhere. In Ekpeye, the Umuebe *Onuobdo* is known as *Edihuru* and Umuenyike is known as *Isiokloko*.[3] It is significant that the Egi group of Ogba call the different *onuobdos* almost the same names which the Ekpeyes call such *onuobdos*.[4]

It has been suggested that the descriptive name "Usomini" (which means "water-side") refers to a group or clan invented by the colonial administrators. The suggestion does not appear plausible because the names of the other two groups viz: Igbru (marshy land) and Egi (dry land) are also descriptive of the terrain they occupy. However, if the suggestion were to be wholly accepted, it would imply that the Usomini group members were non-existent as such before the colonial period, which is preposterous.

The true position, it would appear, is that if the "waterside" people were not known by that name before the colonial times, they most probably regarded themselves purely as "Ogba", and they knew the rest merely as Igbru and Egi respectively. In history, "waterside" people have tended to be more conceited than their neighbours simply because civilisation originated

---

[3] See Table of *Onuobdo* names in the Appendix.
[4] This is one indication that Ogba and Ekpeye are related historically, as claimed in the legends of origin which will be discussed in the next chapter. See Schedule of *Onuobdo* names in the Appendix.

from, and travelled along, the Euphrates and Tigris, the Nile, the Niger, the Ganges, Indus and other waterways before the days of macadam, railways and the aeroplane.

In the case in point, it appears the Egi and Igbru in retaliation called themselves "Ogba" to the exclusion of other groups. For example, the greatest annual celebration among the Egi group today is known as *Egwu Ogba* (i.e. Ogba Festival), although no other Ogbas except Egis participate in it. It is significant, however, that neither of the two groups (Egi or Igbru) disowns or disowned their particular name; and those two groups could not have been enjoying two names apiece (Egi and Ogba on the one hand and Igbru and Ogba on the other), when what is now Usomini group had no separate name at all.

In his Intelligence Report written in 1930, Mr. W.F.H. Newington, Cadet, summarises the information he received on the Ogba traditions concerning the names of the three Ogba groups:

> Their name Egi is apparently an Ekpaffia (Ekpeye) term for farming, and the country is certainly drier here than in the Igbru area which lies to the north of it. Igbru is the Okoba (Ogba) term for swamp, and the nature of the land in which the kindreds of this group lie certainly implies it. The third group, Osomini (Usomini) as mentioned in the previous paragraph has all its towns near water as the word Osomini implies. From the above information it can be seen that the three groups of Okoba are named geographically and not genealogically.

Obviously, the groups and their names were definitely *not* created by the colonial agents! They existed and had their names and culture long before the colonial era.

The Usomini group (excluding Omoku, the present capital which was part and parcel of Usomini Group) comprises Obrikom, Obie, Kreigani, Ohalimini, Aligu, Idu (Osoble), Idu (Obosiukwu),Obor, Ebogro, Okprukpuali, Ebocha Onosi Ogu and Aligu with a combined population of 10,989(1963 Census). Egi group comprises Akabuka, Akabuta, Ede, Egita, Erema, Ibewa, Itu, Obagi, Obiebe, Obigbor, Obite, Obiosimini, Obobru, Obukegi, Ogbogu and Ohalielu with a combined population of 14,990 (1963 Census). Igbru comprises Ikiri, Egbeda, Elieta, Amaah, Elehia, Okansu, Osiakpu, Ohiuga, Uju, Okposi, Obigwe and Ogbidi with a population of 5,270 (1963 Census).

Omoku - Capital of Ali Ogba

The "Capital" of Ali-Ogba today is Omoku, which is situated almost at the northern extremity of the Ogba area. Geographically, Omoku is within the Usomini group. Ogba groups or clans, unlike the *onuobdos*, have spatial identity on the ground. As the "Capital" of Ogba, it has become customary to exclude Omoku from any of the three distinct groups. Today, practically every *onuobdo* is represented in Omoku and each *onuobdo* in Omoku can trace its origin to one of the surrounding Ogba villages.

Ogba people call the whole of their present homeland *Ali-Ogba*, that is land of the Ogbas; a land of high forest and secondary growth, with characteristic wildlife, mahogany and other valuable woods; a land of seasonal floods and heavy rainfall; a fertile land of mixed clay and laterite loams. Modern technology has discovered that all Ali-Ogba is literally sitting on crude oil on which the whole Nigerian economy almost solely depends. According to current oil company records, no local government in Nigeria produces as much crude oil and gas as the Ogba/ Egbema/ Ndoni (ONELGA) local government.

Ogbas regard their land with sincere veneration, as befits a great, mysterious, deity whose favour yields rich harvests and whose anger causes famine, discords, and plague. As the saying goes, *"ali-ogba so eke"* (Ali-Ogba forbids snake). Snakes of all descriptions other than totems are to be destroyed.

Ogba view of Cosmogony

The Ogba ancestors divided the earth into two parts which they called *"Oru"* and *"Igmo"*, respectively. By the former term, Ogbas referred to riverine people.[5],[6],[7],[8]

---

[5] "The Riverine Ibo called themselves "Oru", a name which nineteenth century explorers applied to the Ijaw immediately to the south of them. They are of mixed descent including Bini, Igala and other elements" (Daryll Ford and G. I. Jones)"

[6] "From the mouth of the river (Nun) up to this point (Taylor Creek), the country on either side is named Oru. The people are of the same tribe as those who inhabit the tract of country up to the Rio Formoso, where

By the latter, they meant inhabitants of the hinterland. Both parts represented to them the whole world, which they called "*Oruligmo*" that is, "*Oru*" and "*Igmo*" an idiom still current in Ogba. When an Ogba says *Oruligmo*, he means all the earth, all human beings. Who would object when *Oruligmo* have accepted? Who would venture when they have declined?

The general attitudes and customs of Ogbas themselves appear to be more *Oru* than *Igmo*, though the local tongue is now obviously more *igmo* than *oru*. Indeed the traditional customs are clearly derived from both sources. For example, the proud and graceful *owu* masquerade and *asawa* dances have their origin in *Oru;* whereas the troublesome, though, mysterious and powerful *Okrosu,* comes from *igmo* and speaks *nkaba* (a deeper word for *Igmo*) in a haughty, deathlike manner, through his nose, like the ghost that it is supposed to be!

From their attitude and customs, Ogbas appear to believe that they occupy a central position in the world, between *Oru* and *Igmo*, from where they survey all the activities of mankind, and mock, praise, deride, appreciate or emulate them as the occasion demands. Some of the customs create the vague impression of a people standing between the living and the dead, or between paradise and hell, or between the devil and the deep blue sea.

Geography of Ali-Ogba

In geographical terms, Ali-Ogba occupies an area roughly thirty kilometres by twenty kilometres in the Niger flood plain, with Ekpeye, Engeni and Ijaw areas to the south and southwest;

---

however they are called Ejo or Ojo" (Dr. Baikie in 1854 quoted by E. J. Alagoa in the *Small Brave City State* Ibadan University Press, 1964 page 7).

7 "In the words of Professor Henderson, 'Olu' (or Oru) meant riverine or riverine derived, slave-dealing, kingdom-associated peoples; Igbo meant upland, slave-providing, kingship lacking populations. The Olu, with their well-watered farms and protein rich diet, despised the Igbo, for their food and water shortages, and their role as slave suppliers. To the interior Igbo, the Olu States, with their traditions of origin from elsewhere, were not really Igbo at all". (Elizabeth Isichei, *A History of the Igbo people*. London, Macmillian, 1976).

8 "Igmo" is the Ogba word for "Ibo" or "Igbo". Ogba synonyms for the same word are "Nkaba" and "Isu".

Egbema, Oguta, Awara, to the north and northwest; and Aboh-Ndoni, Kwale and Onitsha to the west and northwest. The chief rivers in the area are the Orashi and the Sombreiro. The greyish and lordly Orashi meanders its way from north to south through Obrikom, Kreigani, Idu. The smoky, transparent and gentle Sombreiro, flowing also from north to south, glides through Ogba towns and villages - Obo, Okprukpuali, Okansu, Ohiuga, Obiozimini to Abonnema, where it rejoins the Orashi and empties soon afterwards into the Atlantic Ocean.[9]

About two miles south of Obrikom, the clear, deep blue River Omoku rises, as it were from the underworld, one mile east of the Orashi, and empties itself into the Orashi at *Onu Omoku*, (i.e mouth of Omoku), after a slow journey of about four miles. *Onu Omoku* is regarded as a shrine, and has a "face" *(ihi erisi)*, where sacrifices are offered by adherents and worshippers at appointed times every year. Omoku town with a population of about forty thousand, nestles smugly on the eastern bank of River Omoku. The western bank is uninhabited and uninhabitable, being subject to annual floods, when the Orashi and the Niger burst their banks and form almost one continuous stream piercing the dense forest at every point.

Traditionally, Omoku people personify their river (the River Omoku) as a fair lady, full of love and kindness, but sometimes frolicsome and often mischievous. They believe that when River Omoku is angry, she burns her thatched houses in the bed of the river, and the thatch can be seen floating on the water surface; that, in her rage, River Omoku would often drown an *isu* person;[10] that when River Omoku is happy, she appears in the *Nkwo* market place in the form of a whirlwind drawing everything into her circle; that occasionally she appears in her true shape and form, as a fair young lady, buying and selling rare commodities in the crowded market place; displaying her wealth, and charm, and feminine elusiveness. Except for the whirlwind, these appearances seem to have become very rare indeed nowadays, due, as they say, to the iniquities of the times.

---

9   See Map of Ali-Ogba.
10 *Isu* persons come from the hinterland and cannot swim

At Idia, about three miles northwest of Omoku and two miles southwest of Obrikom, the River Orashi meets the Onita, a brownish creek about ten miles long, flowing from Ndoni opposite Aboh on the historic River Niger. The banks of the Onita are dotted with "work places", or *Ogboru* of the Ogba (mainly Usomini) people. According to tradition, every February *(Ibegwre)* a great proportion of Ogbas go to live at *Ogboru (iloru)*, and visit home *aliulo* frequently on big market days and on festive occasions. In October they leave *Ogboru* and "return from harvesting yams" *(iloliguiji)*.

Economic and Social Life of the Ogbas

During their prolonged stay at *aliulo*, from October to February, Ogbas devote themselves almost entirely to festivities and ceremonies, mostly in dancing, masquerading and merriment.

The Ogba customs of keeping two homes at *Ogboru* and *Aliulo* began as a social and economic necessity, in an environment marked by long distances; with almost insurmountable transportation difficulties; where the only roads in existence were rough footpaths obstructed by ponds, lakes, creeks, rivers and swamps. It was impractical to travel daily to the distant farmlands and fishing ponds; and the Ogbas would not lightly abandon town life to which they had become accustomed; so they built themselves second homes.

Communication between *aliulo* and *ogboru* was maintained by means of the ubiquitous *ugbakiri*, a small dugout canoe, made from the exceedingly light wood, *ukpo*. Every adult male person was expected to possess an *ugbakiri*, which was usually stored above the fire-place, away from moisture and pests. Because of its shape and paper-weight, the *ugbakiri* can travel as fast on water, as a bicycle on land. Being as unstable as it is light, the *ugbakiri* tends continuously to topple over on water. Thus its operation, like that of a bicycle, requires poise and balance, which are acquired by patient training and practice. An *ugbakiri* operator must perpetually check and stabilise his craft with his paddle by endless contrary body movements. Every adult male Ogba person was an expert *ugbakiri* operator particularly if he belonged to the amphibious *Usomini* group. At the slightest sign of trouble or provocation, an Ogba took to his *ugbakiri* heading for Ogboru, just as a highlander would mount his horse - destination unknown.

Living alternatively at *Aliulo* and *Ogboru*, Ogbas made the best of two worlds. Taking advantage of their extensive fertile lands and numerous rivers, lakes and creeks, they became naturally adept farmers as well as keen fishermen. The sparse population, in an area so well endowed by nature, gained for Ogbas a comparatively high standard of living. Indeed with comparatively little effort, the average Ogba person was on the whole, twice as well off, or half as badly off, as most of his contemporaries elsewhere. But it must not be presumed that poverty was wholly unknown. What was rare in Ali-Ogba was abject poverty, called in local parlance, *Ogboi Onu ntu*, that is literally "ash-mouthed poverty" or poverty so grave that the ash on the lips was seldom washed off in preparation for meals; that is poverty to the point of starvation. It was unheard of that anyone ever died of starvation in Ali-Ogba. Begging and stealing were practically unknown.

Because of their comparative affluence, Ogba people were generally contented and happy; peace-loving, orderly and proud; contemptuous of all forms of menial service other than the properly regulated farming, fishing and trading activities carefully allotted to every man, woman and child in the community by immemorial custom and tradition; excessively conscious of outward appearance with lavish clothing *(awichenya)*, beads *(esum)*, ivory bangles *(odu)* and metal bangles *(mgbrechi)*, head-gear *(ichapo)*, and dye-stuff *(uhie* and *uri)*, traditionally fond of pompous titles and praise names: *(Akpogu)* (thorny skin); *achi ere* (best seller); *Ogbuehi*; (Killer of cows) *Eze nwanyi* (Queen); *Okamadu* (superman); *Ugwodikeji* (Powerful debtor).

The propensity of the generality of Ogba people towards pomposity and adornment of their persons indicates clearly that they must have enjoyed prolonged periods of peace. Nevertheless, some amount of turbulence must have occurred in Ali-Ogba for men usually armed themselves with *akube* (wooden clubs) whenever they had to pass through the dangerous *Orie* market square. On longer journeys, they also carried *okia* (spear) and *omrenyi* (elephant's doom). Every Ogba family had a fence with a strong gate which was always opened with caution, visitors being made to enter into the compound in single file as a security device. The gate was known as Ogba (as in Ali-Ogba) apparently to emphasise its importance to the Ogba people.

Ogbas were not always engaged merely in self-defence and keeping their homes and property secure. A few Ogbas became *Okparionyohia* (warrior-at-large) who carried the war into the enemy's camp. A successful warrior was admitted into the prestigious *Igbu* society whose members alone were entitled to lift their cup of palm wine or another alcoholic drink with the left, instead of the right hand. An *Igbu* person was also entitled, when he died, to lie in state sitting in an upright position, propped up against the wall" "He 's dead, but he won't lie down..."[11]

A man could be suddenly killed, not by an *Okparionyohia* or any other human agency, but by a crocodile, buffalo, tiger, python or another creature into which his enemy is believed to have previously transmigrated. Members of each *onuobdo* are expected to be capable of transmigrating into some particular animal form *(izi anu)*. Members of the Umuenyike *Onuobdo* to which I belong are supposed to be able to transmigrate into insects but I have never succeeded!

There were also some shady characters in Ali-Ogba such as *mgbasi* and *amisu* people (i.e. wizards and witches) who were usually feared and avoided by the community. All deaths in the community were invariably attributed to them. An *amisu* (usually an old woman) was believed capable of transforming herself into an ugly bird known as the *amisu* bird. At the dead of night, several *amisu* birds meet together on the top of an *amkpu*[12] tree at the village square. To provide entertainment at each meeting, some members were required to contribute the "soul" of someone dear to them. Those whose "souls" were contributed

---

11 Popular ballad from *Coming up for Air* by George Orwell (Eric Blair).
12 Cotton tree.

were of course believed to have died automatically. According to traditional belief, any woman would become a witch if she ate food in which the witchcraft had been previously hidden. If the food is first tasted by a male person, the witchcraft would be destroyed and could not be transmitted to a female person subsequently eating it. The cult of witchcraft appears to have been introduced into Ali-Ogba from *Ogbaru* (upper *Oru*). In that area the cult was so strong that the *amisus* had a publicly recognised "Company" under a recognised leader known openly as *Ndiom Osa* in every village.

The methods of *mgbasi* people differed widely from those of the *amisus*. An *mgbasi* was usually a male person. He could not turn himself into a bird; but would kill his enemies by poisoning them. The poison could be hidden in drink or transmitted through dead lizards or dead rats. The intended victim contracted some strange ailment after coming into contact with the demised rat or lizard and died unless he was able to get another wizard able to apply the appropriate antidote. Unlike witchcraft, it is believed that wizardry *(isra mgbasi)* reached Ali-Ogba from *igmo* land.

Though many cases of wizardry and witchcraft were undoubtedly founded on speculation, superstition, or suspicion, there is no doubt that a number of really wicked people of both sexes existed in Ali-Ogba who used subtle or devious means or poisonous concoctions to eliminate their enemies. However, in spite of all the dangers and hazards, surrounding him, it was believed that a good Ogba person never really died. A good Ogba person merely appeared to die but he was quickly reincarnated in the form of a number of young children born into his *onuobdo* after his death, who would bear his name and enjoy the prestige and respect he had established. A bad Ogba man (e.g. one found guilty of murder or some other heinous crime) died *imida* (i.e deepest death) and was incapable of reincarnation.

On the whole, Ali-Ogba appears to have remained relatively calm, considering the general state of turbulence elsewhere at the time. Unlike other areas, there are few accounts of full-scale tribal wars. Indeed, the traditional history deals mainly with the "Abor War" which appears to have occurred in comparatively recent times.

Although only a few pitched battles are remembered in Ali-Ogba, it would appear the slave trade which prevailed in the area from the earliest period of the immigration of the Ogbas created a constant state of undeclared warfare in the territory involving frequent slave raids by the Abor (especially raids by the agents of Obi Ossai of Aboh), frequent private battles, and secret or crafty abductions. Perhaps we can gain some idea of the occurences from certain surviving usages in Ali-Ogba. Today, an Ogba still talks of *Nwadiali* (free-born) and may refer to his sister's off-spring as *Nwonyigmo* (son of an *igmo* and opposite of *Nwadiali*). It would thus appear that slaves were generally obtained from the *igmo* country. Nowadays the term *Nwonyigmo* is always spoken in an affectionate and jovial manner, but originally it may have depicted a state of slavery, degradation, or servitude often emphasized by the description *Nwonyigmo isiekte*, i.e. *Nwonyigmo* with the basket head. An uncle would boast of his traditional right to sell his sister's off-spring (his *nwonyigmo*) into slavery in *Oru* land to make good an outstanding bride price on his sister. *Oru* land is of course near the sea-coast from whence the slaves were transported to the new world.

The horror and inhumanity of the slave trade as observed by eye-witnesses and commentators are fully described in many contemporary works. Ogbas were obviously involved in the slave trade to the extent that their culture and vocabulary have been affected by it. A small number of Ogbas cannot trace their ancestory beyond two or three generations and their attention is always called to this fact (often tacitly) on every convenient occasion.

But the impression must not be created that Ogbas were the chief protagonists or dealers in the slave trade in Eastern Nigeria. In fact the true position appears to be that the part played by Ogbas was comparatively minor in comparison with the activities of other local groups.

In the following sections, we shall examine the role played by each of the major *onuobdos* in Ali-Ogba- their origin and ancestry, their peculiar taboos and totems, their *isiali* titles and their traditional status in a social, political, and religious context. In the end, we may be able to see the Ogbas in their true colours over the ages, as a respectable people observing religiously the intricacies of their complicated *isiali* ceremonies; a proud people enjoying pompous titles and flowery praise names; a merry, imaginative race that loves to sing and dance *asawa, oruorie, oregbu, orabrochi, okrosu;* an ingenious, adaptable people at home with their *Ugbakiri* in *Ogboru*, or *Aliulo;* a graceful and courageous yet bashful people who can wrestle or fight and run away with honour and dignity; a traditionally religious people who see themselves as glorified messengers between the living and the dead, or as middlemen in the traffic between free men and bondmen, or as the fortunate occupants of both the riverine and the hinterland spheres of the universe. We also expect to see some evidence of the tragedies of the age - the superstition, suspicion, indiscipline, fear and hatred. We shall see how the whole complicated edifice was somehow held together through a mixture of the Benin and Oru type of traditional Kingship and the *igmo* pattern of village republicanism.

Chapter 2

The Origin of Ogbas

Predecessors of Ogbas

Although Ogba legends and folklore speak of the arrival of ancestors at an unoccupied land, there is clear evidence that the present Ali-Ogba area was occupied by active groups of people in ancient times. Archaeological evidence[1] shows that the Obrikom (Egbekwu, Obie) area was first inhabited in 3015 B.C. Ikiri was occupied in 2015 B.C. and Omoku in 2815 B.C. By 15 B.C. and 235 A.D., these settlements had become stable as the inhabitants were killing large animals and fish and eating the large African snail. There is a high degree of certainty that yam was the staple food. Iron was known in 235 A.D., and there is strong reason to believe that it aided the clearing of the area for settlement and farming.

Iron was most probably worked at Obrikom as evidenced by the iron slag and iron objects found there. The date 235 A.D. accords with the known dates for iron working in some neighbouring Igbo areas. There is an indication that the settlers enjoyed a considerable amount of leisure as locally made smoking pipes have been found dating before the period of imported tobacco and pipe. There is as yet no clue as to what these ancient people put into the pipes which they smoked; but it is obvious that they did not smoke any imported tobacco. Most probably, they smoked a local weed but such a weed has not as yet been identified.

---

1 Excavations and Conclusions by Dr. Nwanna Nzewunwah (1984) University of Port Harcourt."Extending the chronology of the East Niger Delta" by Dr. Nwanna Nzewunwa published in *Nsukka Journal of the Humanities* Nos, 3/4 June/Dec. 1988. Excavations in Qbriko Ikiri Omoku etc were dated by the ESR (Election Spin Resonance Spectioscopy) method.

Foreign porcelain, J.J.W. Peters gin bottles and other trade goods have been found, dating from the 15th Century onwards which suggest that a sizeable, stable population, capable of dealing with European traders existed in Ali-Ogba during that period.

Ogba nwa Aklaka, Ekpeye nwa Aklaka

See Fig. 2.1 Plantain Farm at Ahiahwo believed to have belonged to Aklaka in the next page.

According to W.F.H. Newington's intelligence report (1930),

> The people call themselves Okoba which means children of Oba who is the common ancestor of the clan. Oba is a younger brother of Ekpaffia, who is the ancestor of the Ekpaffia section of the Division due south of Okoba. Ekpaffia and Oba were the sons of a person called Aklaka who used to reside in one of head towns of Ekpaffia called Olube[2] (corruption of Obiebe?) but his descent cannot be traced by enquiry among Okobas.

Of course Ogbas do not call themselves Okobas but they are so called by some outsiders unable to pronounce the long O sound (O-O) which begins the name "Ogba". It appears that Newington himself was unable to pronounce the word Ogba which he mistook to be Oba.

Ogbas and Ekpeyes have been taught the folklore: *"Ogba nwa Aklaka; Ekpeye nwa Aklaka"*.[3] For many sons and daughters of Ogba and Ekpeye, that is the alpha and omega of Ogba and Ekpeye history. The common ancestor "Aklaka" is said to have come from Benin.

But Ogbas can hardly understand Ekpeye speech, and vice versa. Egi speech, which is an Ogba dialect, is similar in structure and accent to Ekpeye. Mr. W.F.H. Newington has commented on the similarity between Egi and Ekpeye:

> The third group is the Egi group (which) is the Southernmost of the three and bounds Ekpaffia (Ekpeye) on the North. <u>This third group speak a dialect more akin to Ekpeffia</u> (i.e. Ekpeye) (my underlining); and exchange visit with Ubeta, Orupata and Ahoada for dances, plays and wrestling bouts.

---

[2] Olube is a corruption or typing error for a place known as Obiebe near Ahiahuo the traditional place of origin of Ogbas and Ekpeyes.

[3] "Ogba, son of Aklaka; Ekpeye, son of Aklaka".

Fig. 2.1: Plantain Farm at Ahiahwo believed to have belonged to Aklaka

Ogbas and Ekpeyes have many customs in common. For example, they are the only groups in these parts whose wrestlers are not permitted to hold their opponents' legs. This is a distinctive Edo tradition shared with some Yoruba areas but not practised by any other groups in Eastern Nigeria. Ekpeye age-grades are organised in the same manner as Ogba age-grades. Above all, Ekpeyes have *Onuobdos* just like Ogbas, although the same Ogba *Onuobdo* may be known by a different name in Ekpeye. *Isiokloko* in Ekpeye is recognised as Umuenyike (the Nwadei people) in Ogba, and Umuebe is known in Ekpeye as Edihuru. Egi *Onuobdo* names are frequently identical with those in Ekpeye.[4] The existence of *Onuobdos* which are common to both Ekpeye and Ogbas is the strongest single proof of blood and historical relationship between the two groups.

The writer has been informed by the Eze Ekpeye Logbo, (Eze Robinson O. Robinson of Isiokloko *Onuobdo)* that when an Ekpeye woman of standing dies, the *Uma-Ogbani* (female relations moved by the spirit of the late woman) go in a body to the farm of the deceased and harvest some crops which they bring home and cook (for the deceased) just outside her earthly residence. He confirmed that a similar tradition exists in Benin today.

One of the most conspicuous similarities between Ogba, Ekpeye and Benin is the custom of living close together cheek by jowl in towns (like Onitsha and Oguta which also have traditions of Benin origin), unlike most of their neighbours. Another evidence is the traditional dress which will be discussed in greater detail later.

The traditional story of Ogba and Ekpeye is that Aklaka fled from Benin due to the fear and insecurity caused by the depredations of a turbulent prince of the Oba of Benin known as *Ogualo*. Indeed, no traditional story or folklore in Ali-Ogba is complete unless it involves *Ogualo,* the war-like prince, whose foot-print created lakes in the areas he traversed. These stories

---

[4] E.g. Edihuru

also speak of the Oba of Benin himself, who was seen as a great colossus, *Oba Odudu*[5], *Oba ogbu madu ubachi ndu agua*[6].

One gains the general impression that Benin and its Oba were regarded with the greatest awe and veneration over a most extensive territory. Benin king list does not contain the name *Ogualo;* but it contains the name of *Oguola,* who succeeded his father *Ewedo* in C. 1280 A.D.[7] Most probably, *Ogualo* in Ogba folklore is a corruption of the name *Oguola.*

Ogbas and Ekpeyes claim Benin Origin

To this day, practically all Ogba *onuobdos* claim that they and Ekpeyes came from Benin. On the whole, modern historians are very sceptical about claims to Benin origin which create the impression that a people are merely striving to associate their ancestors with a glorious past with which they may, in fact, not have had any connection. Undoubtedly, Benin had a glorious past in political expansion and the arts, but it was also "The City of Blood". On balance, it would be foolish to fabricate a relationship if none actually existed.

The Ogba claims appear amply supported by the customs and usages of Ali-Ogba: In the past, Ogba men and women derived their personal names from their immediate ancestors because of the Ogba belief in re-incarnation. And Ogba towns were named after their founders who were potential re-incarnators. Thus, place and personal names in Ali-Ogba tend generally to embody the history of the people over the ages.

Today, there is an older community known as "Ogba" in the outskirts of Benin City. Ordinarily, this may have been a mere coincidence; but in a society in which place names were derived from founding ancestors who were believed to have been capable of transmitting their names from one generation to

---

5   "Odudu is an onomatopoeic word suggesting fear and terror associated with the title "Oba".
6   Oba, who takes a man's life on the day he enjoys it most.
7   Egharevba, *A Short History of Benin,* Ibadan University Press (Ibadan 1968) page 11.

another by means of re-incarnation, a historical connection seems most probable.

It is significant that the story of the original "Ogba" near Benin is connected with a river of the same name. In the same manner, the "capital" of Ali-Ogba (or the new Ogba area) (i.e. Omoku) is named after River Omoku which rises from a spot near Omoku town. This does not seem a mere co-incidence. Let us consider the story of Ogba near Benin as told by the *Odionwere* of Ogba, Benjamin Erinmwiore Eredia [8].

The story of Ogba is the story of Ogba River from where it got its name. Many years ago, there was a very beautiful lady called *Ogba* from Ikiri[9], a village near Ogba. Her beauty did not only dazzle the then Oba of Benin but made it impossible for him to return to the palace without her. And so it was that she became the Oba's wife.

In the palace, she was the best loved wife so much so that others became jealous and planned to do away with her. They knew she forbade snail and tortoise. To make their charm more effective, they mixed them with other concoctions for a potion which they prepared and kept on her seat.

Ogba, who never knew the "evil plan" of other Oba's wives, innocently sat on the seat. The result was a deformed nose which began to rot away instantly. She was at pains to tell the Oba that that was not how she was when she came to the palace. She wept and as she did, her tears started overflowing the room she was in. She then told the Oba she was going to turn to water, but the Oba told her to move away from the palace as he wouldn't want it flooded.

Consequently, she left for Ezomo's (chief's) compound. While there, the Ezomo observed that his compound was becoming flooded with her tears. He was dumbfounded and quickly ran to the Oba to lodge a complaint. He was told to tell *Ogba* to move away from there to Ozeka village off Ekenuan Road. She did just that, weeping as she went. On reaching the

---

[8] Culled from the *Nigerian Observer* 1st July 1989.
[9] There is also an Ikiri village in Ali-Ogba, the object of this book.

spot, she fell down and turned to water which gradually spread to where we have today Ogba village.

The source is where the Ogba Water Works is located off Ekehuan Road. Hun-n-n-n.

Thereafter, no Benin indigene who came to wash their linnings at Ogba River returned home without the clothes getting dry. Besides, no person from the palace ever drank the water. However, with modernity, they now drink it. In fact, the tap which the Edo speaking people call "Ogba" also got its name from Ogba River.

The Ogba people are of different stock. The Benin people were the first settlers, then the Itsekiris, the Urhobos and recently, a few Igbos.

The extensive ruins around present day Ogba suggests that she once boasted a large population which was most probably reduced by emigration.

The ancestors of Ogbas of the eastern Niger (the subject of this book) were most probably among the early emigrants from Ogba near Benin. Benin history prior to the 10th Century A.D. is still very nebulous. It appears that, emigrants left at different times between the 14th and 17th Centuries. Those who went from Benin to Ali-Ogba either settled down side by side with those whose ancestors had occupied the area in 3015 B.C. or the late arrivals may have displaced the pioneers.

If the original settlers were displaced, they would have formed a separate community or communities somewhere beside Ali-Ogba as happened in Onitsha, Oguta and Aboh, but there are no comparable original groups living near Ali-Ogba today. Consequently, it may be that the original inhabitants were extinct before the Ogbas arrived or they may have mingled with neighbouring groups or the late arrivals may have met them and absorbed them. The last proposition appears to be the most plausible.

Edos (Binis) Claim Origin From Elsewhere

The Binis themselves have also a tradition of migration from elsewhere; so the Ogba migration story is by no means isolated. According to the famous Benin Historian, Jacob Egharevba:

> The Binis came all the way from Egypt to found a more secure shelter in this part of the world after a short stay in the Sudan and at Ile-Ife, which Benin people call Uhe.... The Empire of the first period or dynasty was founded about 900 A.D. The rulers were commonly known as "Ogiso" before the arrival of Oduduwa and his party at Ife in Yorubaland, about the 12th century of the Christian era....

On the other hand, Adiele Afigbo states[10],

> A preliminary excursion into glottochronology of the Kwa language sub-family ... has yielded the suggestion that most of the member - languages of this sub-family (for instance Igbo, Ijo, Edo and Idoma) started diverging from their ancestral root between 5000 and 6000 years ago ... Now linguists are of the view that bearing in mind the distribution and alignment of the languages in the Kwa sub-group of the Niger-Congo family, it is most likely that the members of this sub-group separated in the region of the Niger-Benue Confluence. Art historians are also beginning to draw attention to this same general area, especially to the region between Bida and Kotor-Karifi as one of central importance in the history of the Middle Belt and Southern Nigeria.

Afigbo's story appears to be more credible than the Egyptian story, bearing in mind the crucial issue of racial and cultural differences.

It is curious that in the Ijaw or Ijo group, the word "ama" occurs in practically all dialects. A Nembe praise song quoted by Prof. E. Allagoa states:

> *Kala ekule ama, Nembe, Ama doko doko biekpo.* The suffix 'ama' is noticed in the names of towns such as Degema, Abonnema, Buguma, Sagbama, George ama etc. In Ijaw, *ama* connotes town or city, which is the apex of the Ijaw political hierarchy (i.e. the city state); whereas *ama* in Igbo means the "compound of an individual with a family" - i.e. the lowest level of the political hierarchy. The names of the days in the traditional Igbo four day week (Eke, Nkwo, Ahuo, Orie) are practically identical with the names of the traditional week days in the Edo (Benin) language.

---

[10] Afigbo, A. *Ropes of Sand* (Oxford University Press Ibadan 1981) p.7.

Jacob Egharevba goes on to say:

Though it is impossible to know the precise date of their foundation, some of the important villages which already existed in the first (i.e. the Ogiso) period include the following: Ihimwirin, Avbiama, Oka, Idogbo, Utesi, Ogua, Urhoho, Ute, Eyaen, Aho, Irighon, Azagba, Igo, Egbaton, Ughoton, Udo, Eri, Okha, Umoghumwun, Orogho Uhen, Okenuhen, (Okelure), Okehuwmun, Ikoha, Use, Ego, Ekho, Ebue, Irokhin, Udeni, Ema, Ugha, Orhua, Urhuekpan, Amagba, Ughen, Evbuekori, Ekhua, Ogan, Isua, Uhi, Ekae, Uzeghudu, Iyowa, Omin, Ikoka, Iyekeze....<u>Ogba</u> (my underlining), Ogbokhirima, Okuo, Owe, Ominara, Unuame, Ugolo, Ikpako, Uhogua, Ayen, Osio, Uwan, Egbaen, Idumwonwina, Ohovbe, Ogheghe, Uvbe, Ite, Iguogbe and Izikhiri.

The inclusion of "Ogba" among the villages founded during the Ogiso period is noteworthy.

Now let us read what Ogba elders have to say on the origin of Ogbas:

The general indications are that the different ancestors of the various Ogba *onuobdos* migrated to Ali-Ogba at different times through four main routes - South-northerly, North-southerly, East-westerly and West-easterly during the period 3015 B.C. to C. 1600 A.D. The legendary background of each migration as narrated by the leaders of each *onuobdo* in Ogba is summarised below:

Settlement in Obiebe (near Ahiahuo) - The South-Northerly Route (Ekpeye, Umuezeali, Obosi, Umuekedi, Umuagbda, Umuebe (Edihuru) Uriem.

Ekpeye

Aklaka left Edo and arrived at Obiebe (or the neighbouring site at Ahiahuo). The intervening period was spent in travelling in those difficult times. It is difficult to locate 'Aklaka' in Benin history. The closest evidence appears to be that a man named 'Ekaladerhan' (apparently shortened to Aklaka) was the son of the last Ogiso who founded Ughoton (Gwato). It appears that Ekaladerhan is the Aklaka of Ogba and Ekpeye folklore.

The similarity in the customs and speech of Ekpeyes and Ogbas (especially the Egis) has already been described. Mention has also been made of the similarity between the custom of Engennis (on the western side of the Orashi, South of Ekpeye land) and Ekpeyes, which suggest that Aklaka and his co-travellers may have stayed in Engenni territory for some time and that they crossed the Orashi at a more southerly point (e.g. Engenni) before moving northwards (i.e. in a south-northerly direction) to occupy their present home lands.

Umuezeali

According to Umuezeali legend,[11a] Aklaka had two sons, Ogba and Ekpeye. Ogba was the father of Nweke, who was the father of Yaha (Uyaha), who was the father of Ezeali. However, from evidence elsewhere, "Ezeali" or "Ezeani" or "Ezeala" is a title usually given to first arrivals at a new habitation in recognition of their status as landlords. Consequently, the name Ezeali may be considered as "cognomen" - or descriptive nickname which has over the years replaced the original name of the founding *Onuobdo*.

The Umuezeali *Onuobdo* are recognised today as the earliest arrivals and "landlords" of Ali-Ogba. In view of the archaeological evidence[11b] that parts of the Ogba area were inhabited as early as 3015 B.C., it may be presumed that Umuezeali actually arrived Ali-Ogba at that date. On the other hand, they may have arrived during the general exodus from Benin to the lower Niger Basin between the 14th and 17th centuries. In that case, they should have met earlier inhabitants of the Ogba area, but traditional oral history does not say so.

The legend and family histories of various Ogba *Onuobdos* indicate that Umuezealis were not the only group that came by the Engenni (or the south-northerly) route. The following summaries tell the stories of other onuobdos according to their oral historians:

Obosi

On a certain day, after the death of Oba Oguola but before the reign of Oba Ewuare the great, Oba Ohen who was continually fighting with the Uzama and Town Chiefs, summoned them (the

---

[11a] According to account given by Chief Mark Ogwe, Head of Umuezeali *Onuobdo* at Obigwe, on 10th January 1980.

[11b] Excavations by Dr. Nwanna Nzewunwah at Obie (Obrikom), Omoku, and Ikiri indicate that these places were inhabited in 3015 B.C., 2815 B.C. and 2015 B.C. respectively.

Uzamas and Town Chiefs) to his palace. When they had assembled, he proclaimed quietly behind the royal "curtains":

> There shall be no fighting tomorrow. Instead, we shall appease the gods. They are calling for sacrifice, and I hereby order that sacrifice be offered to them tomorrow at mid-day.

Replying, the Iyase, the senior *Uzama Nihiron* or Town Chief, whose successors were destined to become the commanders of the Benin Armies in course of time, suggested an alternative line of action, and thereby incurred the wrath of the Oba. At once, with his *ada*, the Oba cut off the Iyase's head, there and then, in a feat of royal anger. The Uzamas and Town Chiefs were shocked and enraged beyond control, and they openly accused the Oba of murder and dictatorship[12].

Now, the Uzamas were hereditary Chiefs who had large numbers of their own followers. When the Uzamas emerged from the palace, the crowds became aware of the tragedy which had occurred. Spontaneously, they acted at once to avenge the murder of the Iyase. They stormed the palace, and, by throwing stones, killed Oba Ohen by their own hands.[13]

Meanwhile, the Oba's (Ohen's) son, was away fighting battles in distant lands. Soon, news reached him about his father's death and the circumstances in which it had happened. He immediately stopped warring and began his return journey to Benin, spoiling for vengeance.

Just like the Uzamas, the late Oba and his son had their own close relations who would stand by them through thick and thin. Thus, the Benin community was divided into two opposing camps, the Obas and the Uzamas. The stage was set for a war that was destined to last many generations.

---

12 Based on accounts given by Chief Akoji Oburu, Otigbu Anyinya and Ojoka of Obosi, in his residence on the 20th of November, 1979.

13 A.F.C. Drydor, in *Benin and the Europeans* (Longmans London 1969, Page 8), has commented: "The century and a half which by Egharevba's computation, came between the death of Oguola and the accession of Ewuare are among the most obscure periods in Benin history. The rulers are shadowy figures to whom tradition attributes no notable achievements... <u>One of them, Ohen, is said to have been stoned to death</u>..... (my under-lining).

As the war in Benin raged, Ohen's son dealt death and destruction on all sides and even neutral but politically prominent citizens had to flee in fear for their lives. Obosi (the ancestor of the Obosi *Onuobdo* in Ali-Ogba) and Ossamara, sons of Igoro, left Benin in the company of a host of refugees. They moved due east, arriving eventually at Ida where they settled for a considerable length of time. Apparently, the name "Igara" used by Ogbas to describe the people of Ida is derived from "Igoro", the name of the father of Obosi and Ossamara. (There is a sub-*onuobdo* known as Umu-Igro in Obosi today).

Being based on the River Niger, Obosi and Ossamara became great navigators, trading along the banks of the River Niger. It was obviously easier to sail downstream than vice versa. In this way, Ossamara later founded a town of the same name (Ossamara) in the lower Niger region. Obosi probably founded Obosi near Onitsha and sailing further south, also founded another place named Obosia.[14] He eventually discovered that Aklaka who had settled down with his family at Obiebe not far from Obosia was a fellow emigrant who left Benin about twenty years previously. A strong bond of friendship quickly developed between Obosi and Aklaka.

Umuekedi

Igwe, the ancestor of Umuekedi *Onuobdo* left Benin as a result of the troubles of Oba Ohen. He and his close relatives probably left Benin soon after Obosi had left. They settled for long in Ekpeye territory. Igwe was accompanied by his son, Eke. After a short time, Eke got married and had two sons, *Ogbowu* and *Ngbagba*. Other close relations whose descendants are members of Umuekedi were *Odogwu* and *Eriehi*.

Umuagbda [15]

Nweze the father of Agbda (ancestor of Umuagbda) was the brother of *Ogidi, Nchikere* and *Olodi*. The father of Nweze was

---

[14] Now extinct.

[15] Based on account given by Chief Sunday Onyeocha Amadike the *Iyasara* of Umuagbda, in Omoku on 24th October, 1979.

Akwu, who had left Obio for Obiebe in the company of his father, Ogba. Akwu died in Obiebe. Other movements of Umuagbda will be narrated later.

Umuebe (Edihuru)[16]

Edihuru (the ancestor of Umuebe) appears to have left Benin in the company of Ebe nwa Ali who was the father of Egburu, Okoya, Ossia, Akoluka and Enyabi in that order. They took years to arrive at Ali-Ogba. The first place where they settled in Ali-Ogba was Erema in Egi. From Erema they went to Ohiuga, Elehia and Ikiri. Umuebes sought sanctuary in Obigwe along with other Ogbas when the Mboaki tragedy[17] occured.

Uriem[18]

Uriem (the ancestor of Uriem *Onuobdo),* one of the descendants of Ogba was living at Obiebe when Ekpeye, Ogba's brother, was also living there with his sons and daughters.

Before Tragedy Struck

From the above accounts, it is apparent that before the *Mboaki* tragedy, Ogbas who came by the south-northerly route settled in small groups as shown in the southern section of the following sketch: (See Figure 2.2: Sketch of Ali-Ogba showing the South-Northerly route in the next page)

Aklaka, the ancestor of Ogba and Ekpeye settled at Obiebe (Ahiahuo) Umuezeali (among the descendants of Aklaka) also settled at Obiebe (Ahiahuo). Obosi (the ancestor of Obosi *Onuobdo)* followed the same route, one or two decades later, and settled at Obosia. Igwe, the ancestor of Umuekedi, and his son, Eke, arrived almost simultaneously with Obosi and settled at Obiebe. Umuagbda, led by Akwu, father of Nweze, first settled in Obio and Obiebe. Edihuru, accompanied by Egburu, Okoya, Ossia and Akoluka settled in Erema. Uriem also lived in Obiebe.

---

16 Based on account given by Chief Mark Obiohuru, the *Omodi* of Edihuru at his Usomini quarters in Omoku on 9th March, 1980.
17 See episode narrated under 'uriem' below.
18 Based on account given by Jumbo Nwaogbaligwe leading member of Uriem *Onuobdo* at his residence in Okposi on 26th January, 1980.

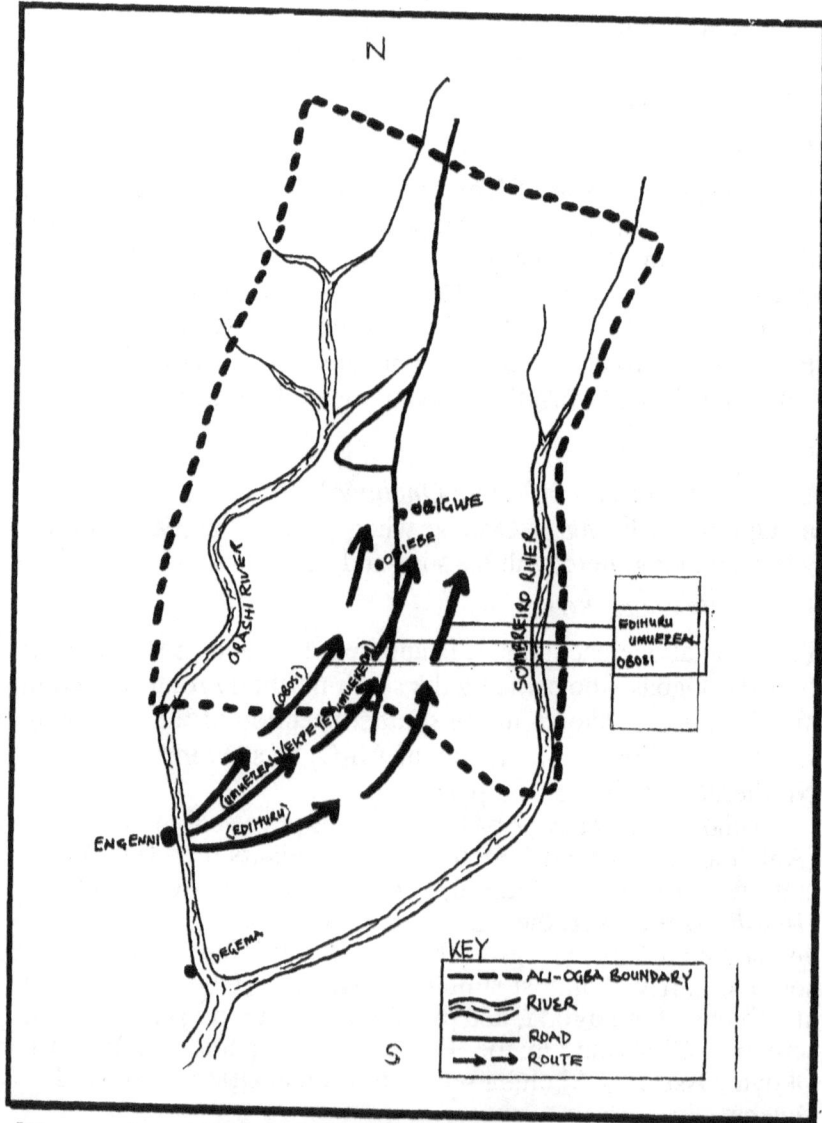

Figure 2.2: Sketch of Ali-Ogba showing the South-Northerly Route

The greatest concentration of the sons of Aklaka and their families, numbering perhaps up to one hundred souls[19] in the earliest period was to be found in other pioneer settlements. Obosia, Erema, Obio, Ahiahuo, contained smaller populations totalling altogether another one hundred souls approximately. The most significant factor is that these settlements were all located more or less on a circle, with Obiebe as centre, less than an hour's walk and within loud earshot from one another. Consequently, there was frequent communication and interaction between them all.

The Mboaki (grinding stone) tragedy and the flight into Obigwe (Haven of peace)[20]

Within the first century after the arrival of Ogba and Ekpeye in Ali-Ogba, a very unfortunate incident occurred in Ahiahuo (Obiebe) - one of the sons of Ogba accidentally pushed a son of Ekpeye down and he hit his head against a grinding stone (Mboaki). The fall was so serious that within minutes, the victim was stone-dead. Ekpeye and Ogba were out on their farms when the tragedy occurred.

When every effort to revive Ekpeye's son failed, wailing and weeping rent the air and on hearing it, the two brothers rushed home to know what had happened. Immediately, Ekpeye recovered from the initial shock, he swore instant vengeance. The law of the age was an eye for eye. The sons of Ekpeye pursued the sons of Ogba helter-skelter in all directions. News of the hostilities spread like wildfire. Ogbas from the different settlements fled for safety and eventually assembled in Obigwe, the "sanctuary" or "haven of peace" where no one could touch a refugee without incurring the wrath of the gods (according to contemporary belief and practices).(See Figure 2.3: Sketch of Ali-Ogba showing flight into Obigwe (Haven of Peace or Sanctuary) in the next page.

---

19 Based on recent census figures, allowing for two to three percent of annual population increase.
20 The Mboaki tragedy may have occurred in C. 1390.

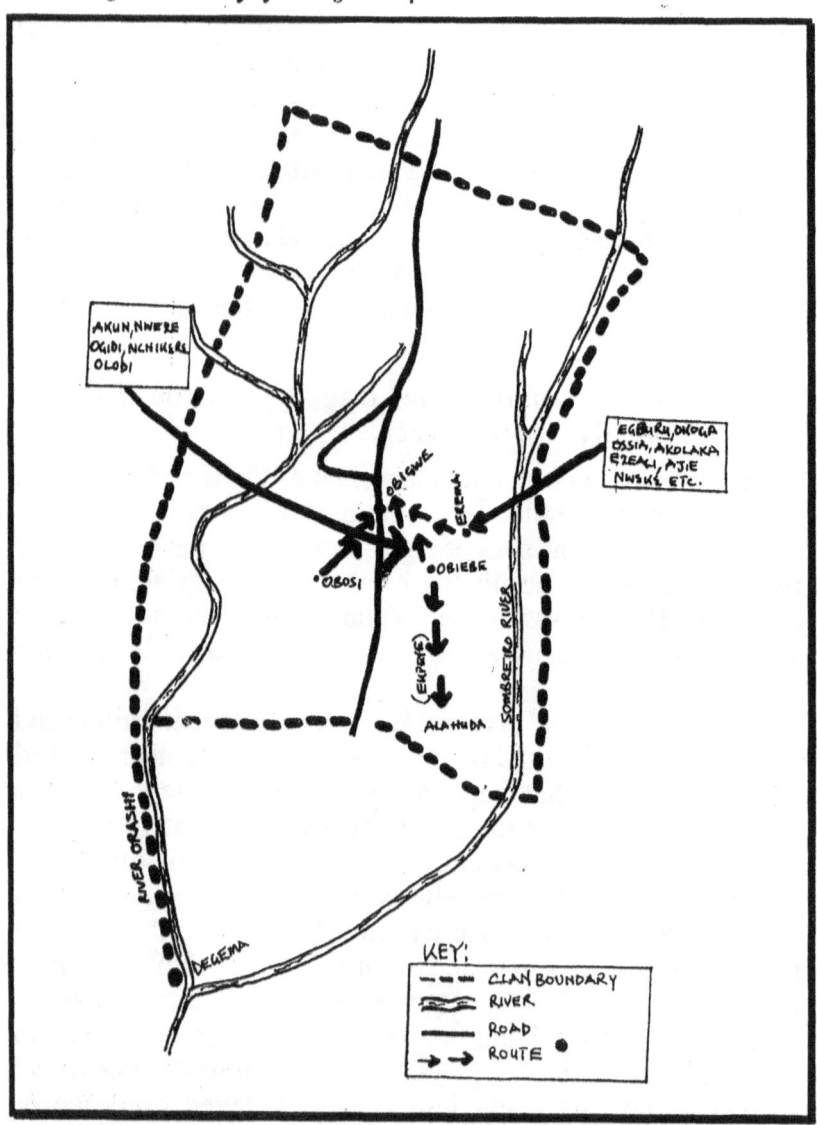

Figure 2.3: Sketch of Ali-Ogba showing flight into Obigwe (Haven of Peace or Sanctuary)

From *onuobdo* histories, the refugees who fled into Obigwe included Uriem from Obiebe; Egburu, Okoya, Ossia, and Akoluka from Erema; Akwu, Nweze Ogidi, Nchikere and Olodi from Obio; Igwe, the ancestor of Umuekedi *onuobdo*, and his son Eke and grandsons Ogbowu and Ngbagba, together with other close relations Odogwu and Eriehi; Olodi, the brother of Ossamara (both sons of Igoro), from Obosia; Yaha (Uyaha) and his son Ajie-Nweke and grandson Ezeali. Nweke the father of Yaha and the son of Ogba, and his father, Ogba, were too old to flee and died soon afterwards in Obiebe. Yaya, the father of Ezeali immediately established the *Ihialikogba* shrine where the *Ohuos* of all the refugees *onuobdos* were assembled and worshipped. Every new *onuobdo* or branch of *onuobdo* which arrived subsequently at Obigwe brought its own *Ohuo* (or family Idol) and deposited it at Ihiali-Kogba.

It is said[21] that Ezeali had the power to "discuss freely with the land- he spoke to the land and the land replied and advised him. Anything he told the land to do was eventually done; and whatever he reported as having been communicated to him by the land was unquestionably believed by the people. Consequently, he wielded great power among the people and was held in high esteem throughout the land. In any dispute whatsoever, the decision announced by him after striking his Ohuo and Ogbachi[22] on the ground was accepted as the last word by everyone.[23]

---

21 According to the traditional belief of Umuezealis based on account given by Chief Mark Ogwe at his residence in Omoku on 16th January, 1980.
22 Traditional symbols of authority within an extended family.
23 Verbatim translation of text by Chief Mark Ogwe, oldest member and head of Umuezeali *onuobdo* on 10th January, 1980.

The North-Southerly Route to Obrikom: (Umuenyike/Umudei (Isiokloko)[24]

(See Figure 2.4: Sketch of Ali-Ogba Showing the North-Southerly Route in the next page)

At roughly the same period when the "Umuezealis" led some groups to Ali-Ogba through a South-northerly route, some members of the Umuenyike (i.e. Umudei or Isiokloko) *Onuobdo* were leading other groups to Ali-Ogba through a north-southerly route. Ikpulada, a turbulent noble left Ogba near Benin in the company of his son, Yudara and his brother, Ajayi and members of their families. Many other families fled Benin at this time due to the same troubles. The fugitives headed towards the Niger in the south east because that direction promised them peace and prosperity. When they arrived at Oko on the western bank, they were faced with the problem of crossing the Niger. Fortunately, through the assistance and co-operation of the Oko people, they were able to cross to Atani on the opposite bank by means of wooden crafts.

Now, Ikpulada came from the "dei" family, a traditional title which implies "well-born, dignified", "royalty". From neighbours in Atani, Ikpulada learnt that there was an Umu "dei" extended family in Uguta not far from Atani. He realised at once that the members of that family were his "brothers" and "sisters". He decided to travel to Uguta. At Uguta, Ikpulada and his followers met the Umu-"dei" kingship family who received them with fraternal warmth and hospitality and helped them settle down. At Uguta, Ikpulada and his son were re-united with some members of their family who had left Benin at various times in the past as a result of the prevailing political turbulence.[25]

During their stay at Uguta, Ikpulada and his group engaged

---

[24] Based on accounts by H.R.H. John Wokocha Ellah *Eze Ogba Nwadei Ogbuehi* and Mrs. Christiana Wokocha Ellah (nee Adah Osiah) and Lazarus Ezi Osere, *Okiye* of Umuenyike in Omoku, on 26th September 1979. Umuenyike is called "Isiokloko" in Egi and Ekpeye.

[25] The respected Nani Ojiako of Oguta chieftaincy dispute fame (1959) is an Umudei son. Other Oguta families such as Umuajie have Ogba connections which are still maintained today.

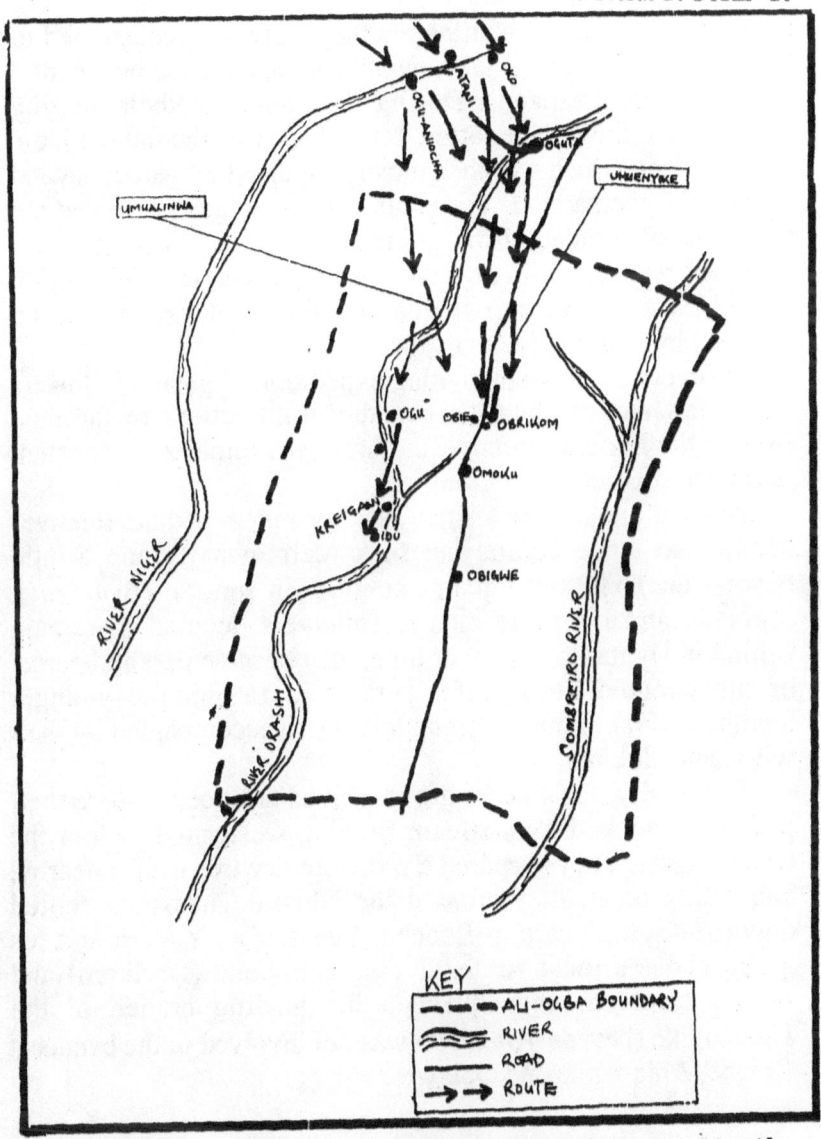

Figure 2.4: Sketch of Ali-Ogba Showing the North-Southerly Route

themselves mainly in hunting, as they were not accustomed to fishing in the Ughamini lake, which had become the occupation of many Uguta citizens. During the course of their hunting expeditions they were often ferried across the lake to the opposite land which was then mostly occupied by game, beyond Orsu and Egbema land. The greatest terror which prevented the followers of Ikpulada from going farther afield than Orsu and Egbema was an animal described as *Nwarigasi*[26] which resembled a chimpanzee and had the power of killing even an elephant by striking it with its bare hand.

On every subsequent hunting expedition, Ikpulada followers heard new stories about the wonderful attractions of the land beyond the Ebocha stream. But *Nwarigasi* remained a constant terror and obstacle.

At last, Yudara and a small band of his immediate relatives decided to leave Uguta and seek their own fortune South, beyond the Orsu and Egbema country, in spite of *Nwarigasi*. Ikpulada and his more elderly followers decided to remain behind in Uguta. In course of time, they became part and parcel of the Umudei family of Uguta. Yudara and the younger members of the Ikpulada group left Uguta accompanied by their wives and children.

Eventually, the Yudara group arrived at Ebocha where their path was blocked by a stream flowing westwards to join the Orashi River. They prepared a raft from dry tree trunks nearby, and riding on it, they crossed the Nkissa. Then, they settled down for some years in Ebocha. Eventually, Yudara and his group chose a most strategic area at Egbeku (Obrikom) and settled there. In consequence, this leading branch of the Umuenyike (Nwadei) *onuobdo* was not involved in the events at Obiebe, Ahia-Ahuo and Obigwe.

---

[26] Apparently extinct.

Umualinwa [27]

One of the other *onuobdos* that came by the North-southerly route was the Umualinwa *onuobdo*. Alinwa or his ancestors left Benin in the company of Chi the ancestor of Umunkaru and Umuoyro.

While Chi and his followers stopped in the Aboh towns of Adiawai and Utuochi and approached Ali-Ogba by the West-easterly route, Alinwa and his sons and grandsons (Ebu, Ogoyi, Obdo and Udaramata) came through Ogwu Aniocha, another Aboh town near Ihiala.

From Ogwu Aniocha, the Umualinwas migrated to Oguta, and thence to Osu-Ofuru, Odumadu and Obrikom, in that order.

A few years after their arrival in Obrikom, many Umualinwas moved closer to the Orashi River and established the Onosi *Ogu* settlement in commemoration of their old home at *Ogu* Aniocha. [28]

Meanwhile the families of Agburu, Okpraoma and Obosi had settled down in Omoku for more than a century. Umualinwas approached them to request for land on which to settle in Omoku and were readily offered a place in Obakata quarter.

> In those days, people were always happy to welcome newcomers because greater population brought greater strength and protection.
> In fact, many communities went so far as to prepare a charm called *Udomadu* in order to attract more people to live with them.

The West-Easterly Route - (Umunkaru, Umuoyro)[29]

(See Figure 2.5: Sketch of Ali-Ogba Showing the West-Easterly Route in the next page).

---

27 Based on account by Chief Will Orike, second *Okiye* of *Onuobdo*, in his house on 19th November, 1979.

28 Onosi *Ogu* is the present site of the Agip ferry to Ogbogena on the River Niger.

29 Based on account given by Nwokogu Adah, head of Umunkaru *Onuobdo*, Benedict Osiagor (the Akogu), and pius Adah, a prominent member of Umunkaru *Onuobdo;* Godfrey Onwugbonu oldest member and head of Umuoyro, at his Usomini quarter residence at Omoku on the 6th of March, 1980.

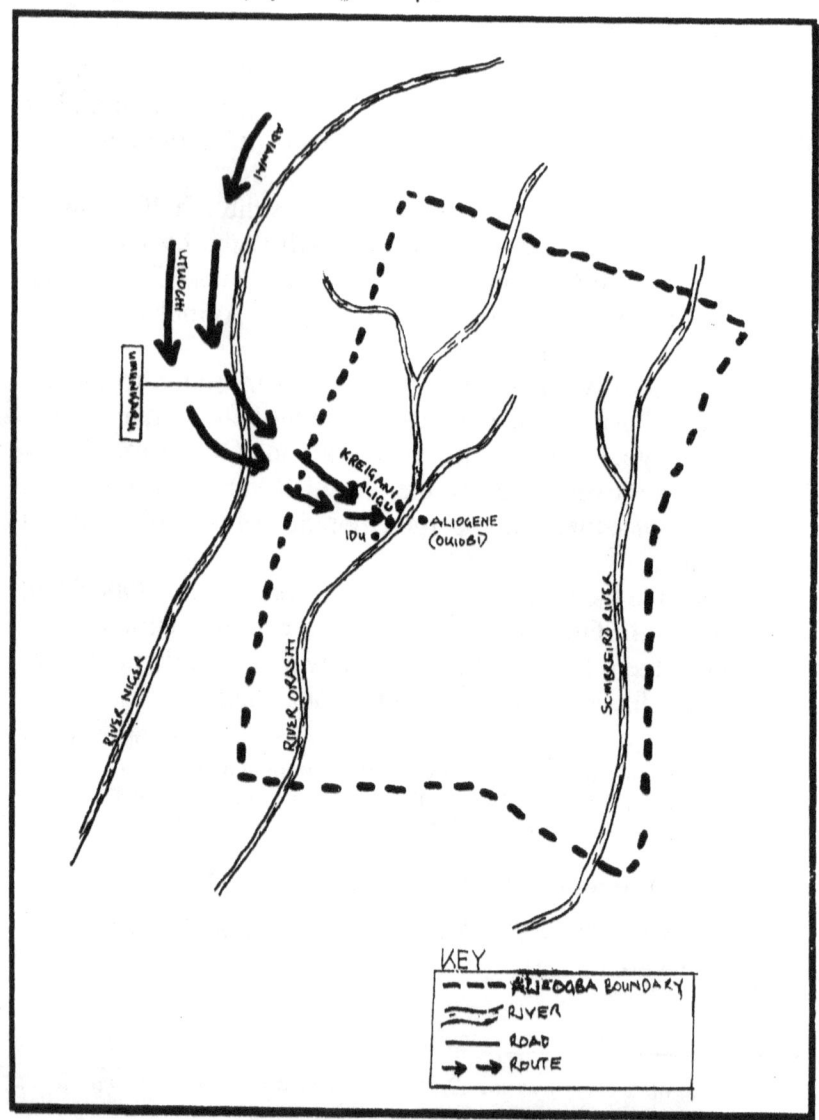

Figure 2.5: Sketch of Ali-Ogba Showing the West-Easterly Route

Chi the ancestor of Umunkaru left Benin most probably during the turbulent reign of Orhogbua. Chi and his followers stopped in various places for varying periods of time, but eventually they reached the present Adiawai, an Aboh town in Delta state, which observes close relationship ties with Umunkaru to this day. The bird *Abba* is sacred to both Umunkaru and Adiawai citizens.

Obviously, some members of Chi's team must have dropped out at Adiawai, through exhaustion or other causes; but the main body of emigrants carried on and crossed the Niger and the Orashi Rivers until they arrived at Okpulo or "everlasting home" (near present-day Aligu). There, Nkaru and his elder brother were born. The ruins of Nkaru's house and his shrine can be seen at Okpulo today.

Nkaru eventually made friends with Isoma (Ebelechi) of Ihiukwu who had already settled down at Omoku. Later, Nkaru went over to Omoku with his family. At first, they were guests of Isoma, but soon, they built their own house near the Ahia-Orie - Usomini road. Nkaru had three male children -Okpra, Ezema and Nkweke-Owre. The descendants of the three sons make up the Umunkaru today.

Umuoyros are related to Umunkarus through their common ancestor, Chi or one of his descendants. After the migration of Chi from Benin, he and his followers stopped at different spots along the banks of the Niger. The Umunkarus are the descendants of Chi's followers who stopped in Adiawai, while the Umuoyros are the descendants of those who stopped at Utuochi, another Aboh town. To this day both the Iguana *(awu)* and *Abba* are taboo to Utuochi citizens as well as to members of the Umuoyro *onuobdo*.

When Oyro arrived in Ali-Ogba, he first settled with his family at Ali Ogene (also known as Okiobi or present day Onuomoku) near to Aligu where his relatives (other members of Umunkaru *Onuobdo*) had settled.

The East-Westerly Route - (Umuagbda Onuobdo)

It has already been narrated that Nweze the father of Agbda and his father (Akwu) and his brothers Ogidi, Nchikere and Olodi had settled in Obio and Obiebe. Therefore they came originally via the South-northerly route, like the Umuezealis; but unlike other *onuobdos*, they had "a second coming", via an East-Westerly route, after the foundation of the Ogba "Capital City" Omoku. Details of the latter movement will be narrated later.

Dispersal from Obigwe (Diaspora) and Foundation of Omoku, the Capital of Ogba

(See Figure 2.6: Dispersal from Obigwe (Diaspora) and Foundation of Omoku, the Capital of Ogba in the next page).

Within a few generations after Ogbas had arrived from the four cardinal points and taken refuge in Obigwe and Egbeku (Obrikom), many were again dispersed to other parts, mainly to the North-east and North-west, especially Omoku all within Ali-Ogba. After the dispersal, Obigwe became almost the least populated among Ogba villages, and has remained so ever since.

The greatest factor which led to the dispersal was the frequency of Aboh slave raids[30] which attacked Obigwe through *Uhwo-K-Obigwe,* then a large and navigable tributary of the Orashi River.

Two of the sons of Ezeali, (Agbru, Ngah and Okpraome) left Obigwe and founded Omoku.[31] They were great hunters. During a hunting expedition, they discovered[32] Omoku and decided to settle there with their families. Agbru, the elder brother settled in Obieti (middle quarter in Omoku) and Okpraome settled in Obakata (the Northern quarter). Ezeali, the father of Agbru and Okpraome died at Obigwe. According to Umuezeali folklore, when Ezeali was about to be buried, his sister made up a fetish comprising kola-nuts, a knife and a gong and put them in his grave and said that since Ogbas failed to look after their brother (Ezeali), which was the cause of his death, no head or leader of Ogba should ever live to a great age. She

---

[30] The atlantic slave trade which stimulated these raids was well under way in the 15th century.
[31] Continuation of text of interview granted by Head of Umuezeali *Onuobdo*, Chief Mark Ogwe, on 10th January, 1980.
[32] The original settlers either died out or departed or were absorbed.

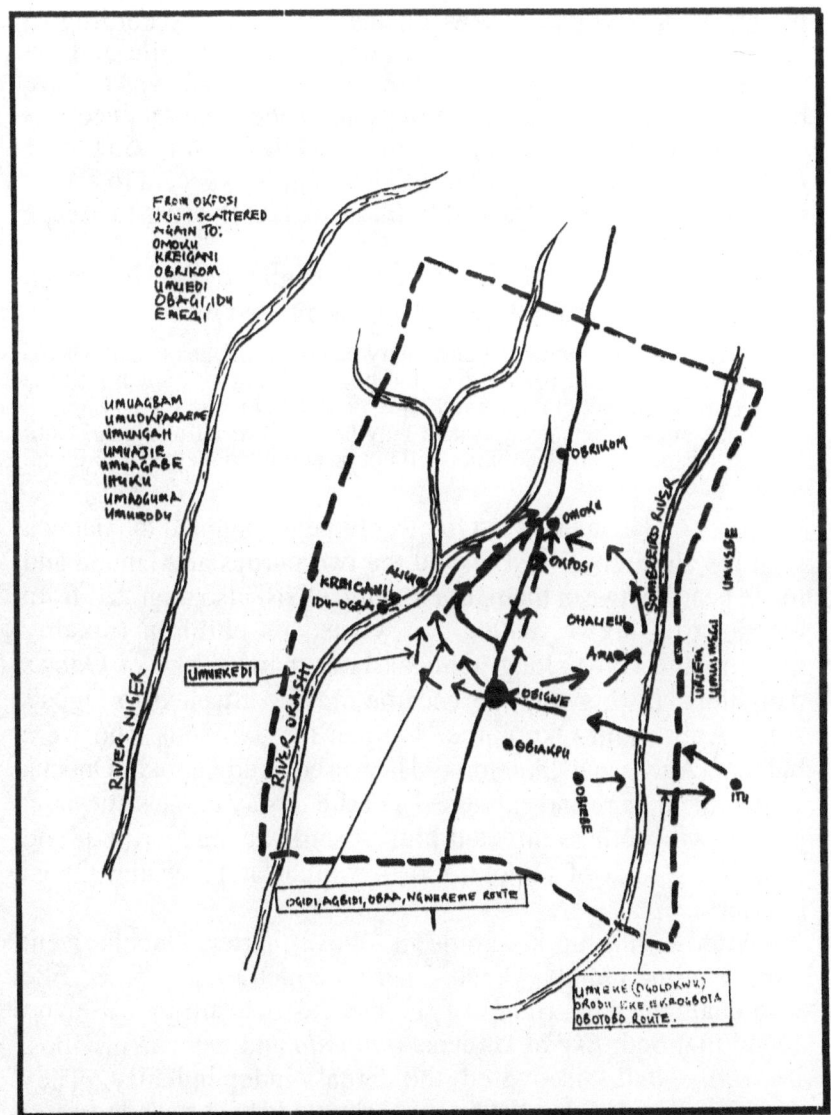

Figure 2.6: Dispersal from Obigwe (Diaspora) and Foundation of Omoku, the Capital of Ogba

planted *Ene* and *Okpu* trees on the grave site. According to Umuezeali chroniclers, when the trees died, the knife and the kola-nuts and the gong placed in the grave were believed to have been found in the trunk of the trees and have been retained this day in the custody of the oldest man in Obigwe. Any king to be crowned in Ogba, who wishes to last long, is expected to send a cow or a goat to be sacrificed to *Ihiali-Kogba* in order to escape premature death.

There are other ways in which the position of the Umuezeali *Onuobdo* as the landlords of Ogba is recognised today:

> One of the most important customary practices in Ogba is that when a non - Umu-Ezeali person dies, the body will not be buried until the Umu-Ezeali people received one goat known as *Ewu-ekeja*.[33] Sometimes, a money equivalent may be paid instead of a goat. Until this custom is satisfied, burial will not be permitted by the Umu-Ezeali people.

After Ogba had fled to Obigwe, Ekpeye migrated to Alahuda with his children. Obosi visited the two parties at Alahuda and made peace between them. Eventually, Obosi also migrated from Obosia to Obigwe, taking his wives, his children (notably Onocha and Ugo) along. Onocha later married one of Ogba's daughters. In this way, he became closely attached to Ogba's sons, Agbru and Okpraome.[34] When the two sons who were hunters (Agbru and Okpraome) later discovered Omoku, Onocha visited them there and expressed a desire to stay in the same area; so the two brothers directed him to settle at the Northern end near the source of Omoku Creek which later became Obosi quarters.

After setting up his home in Obosi quarter, Onocha went fishing in the Omoku Creek. There, he met a man named Eke who challenged his right to fish. The elders heard the case and found that both *Eke* of Umueke *onuobdo* and Onocha of Obosi *onuobdo* had discovered the Creek independently. They therefore decided that both parties should have a right to fish in the Omoku Creek but that each should use a different fishing

---

[33] A goat in recognition of authority over land.
[34] According to Ezeali account, Agbru and Okproame are supposed to be great-grandchildren of Ogba.

gear. To this day, Obosi have the sole right to use the *enuma ogwudu* for fishing in the Omoku Creek while Umu-Eke (Eke's descendants or *onuobdo)* have the exclusive right to use the *eri ogbasi.*

Umueke[35]

A few years after Agbru and his brother, Okpraome had settled in Omoku, Eke the son of Ogolokwu, a son or grandson of Ogba, arrived at Omoku. Eke's presence became widely known in Omoku as a result of his dispute with Obosi in connection with fishing rights over the Omoku Creek.

According to the Obosi narrative to which reference has already been made, which is confirmed by Umueke, Obosi gained an exclusive right to use *enuma ogwudu,* while Eke acquired the right to use *eri ogbasi* in fishing in the Omoku Creek.

Eke's father, Ogolokwu, had settled in Obiebe where he found *Ogbo - ka - Ogolokwu* (or Ogolokwu quarter). It would appear he (or his parents) left Benin more than a decade earlier. Ogolokwu had five sons viz:- *Orodu, Eke, Akocha, Ekeagbota* and *Obotobo*. These sons were the founders of the five sub-*onuobdos* known by their names. The five groups are often described collectively as "Agwolo" or "Egboha". It appears that Ogolokwu reached Itu before coming to Obigwe in the Ogba area where he deposited his traditional *Ohuo* as other *onuobdo* leaders were doing. It is from Obigwe that his sons migrated to Omoku and elsewhere.

The first son of Ogolokwu to leave Obigwe was Eke. Eke appears to have arrived at Omoku about six years after it had been discovered or rediscovered and occupied by Agburu and Okpraome.

After leaving Obigwe, he spent much time hunting and discovering Rivers and Creeks. He was the first to discover the Orashi River and cross it. Thereafter, he spent months hunting in the marshy region between the Orashi River and the eastern

---

[35] Based on account by Victor Eke Osi, "Owerre" of Umueke, at his residence in Usomini quarters on 10th November, 1979.

bank of the River Niger. This was during the dry season, otherwise the high flood in the area would have prevented him from hunting. Fortunately for him, he killed so much game that he did not know how he could carry it away. So he built a strong, large, wooden platform *(imasi ogo)* placed the animals on it, and made a big fire below to dry the animals. His food being thus assured, he planted his *abigwe*[36] in the ground. This device it was believed attracted a large crowd of people. Among them, a man named Obinwa, the ancestor of Umuobianwa, came with his wives and children and made his home at the spot where the *abigwe* had been planted. To this day, a member of Umueke *onuobdo* is received with fraternal affection in Umuobianwa village.

Eke spent some time discovering creeks and rivers in the vicinity of Umuobianwa near Emegi.[37] Today, at least four creeks in that area belong to the Umueke *Onuobdo* and their rights and privileges are traditionally respected and protected by the Emegis.

Years later, Eke crossed the Orashi again and discovered the Omoku Creek before he arrived in Omoku, hence his dispute with Obosi in connection with fishing rights in the Omoku Creek which led to the decision narrated earlier. That the right of Umuekes to operate *eri* in the *eri Ogbasi* Omoku Creek has been honoured and protected to this day in spite of "economic temptations" is a testimony to the high moral standards observed in traditional Ogba society.

It is narrated how Eke at a later stage persuaded his father, Ogolokwu, to come to Omoku to settle. Soon afterwards, Ogolokwu died. According to traditional sources, some payment was to have been made to Umuezeali before he could be buried; but Eke argued that if he paid before any burial, Umuezeali must pay before fishing in the Omoku River or drinking from it. Eventually, it was decided that no payment should be made by either party and that has remained the tradition till this day.

---

[36] Enchanted iron rod.
[37] Emegi is called **Biseni** by her indigenes.

Umuorodu [38]

Eke's (ancestor of Umu-Eke's) senior brother Orodu, apparently left Obigwe about the same period as Eke, but unlike Eke, he headed almost straight for Omoku in the company of his bossom friend, Agbru, who was setting out at the same time in the company of his junior brother Okpraome. In due course, Orodu succeeded in acquiring certain rights over the Omoku Creek, most probably through the exploits of his brother, Eke. The fact that Umueke are the recognised priests of the *"erisi Omoku"* goddess suggests that they have a superior claim. For the same reason seemingly, Umuorodu are exempt from the custom which requires other Ogbas to send a goat and drinks to Umuezeali and seek their permission before they can bury their dead in Omoku.

Ngbagba of Umuekedi had migrated to Obigwe when other Ogbas were taking refuge there. During the course of a hunting expedition, he discovered Kreigani and moved his family there. Soon after settling down in Kreigani, Eke discovered the land on the opposite bank of the Orashi River and declared it his own.

Meanwhile, Eke's first son, Obunwa, who was a keen hunter like his father, reached Omoku, and found that Agburu and his brother, Opkraome had settled there. The two brothers had prepared a charm known as *Udo madu* (or drawer of persons) which they placed in a traditional pot (called *Okwu* in Ogba dialect). The name "Omoku" is a corruption of *"Umuokwu"* (or sons of *Okwu*) a phrase used to describe those who were affected by the *Udo madu* charm and made to go and settle in Omoku. As the narrator says, one of the earliest persons who may have been affected by the charm was Obunwa. He moved with his family to Omoku.

By this time, Obunwa's father (Eke) and some of his other relations had discovered more lands to the West and North on the west bank of the Orashi River opposite Kirigeni. They travelled far and wide in the narrow stretch of swamp land between the Orashi and the Niger River. This brought them into

---

[38] Based on account by S. Okroma and Thompson Ezegbirika, oldest members and heads of Umuorodu, in their houses on 8th November, 1979.

early conflict with the Abohs who were moving Southwards and Eastwards on their own expeditions. The Abohs were hunting for beasts to kill as well as men to enslave. Thus, Umuekedi became inevitably involved in some of the early battles in the Aboh - Ogba war.

Ihiukwu [39]

Cha, Cha, Cha, Chro. Ko, Ko, Ko Kroo. Ebelechi (Isoma), brother of Dike and Okiriekwota, knew from the *Okwa* and *Eklu* birds that day - break was at hand. Rising from his mud-bed, he armed himself with *akube, omrenyi* and *okiya*[40] and stepped out of his thatched hut in Obigwe, followed by his dog, Ogbuanu, without taking leave of his two wives and nine children. It was Eke day, when farming and trading are forbidden in most of Ebelechi's land.

Ebelechi made his way northwards through thick forest, and when the golden sun began to appear at his left hand, he arrived at the bank of a wide shallow stream[41]. He crossed the stream easily and arrived at the northern bank. There he saw some game, a company of frightened antelopes, but they quickly fled, swimming across the stream in the opposite direction. Having no firearms, he could do nothing. His opportunity would come when he is able to get close enough, when he could use his *Okiya*[42] or *Omrenyi*[43] or even *Akube*.[44]

He continued his journey cautiously, peering into every thicket in search of any beast or man that may be lying in ambush. Then came the greatest shock of his life - he saw a buffalo lying down under a large cotton wool tree, fast asleep in the lazy afternoon heat. He thought it safe to let sleeping buffalos lie, and pressed on his journey to the unknown.

---

[39] Based on recorded accounts given by Chief David Ojadi, Albert Nwoko, Jeremiah Elebah (oldest member and head of onuobdo), Wilson Onyige and Bathwell Ibra, on 16th November, 1979.
[40] A club, a knife called "elephants' doom" and a spear.
[41] This has now become grassland known as "Uhwo ka Obigwe"?
[42] Spear.
[43] Elephant's doom (sharp long iron knife).
[44] Long, heavy, heard, wood.

Before long he heard the sound of an angry leopard growling in the distance. Following age-old traditions, he climbed to the top of a pear tree nearby. From there he watched the menacing quadruped as it prowled around. An angry leopard will attack anyone (especially if it had been previously provoked by any member of the human race). It may even climb a tree!

When the ferocious danger was over, Ebelechi climbed down from his hiding place and continued hunting. The sun had now begun to set at his right hand. A pack of deers on the move soon attracted his attention. As it happened, they were moving in front, ahead of him; so he determined to track them down. He would walk stealthily on his toes, like a ghost, bending his body and holding up his head. As he got closer, he would crawl on all fours like a beast himself; but just before the beasts came within range, they would bounce off systematically in apparent obedience to some animal instinct of self preservation. Then, he would commence trailing them all over again.

Before Ebelechi realised it, the sun was already sinking into the ground. Going forward became as difficult as going back. And it was quiet all around but for the sound of the frolicsome deers. Then some faint human voices became audible to him. In the near distance, he could discern some signs of smoke. Only human beings use fire, he thought to himself - so there must be some habitation nearby. Of course this could spell danger, depending on the disposition of the inhabitants!

Ebelechi pressed on more cautiously. Soon, he was able to count one major thatched house, and five smaller ones, built around a quadrangle with only one single entrance secured by a stout *Ogba* or traditional wooden gate. This turned out to be the compound of the oldest member and leader of the Umuezeali *Onuobdo* who were already resident in Omoku. He went within an *Okiya* length from the Ogba leading into the compound. Then he raised the traditional emergency cry: *"odi onye dinimnio"*.[45] An elderly voice asked who he was and, in reply, he described his *onuobdo* and ancestors and explained his predicament. Two stalwart sons of Agbru, armed to the teeth, went to open the Ogba. One of them moved the Ogba inch by inch, while his brother stood guard, with his *akube* at the ready. Meanwhile,

---

[45] There is no one to save me.

they maintained an unending stream of questions and answers with Ebelechi to make sure he was a friend and not a foe.

Eventually, the armed sons of Agbru came face to face with Ebelechi. They ushered him into Agbru's presence, practically under guard. Agbru knew at once, almost by instinct, that Ebelechi did not come to make war but peace. *Oji* and *Osoji*[46] were produced. They were first offered to the land, then to the ancestors, who were enjoined to reward good and punish evil. Then Agbru and Ebelechi ate a piece each and the sons of Agbru ate some as well. The weapons were then laid on the ground and Ebelechi was received as an honoured guest.

Ebelechi was very well treated by his host who showed him the riches of the land: the clear streams, wild game, fertile lands and abundant fish. Consequently, Ebelechi was in no hurry to return to Obigwe which was under constant threat from Aboh slave raiders. After some market days, his closest relatives in Obigwe became worried about his safety; so they sent out expeditions in search of him. The first expedition comprised his eldest wife, two of his senior sons and a nephew. When they arrived at Omoku, they found the place congenial, and practically flowing with milk and honey; so they stayed on. In this way, the Ebelechi group grew larger season after season.

Ebelechi's relations often hunted together as a group. In the turbulent days, it was safer for relatives to hunt in groups and protect themselves against dangerous men and beasts. On one occasion, Ebelechi and his group uprooted a giant tree at *Uhwesi Omoku* and were thenceforth nicknamed "Ihiukwu", said to mean "a great thing". The current Ogba equivalent of the nickname should have been "Whukwu" (something great!). *Ihiukwu* in current Ogba actually means 'large face'.

Umuogidi[47]

Ogba community is strictly patrilineal. A sister's son is regarded almost as a pet, as *nwoyigmo*, as someone to be loved and protected, but not to be taken into account in matters of inheritance in his mother's family. In the Isiali, ceremony, *nwoyigmo* "bows" to every member of his mother's family. But

---

[46] Kola nuts and pepper.
[47] Based on accounts by Ebenezer Osima, Iyasra of Umuogidi, and Johnson Ogidi of Umuogidi, at Omoku on 14th March, 1980.

maternal uncles will put themselves to every inconvenience to ensure the comfort of their *nwoyigmo*.[48] When *nwoyigmo* brings *whekanu*"[49], his *nwadiali* blesses his industry with the sign of white chalk drawn on his *(nwoyigmo's)* right hand accompanied with some handsome monetary or material present. If *nwoyigmo* has special problems which his own family cannot solve, he goes confidently to his *nwadiali* for help.

Ogidi, the son of Ogidi of Osiakpu (and grandson of Odukwu Obaa), whose half-brothers were Ichikere, Iyasra, Agbidi, Obaa and Ngwerema, left Osiakpu for Idu Ogba. The date of his departure is uncertain but it is believed to have occurred about ten years after Umuezeali and Obosi had settled at Omoku. Ogidi would eventually take refuge with his mother's relatives, (his *nwadialis*, the Obosi's) in Omoku. Meanwhile, he left his children (Adina, Idibia, Okarawor, Eleah and Onyije) in Osiakpu. The latter's descendants are the members of Umuogidi *Onuobdo* in Osiakpu today. Ogidi went to Idu Ogba in the company of his half brothers. After a brief period, he suspected that his half brothers had conspired to kill him, so he fled from Idu Ogba to Ozra - Enwo, accompanied by another member of the Umuogidi *Onuobdo* known as Igwe - Emegi. Ogidi stayed long enough in Ozra - Enwo to establish his claim to that land which is traditionally recognised as Umuogidi land to this day. Soon, he was in contact with his *nwadialis* (the Obosi's) living in Obosi quarters of Omoku. His maternal uncles offered him protection and invited him to come and stay with them in Omoku.

While Ogidi was living with his Obosi relatives, he went fishing at Ubomukwu (on the Omoku River) and there he encountered the Abohs on one of their periodic raids. A great struggle ensued in which he defeated and drove away the Abohs and claimed *Ubom Ukwu as his own*. That land has remained the property of Umuogidi to this day. At first, it was supervised by Ogidi's friend, Igwe Emegi, from Ozro Enwo, but when he died Ogidi took over direct supervision.

---

[48] Sister's son.
[49] According to Ogba tradition, the first animal *(whekanu)* killed by *nwoyigmo* should be taken to his *nwadiali* (mother's brothers).

Another conquest won by Ogidi is a lake called Abraka-Umuogidi. Here again, Ogidi saw Aboh people fishing and attacked them. He killed many of them buried their bodies beside the lake and took over the lake. As a result of the resounding victory, Umuogidi acquired the praise name *"Umu-Ogidi-Ojl-Madu-esi-eje; eje rima-madu-wre-azu-kwu-ugwo"*.[50]

Dispersal of Uriems-[51] The Tragedy of Eyio's wife and the exploits of Umeri Nwube

At first, when Uriems left Obigwe they fled due north and founded Okposi under the leadership of an ancient mystic known as Umeri Nwube.

Soon, a tragedy occurred which scattered the Uriem community through the length and breadth of Ali-Ogba: Eyio, an Uriem from Dibia Nwoloko's family, had told his wife to fetch water and prepare food, but she was reluctant to do so. Eyio then threatened that if he should prepare the food himself, his wife should not attempt to eat it, unless she wanted to die. Thinking that her husband was joking, Eyio's wife attempted to eat the food and was promptly murdered by Eyio. The whole community was thrown into the greatest confusion. Almost all Uriems fled from Okposi and went in different directions in search of safety. The event resulted in *Ito-Abohuo* or dissolution of the traditional unity shrine which bound all Uriems together. Thereafter, Uriems were separated into Umu-Olota and Okposi-Obodo.

Some Uriems went to Umuedi and established a branch of the Uriem *Onuobdo* which exists there today. Orikuku Nwadiokpa went with his family to Omoku to reside there. This gave rise to what is known as Uriem - Ahia - Orie in Omoku today. Ube of Uriem Ahia - Orie is a direct grandson of Orikuku Nwadiokpa·Osu Nwile is another leader of of Uriem Ahia orie who migrated from Okposi.

---

50 Umuogidis who use men to dam a river; the dam eats the men; and pays back with fish.

51 Based on account given by Jumbo Nwaogbaligwe, a leading member of Uriem *Onuobdo*.

Other Uriems went to Obagi and thence to Idu on the Orashi River. Some went to Kreigani, while Ossia and Orukwowu accompanied their senior brother to Emegi. A few Uriems later went beyond Omoku to Obrikom.

Apart from the murder of his wife by Eyio and the consequent *Ito-Abohuo* which caused the *dispersal of Uriems*, Umeri Nwube who had led Uriems from Obigwe to Okposi turned out to be a great mystic whose activities scared away some of his relatives: Umeri Nwube claimed to have visited heaven and seen God! It was claimed that God sent a rope down from heaven by which he climbed to heaven. But Umeri himself said that he was not given any rope; that he showed a leaf to his people as the ladder by which he would go to heaven; that he disappeared on setting foot on that leaf; that he stayed in heaven for thirty-two days i.e eight *Ekes* plus eight *Ories* plus eight *Ahuos* plus eight *Nkwo;* that he returned to earth through the leaf; that he was warned not to narrate all he saw in heaven and given great powers.

Umeri Nwube is supposed to have used his powers on the following occasions:

> First, he produced a charm for population growth. He said that no child born in Okposi would die and all the new-born children in Okposi survived during his time. The charm was planted in front of his house in Okposi. A woman could not pass in front of the charm during her menstruation period, otherwise the period would continue indefinitely until adequate sacrifice was offered.
>
> Indeed any woman of child-bearing age could not pass in front of the charm otherwise she would stop bearing children, unless adequate sacrifice was offered. Up till today, no one is permitted to carry firewood tied *in a bundle* across the charm.
>
> Secondly, he had the power of a seer. Whenever he said that so and so was going to die or was dead, it turned out that he was right.
>
> Thirdly, he brought a palm fruit which he planted in the ground. Before he planted it, he claimed that it would have two branches, and that one branch would produce a high-grade palm oil known as *Osukwu*, while the other branch would produce a poorer type known as *okpurukpu*. The palm tree produced as he had said.
>
> Fourthly, after visiting his mother's relatives in Ikiri, he tripped up and fell down on the road to Okposi near a place called *Ahia Uzor*. In his

rage, he turned the land on the left and right hand sides of the road into "desert" and it is still so today.

Fiftly, when one woman complained to him that she was barren and another one complained that she lost all her children in infancy, he prepared a concoction for both of them. The former despised the medicine but the latter took it and all her subsequent children survived. One of her grand-children who is alive today is known as Isaiah Nwaojadi.

In view of these powers, Umeri was greatly feared. Anyone he cursed and asked to "go into the bush" went and committed suicide in the bush.

These fearful claims of real or imaginary dreadful powers must have contributed towards the dispersal of Uriems to various parts of Ali-Ogba.

Movements by Umuokrocha, Umuimegi, Umuohali, Umuossia

Umuokrocha [52]

Okrocha was a descendant of Uriem. He was born in Obigwe and he grew up to be a fearless and dedicated hunter of animals and men. An *Nkwrizu*[53] hardly passed in which he did not bring home at least one human head. In fact, he used human heads as his drinking cup.

Following the tragedy of Eyio when Uriems fled in different directions, Okrocha left Obigwe and migrated to Ogbuta near Ubomta on the Omoku Creek. Members of the Umu-Emeri *Onuobdo*, who were already settled there, welcomed him happily. From Ogbuta, Okrocha and his children (Umuokrocha) migrated to Omoku.

Umuimegi[54] (Umuolota)

Imegi, a wealthy and powerful farmer and hunter of repute, whose family had taken refuge in Obigwe along with other Ogbas ten years previously, decided to migrate Northwards to

---

[52] Based on account given by Chief Ibra Nwaegburi, oldest member and head of Umuokrocha, on 15th March, 1980, at his residence in Usomini.

[53] Native week comprising four days.

[54] Based on account given by Chief Lawyer Eluozo Ajie of Umuimegi, in his house in Omoku in January, 1980.

Okposi. At this time, Ogbas were leaving Obigwe because of troubles from Abohs. Imegi and his sons and followers settled at Okposi for many years. Here, they worshipped a common shrine which made them abstain from *mma ekwu* palm fruit. The ruins of their houses in Okposi can still be traced today.

After the tragedy of Eyio's wife, many Uriems fled in various directions. It has already been narrated how the tragedy of Eyio's wife resulted in what is known in Uriem history as :*Ito - Abo Ohuo* which divided that *onuobdo* into Umuolota and Okposi *obodo*. Umuimegi and Umuolota are in fact one and the same people. When Umuimegi (alias Umuolota) left Okposi, they went to Ogbuta near Onu-Omoku and settled there for many years.

Umuohali[55]

'Ohia', corrupted to 'Ohali', was one of the sons of Ogba born at Obigwe. One of Ohia's (or Ohali's) descendants, Ubo, had two sons (Okroma and Nna) who established the headquarters of the Umuohali onuobdo at Ohalielu. Another descendant of his, Onyije, the son of Egbrika, settled at Ama.

Eventually, some Umuohalis, like other Ogba *onuobdos*, went and settled in Omoku. They occupied a place in the Usomini quarter. Later, some of them settled in Obakata as well". The political issue of the royal "transaction" between Umuohali and Umuebe (Edihuru) will be discussed in the next chapter.

Umuebe (Edihuru)

Like many other Ogbas, Umuebes moved again from Obigwe when that "sanctuary" was no longer safe. The four brothers of Ebe nwa Ali left Obigwe and headed in different directions. Ebe nwa Ali migrated to Ikiri with his sons Egburu and Okoya. Ebe had married the daughter of an Eze Ohali. That daughter was the mother of Okoya. Egburu, the elder brother of Okoya had a different mother (as Ebe had many wives).

---

[55] Based on accounts by Osi Nwa Orji, oldest member and head of *onuobdo*, Gilber Nwajari, leading *onuobdo* member and Mark Obiohuru, *Emodi* of Edihuru, at his residence in Usomini on 9th March, 1980.

Umuossia

As has already been narrated, Ebe nwa Alia migrated from Erema to Obigwe in the company of his sons Egburu Okoya, Ossia, Akoluka, and Enyasi. Later, Ossia and his family migrated to Elehia, and thence to Omoku. The only families who arrived at Omoku before Ossia and his family were Umuezeali, Umuodogwu and Umuogidi.

The "Second Coming of Umuagbda[56] From an East-Westerly Route

(See Figure 2.7: Sketch showing the coming of Ogbas from the East-Westerly Route in the next page). Nweze of Umuagbda had migrated to Obigwe, accompanied by his brothers, Olodi, Nchikere and Ogidi, and his own sons. After Nweze had arrived at Omoku from Obigwe, he had to flee the town very soon due to troubles from the Abohs who were coming to Omoku annually to enslave all the first born sons. Nweze refused to give up his son, Agbda, in any circumstances. He took him away to a site lying between Omoku and Ebogro which has remained Umuagbda land till today.

After two or three years respite, Ogbas who had surrendered their sons to the Abohs discovered where Nweze and his sons were hiding and decided to disclose it to the Abohs. Friendly sources leaked the plan to Nweze and once again he planned an escape. This time he went with his son to reside at a place called Njita on the Egbada road which also became Umuagbda land. Within another year or two, there was another rumour that the Abohs would be conducted to Nweze's hide-out; so he moved as far as possible near to the very banks of the Nkissa or Somebreiro River.

But even the most distant hide-out could not provide a safe sanctuary for Nweze and his son. He had no option but to plan how to cross the Nkissa river. In the absence of a canoe, he constructed a suitable raft on which he and his son crossed to the eastern bank of the Nkissa. As he found many *"Uju"* plants

---

[56] Based on account given by Chief Sunday Onyebucha Amadike, *Iyasra* of *Umuagbda,* in Omoku, on 24th October, 1979.

The Origin Of Ogbas 51

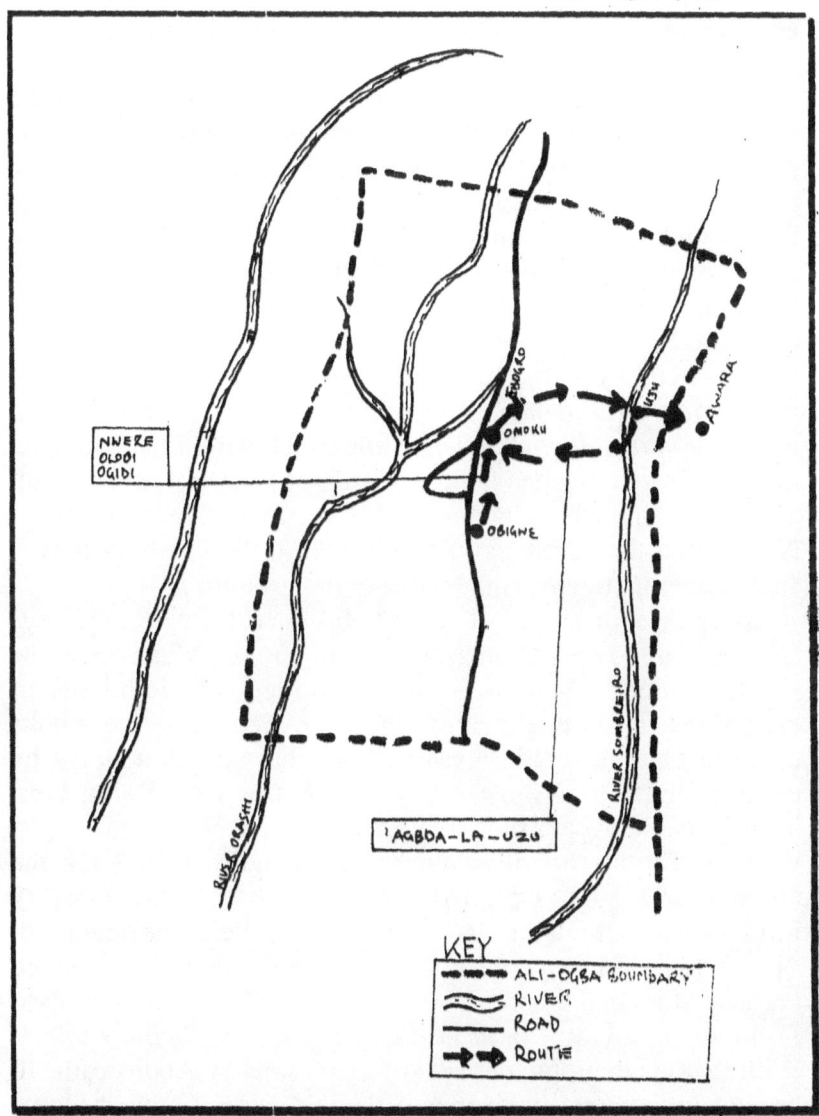

Figure 2.7: Sketch showing the coming of Ogbas from the East-Westerly Route

growing there, he called the place Uju, which is still a thriving village to this day.

But although he had travelled far enough and crossed the Nkissa (or Sombreiro) inorder to avoid the "impertinence" of the Abohs, Nweze's mind was not yet at rest . He still had grave fears that his new home would be disclosed to the Abohs by fellow Ogbas whose sons had been taken away. Although the river could help in checking the progress of his pursuers, he knew that the Abohs were adept swimmers who could easily cross the Nkissa.

Worried by these anxieties, Nweze went to a nearby village in *Awara where he met an igmo man who was a blacksmith as well as a native doctor*. After telling him his troubles, the *igmo* man, according to legend, quickly prepared a terrible charm with a live crocodile which he threw into the Nkissa river and assured Nweze that the Abohs would be killed to the last man if they should attempt to cross the Nkissa to molest him.

Nweze went back to Uju and abstained from many things from which the *igmo* man asked him to abstain. Meanwhile, the single crocodile increased and multiplied into hundreds of crocodiles. As was expected, the following year, the Abohs came to Omoku for the usual tribute and were conducted by certain Ogbas to Nweze's new hide-out at Uju. Being born swimmers, the Abohs quickly jumped into the Nkissa and began to swim. By the time they reached the middle of the river, the crocodiles, it is narrated, had done their work. Each and every intruder was believed to have been dismembered or devoured! "The colour of the river changed from smoky grey into deep red because of human blood", it is said. The incident is immortalised in the Ogba saying, *"mini eruka nka Nweze erubrilla ozo"*. [57] With that incident, the demand of Ogba sons by Abohs came to an end automatically. Henceforth, the name, Ogba, became associated with the crocodile in Aboh minds. Abohs believed Ogbas could do whatever they wanted with crocodiles.

---

[57] May Nweze's tide never occur again.

When it became apparent that the Abohs would not come again, the son of Nweze, Agbda, prepared to return to Omoku (his father having, in the meantime, died in old age). Agbda was welcomed back as a hero and called certain praise names. In respect of the crocodile war, he and his descendants are known as *Umu-Omela ekiri*.[58] Before leaving Uju, Agbda and his sons had been trained as blacksmiths by the *igmo* man. This earned them the praise name *"Agbda luzu"*[59]. On their return, the members of the Umuagbda *Onuobdo* produced iron implements of all kinds - guns, gongs, spears and matchets. For these accomplishments they, were honoured with the highest political position in Ogba, excelled only by that of traditional rulership. The Umuagbdas have the title "Iyasra" (or prime minister) and are called *"Umu okwu oto ekle eze"*.[60]

General Observation

The stories told in the above oral histories are not to be accepted as gospel truth. They have passed from generation to generation and a considerable level of distortion must be presumed. But there are certain features which emerge which can be accepted as historical truth especially those aspects which can be verified today. Although all *onuobdos* claim "Benin" origin, the narratives disclose that there was much wandering about before most of the *onuobdos* arrived in Ali-Ogba. Some *onuobdos* may have been accompanied by strangers whom they met *en-route*.

As Ogbas left their original home due to internal strife and danger, they must have instinctively followed a route where they met with the least opposition and which led to a land with desirable economic prospects. The Ali-Ogba area was sparsely populated and was close to an area already inhabited by the ancestral relatives of Ogbas e.g. Ekpeye and Oguta.

The merits of the saying *"Ogba nwa Aklaka, Ekpeye nwa Aklaka"* appear quite obvious. Ogba and Ekpeye have outstanding cultural peculiarities and affinities which make it

---

58 Sons of those whose strength lies in eddies of water.
59 Agbda the blacksmith.
60 Those who greet royalty, standing.

imperative to recognise their common brotherhood. And yet, it is obvious that the two peoples are not as close as they might have been, thus giving credence to the story of the *Mboaki* Tragedy. Perhaps, the dispute between the two groups was more serious than what has been narrated. It almost certainly involved homicide but its true causes and dimensions may have been dimmed by lapse of time.

Arising from the *Mboaki* Tragedy was the flight into Obigwe. In this instance, the "holy city" of Obigwe is a living testimony. *Ihialikogba* still exists in Obigwe for all to see. There are other signs also to prove that the town was highly populated at one stage in its history. Today, Obigwe is almost the least populated town in Ogba although its ancient religious character is still highly respected. The causes of the depopulation of Obigwe have not been highly articulated in the oral histories probably because Ogba oral historians are reluctant to accept that the Abohs were at any stage in history a thorn in the flesh of our ancestors.

The only Aboh story that is commonly told is the instance in which Aboh war canoes were sunk at Onuomoku and the Abohs were murdered or drowned to the last man. However, the cases of Umuagbda who were christened *Umu-Omelekiri* and Umuogidi who became *Oji madu esi eje, eje rima madu wre azu kwu ugwo* disclose clearly that Ogbas were constantly threatened by Abohs. Since Obigwe is on the bank of a former waterway, now a swamp known as *uhwokobigwe,* (and the Abohs had harrassed people along waterways), it appears quite certain that they must have contributed greatly to the dispersal from Obigwe or Diaspora.

After the diaspora, came the growth of Omoku from a small Usomini village to a capital city. The peculiar pattern today in Ali-Ogba is that every *onuobdo* in Omoku can trace its immediate origin to one of the neighbouring Ogba villages which number roughly forty-one at present.

The land-ownerships and water-ownerships disclosed in the oral traditions are strictly respected and observed to this day. On the other hand, such stories as the one in which Ezeali held frequent dialogue with the land, or the case of Umeri Nwube who visited heaven and returned to earth to perform wonders must be taken with a grain of salt. As for the migrations themselves, I have no doubt in my mind that some wide-spread movements occurred, but the details may not be as accurate as one would have liked, due mainly to the time lag. After all, throughout the world, human history before modern civilization was everywhere characterised by migrations and conquests. But only the most famous examples are recorded - the exploits of the Jukuns and the Jihad, the Danish invasion and the Norman conquest. It must be conceded that small groups like the Ogbas were not standing still while the rest of the world moved round, propelled by economic and political forces. Consequently, the stories of origin of Ogba *onuobdos* appear generally credible, except in matters of detail and in areas involving superstitious belief in fetish and miracles.

Chapter 3

Political Organisation of Ali-Ogba

When Ogbas eventually settled down in Ali-Ogba, they established a political structure which is broadly similar to the Benin structure which is marked by "King and Cabinet". The traditional cabinet posts reflect political offices, titles, rights and privileges acquired by different *onuobdos* when they settled down in Ali-Ogba. A semblance of these positions, titles, rights and privileges has been retained by the various *onuobdos* to this day through *Isiali* and the observance of other customs and traditions which are graphically indicated in the Table of Titles in subsequent pages.

The most outstanding feature of the titles is that they depict a monarchical hierarchy complete with cabinet and departments of state. Elizabeth Isichei has said in her *History of the Igbo People*[1].

> In the sixteenth century, a number of new states were established on the Niger, some of which rose to a position of great wealth and power, as the slave trade rose to a climax in the seventeenth and eighteenth centuries... They (grew) up on the fringes of Igboland, at cultural meeting places with other peoples, often as a result of migration from elsewhere. They have distinctive types of political institutions. They are closely linked with trade routes, and with the expansion of the slave trade.

Ali-Ogba satisfies all the enumerated characteristics as it shares a common boundary with Ijaws, has a history of migration from Benin, has distinctive political (kingship) institutions and is closely linked with trade routes and with the expansion of the slave trade.

Elizabeth Isichei, *A History of the Igbo People*, Macmillan London 1976 page 51.

Adiele Afigbo[2] paints a slightly different picture of the same events:

> In the West Niger and Riverine area it (the 16th Century) was a period during which villages and village group heads under the impact of Benin and of expanded trade on the Niger built up their positions into village monarchies, and as part of this process constructed elaborate ideological charters linking them in different degrees with Benin, Ida and Nri.

It would appear that both views (Isichei's and Afigbo's) have relevance to the Ogba political structure which is seen as a combination of Benin monarchism and Igbo republicanism. Although some Ogbas had arrived at their new home some centuries earlier, it would appear that their "monarchies" had not been fully established by the early sixteenth century. It was mainly the money derived from the slave trade that was used in bolstering up the stature of these monarchies to heights which were staggering in contemporary eyes.

Let us now examine more closely some aspects of the cultural and political legacies of the Ogba people depicted in the table of titles beginning with *Isiali*.

Isiali

As indicated in the Table of *Onuobdo* Titles (pages 58 & 59), every Ogba *onuobdo* had a traditional position in the political organisation of Ali-Ogba which is preserved to this day. When a member of an *onuobdo* "bows" in the *Isiali* (or formal greeting) ceremony, he or she is "praised" with the appropriate title of his or her own *onuobdo*. According to tradition, the person bowing responds loudly to at least two "praises" (sometimes more) before a ceremony is considered properly accomplished.

The *Isiali* or greeting ceremony is an important affair which must be mastered by anyone anxious to retain his self-respect as a full-fledged Ogba indigene. To carry out *Isiali* correctly, you must know the exact *onuobdo* of the person you are about to greet. You must also know the appropriate greeting for his *onuobdo* in terms of praise names or titles of distinction.

---

2   Adiele Afigbo, *Ropes of Sand* Oxford University Press Ibadan 1981 page 27.

Table of *Onuobdo* Titles

S/No.	Onuobdos	Political Titles	Okrosu Titles	Other Titles	Totems & Taboos	Shrines	Remarks
1	Uriem Umu'riem UmuOkirie UmuImegi UmuOji-nw'Okara Umu-Okorocha	Ajie Ikeoha (Commander)	Onuotu, Ogbowu		Leopard, Squirrel, ubelebe, mmakwu Awu(Iguana) Okro	Mkpitima Ema ka Ogbuta	Land beween Omoku and Okposi called Onu-uzor egbaeru belongs to all Uriems. Wonder man, Umeri Nwaube who visited God was an Uriem.
2.	IMEAGI Umu-Chikere Umu-Iyasara UmuOgidi Umu-Agbda Umu-Ikemta	Iyasara (Prime Minister)	Ogbowu (In Uju)	Iyasra greets Royalty standing. Agbda	Crocodile, Tiger	mgbrocha, Ohuocha Oche	Titles derived from the action of Nweze of Uju - Agbda luzu, Umuokwuoto ekleze.
3.	Umu-Alinwa	Ewo (Peacemaker)		Ijere	Elephant mushroom, ona uga	Odu Ka Ajie	Came originally from Ogu Aliocha near Isala refuse to fight Aboh war. Umu aju aju ohu. Denied Ogudu.
4.	Umueke UmuOrodu UmuEkeagbota Obotobo Umuakocha Umu-Usoma	Owerri (Guard, Commander) (Umuorodu: Igbazu keze (Aide-de-Camp))	Ogbowu Onuotu. Orodu exempt from initiation fee and burial fee.	Eze Ngwo, Umu-ogbu-ebirisi.	Python, Okuegbe Nrebruhie, Lizard, ukawu, ogbor fishes.	Erisi Omoku (Umueke are juju Priests of Erisi Omoku)	Relatives of Umuobianwa across the Orashi. Discovered Omoku River. Umuorodu must first shoot at Nchaka or Ogudu and follow Ihiukwu at Ogudu.
5.	Umu-Enyike	Nwadei, Nwogbuehi "king" Akpe(females) only	Isiji	Eze awo, Umu-Chukwu oriogba maya eriwo	Ijere (ants) mushroom ona	Egmoka Enyike Chuku Odu-ocha	
6.	Umuekedi (Umueriehi)	Ochi-Agha (General)		Onuotu	Cow Rabit		
7.	Umu-nkaru	Akogu (Loyal Leader)	Onuotu		Aba, Python	Awiya ocha Akpu eze	Umu-Okapre muenya Umuodil'ura ka Ebo gra
8	Umuoyro	Oyro	Onuotu		Aba Iguana Python	Orji Aligu	Oyro came from Utuochi in Aboh. His younger brother was Akogu who settled in Aligu.
9.	Obosi (Umuoba)	Ojoka (hawk)	Onuotu		Python, Ede, Iguana	Ochi-k'-Obosi	

10.	Ihiukwu	Isoma (Brave Leader)	Ogbowu in Obieti	Isoma		Ema-ka-Dike (egbu akwra akwru)	Umu Ogbu-ebiringa. Leaders of Ogudu procession. Isoma, entitled to kill public cows with one stroke. Keepers of records. Contemporary of Agburu. Leaders of Ogudu, introduced echiwa?
11.	Umuebe Umuokoya	Nwa-ogbuehi "King"	Ogbowu, Onuotu		beetle (ebe) mushroom ona	Odu Ocha	
12.	Umuossia	Omodi		Oche akun	Cocoyam, Crayfish, beetle, Okwu egbe	Agbo-eti Ogwe, Utu and Nde-eze	
13.	Umu-Ezeali, (Umu-Okpraeme, Umun-Nga, Umu-Agburu)	Okpraeze (Prince), Umu-agburu greeted Ezeali.	Ogbowu	UmuOgu-niali oku (Priest of the land).	Python	Ihi-ali K'Ogba at Obigwe.	
14.	Umuohali	Ewo (Peace maker),	Akube, Nkpodu	Ijere	Python, Snail, Iguana	Otu Ohali Uzor Oru	Umu-oji-eze eme ogo. Owu otu Ohali may be related to Umu-alinwa: Shrine in Ohali-Elu.

Every *onuobdo* has its own distinct titles which have political, social or economic implications, which must be correctly recounted.[3] You must know the age-grade of the person to be greeted because a member of a younger age-grade should "bow" or commence the greeting ceremony (i.e. *iduisiali*), other things being equal. But other things are seldom equal in Ali-Ogba. Whatever may be a person's age, he will "bow" to every member of his mother's *onuobdo*, except the very young.

A man and his agnatic relatives will "bow" to the agnatic relatives of his wife or wives. A man will "bow" to the wife of an elder member of his own *onuobdo*. All female members of

---

[3] See table showing the distinctive titles and sayings depicting the social and political status of each *onuobdo* as preserved in the *Isiali* ceremony. The political title *"Iyasra"* (or Prime Minister) is obviously copied from the *"Iyase"* of Benin. In certain respects, the political organisation is similar to that of Benin. Onitsha, Aboh and Oguta, with histories of Benin origin, have counterparts resembling the *Iyasra* title, with slight modifications.

an *onuobdo* should "bow" to all male members of the same *onuobdo* irrespective of age, except those from their own immediate extended family. Members of the same age-grade *bow* almost indiscriminately among themselves. These rules vary slightly among the three major clans or groups (Egi, Igburu and Usomini) in Ali-Ogba.

The Usomini version of *Isiali* involves only a fraction of the ceremonies associated with Egi *Isiali*. The latter is cheerfully hedged about with unparalleled ceremonial embellishment and camaraderie. An Ogba "king" or traditional ruler does not respond to *Isiali*. Instead, a visitor praises the "king" with his royal title (e.g. Eze Ogba Nwadei Ogbuehi), bowing or genuflecting slowly. The ruler replies by praising the subject with the traditional title of his *onuobdo* (e.g. *Akogu, Iyasra, Ogbuehi, Adeze,* etc). In this way, the essential features of Ogba political history has been preserved without written records. We may now examine the implications of these titles and the political position of each *onuobdo*.

Landlords (Ezeali) - Umuezeali

The earliest arrivals, the Umuezealis are the recognised traditional "landlords" of Ogba, entitled to all the rights and privileges attached to that position. Umuezealis bear the political title of *Okpraeze* or *Ezeali*. The most important rights appear to have been religious in character. Umuezealis are the priests and custodians of *Ihialikogba* (the "face" of Ali Ogba) located at Obigwe, which contains the *Ohuo* (or symbols of traditional authority) of most of the Ogba *onuobdos*, especially those that came from the southern routes.

To this day, Ogbas observed the *Whekeja* tradition which is a monetary payment made to the Umuezealis before a corpse is buried. That the Umuezealis were the first Ogbas to arrive at the parts of Ali-Ogba which they occupy has never been in doubt. What remains to be established is the identity of those who lived in the Umuezeali areas almost four thousand years before the arrival of the Umuezealis. Archaeological evidence indicates that the Umuagbru (Umuezeali) quarter in Omoku was occupied in

2,500 B.C. The original inhabitants were most probably absorbed, or they may have fled or they may have died out.

"Kingship" Title (Eze-Ogba, Eze-Ohali) - Umuebe, Umuenyike and Umuohali

From the available oral and documentary evidence, the rulership positions of Umuohali and Umuebe require clarification: Ogba tradition describes Umuohali as *Umu Oji eze emeogo* i.e. those who make a gift of kingship or those who give kingship away as a gift. It is narrated that Okoya's mother, an Umuohali princess, obtained kingly clothes from her mother, a widow of the Eze Ohali and gave it secretly to Okoya, her son with Ebe Nwali of Umuebe.There are slight variations in this story but all the versions agree that kingship was conferred on Okoya, a "son" of Ebe Nwali of Umuebe through the gift of an Umuohali kingly cap or kingly clothes or some other form of kingly regalia.

In other words, kingship came to Umuebe through a woman (viz the mother of Okoya) and through the gift or acquisition of regalia. For a strictly patrilineal society, accession to a throne through the female line would appear most irregular and untraditional. Although, Ogbas may pet and pamper their *Nwoyigmo,* he does not *inherit* anything from his *Nwadiali.*

Nwoyigmo receives a present *(Whekanu)*from *Nwadiali* on special occasions, but we have not been told the special occasion or the special act performed by Okoya which warranted such a rare and precious *Whekanu* as kingly regalia. According to some sources, the kingly cap or regalia may in fact have been stolen or acquired by subterfuge from Umuohali, a situation which would automatically vitiate and invalidate the whole transaction in native law and custom.

Furthermore, can the gift of mere clothes confer or transfer rulership status in Ogba Society? The history of conferment of political status in Ogba shows that political positions such as Iyasra, Isoma and Ajie Ikoha were acquired through notable performances in war by the various *onuobdos.* How can an *onuobdo* acquire the highest of all Ogba political positions (that of paramount rulership or kingship) through the doubtful procurement of regalia?

Assuming that kingship could be conferred through the gift of kingly regalia, any king worth his salt would own more than one set of regalia, so that after giving out one set, he would still have other sets which would make him superior to his beneficiary, not vice versa.

According to available oral evidence, Okoya sneaked away from Ikiri and went to Omoku, wearing the royal regalia supposedly given to him by Umuohali. Immediately, the people in Omoku saw him, he was acclaimed king, which appears preposterous. At this time, Omoku was one of the smallest villages within Usomini. So, Okoya was actually encroaching on the territory of the *Eze Ogba Nwadei Ogbuehi* (the head of Usomini) with headquarters in Obrikom. We are informed that Okoya was permitted to live in Usomini by the Nwadei Ogbuehi upon the performance of certain traditional rites. Of course, the Umuebes vehemently deny having performed any such rites; but they fail to explain how else an Igburu immigrant from Ikiri was able to establish himself as king of Omoku within the Usomini area.

The Aboh/Ogba war seems to have occurred a few years after the arrival of Okoya in Omoku where it is said he was acclaimed king. Strangely enough, when the Abohs attacked, instead of retreating to Ikiri or elsewhere, "King" Okoya hid himself in a bunker underground. The Abohs arrived and found Okoya's dog (a bitch) barking near a freshly closed pit. There must have been some ventilation to prevent "His Majesty" from suffocation. The Abohs found Okoya in the pit and promptly decapitated him. What a pity!

The story of Okoya's decapitation is confirmed by all the sources. Because of this tragedy, to this day, a bitch is not allowed to enter Omoku, under pain of instant execution. They say a bitch "betrayed" Okoya. The traditional taboo which is still observed against a bitch in Omoku makes the decapitation story incontrovertible. The fact that this sanction against a bitch did not extend to many Ogba villages outside Omoku seems to confirm that Okoya's jurisdiction did not extend to all Ogba.

The penalty imposed by Ogba tradition against bitches as a specie appears most unfair and unjustified as the poor animal was merely reacting to its natural instincts. It is the royal strategy of hiding in a bunker that Ogbas ought to worry about. Hiding of royalty in a bunker does not appear particularly courageous or ingenious.

Traditional chivalry requires that royalty should not flee from danger. He should be the real leader of his people in peace and in war. A royal personage must be seen to face danger boldly, with spirit and determination; not timorously like a frog hiding in the ground.

If Okoya could not face the enemy, why did he not retreat in dignity to Ikiri from whence he came? We may here recall the circumstances under which he may have obtained the "kinglet regalia" or royal "cap". Apparently, he was afraid of encountering the injured parties viz his elder "brother" or "uncle" Egbru who was entitled to be king under primogeniture and the Umuohalis from whom the regalia were most probably obtained surreptitiously.

Ogba oral historians, it would appear, have left a number of vital questions unanswered in connection with the Umuebe rulership position. Was it a mere co-incidence that the Eze Ogba decapitated by the Abohs was Okoya (a typical Aboh name) in an age when the Abohs were the greatest power on the Niger making constant slave raids into Ali-Ogba? Is it possible that Okoya was actually placed in Omoku by the Abohs as their agent or surrogate and that he failed to live up to expectation giving rise to the attack and decapitation?

What in fact were the reasons for the attack? No oral historian has given us tangible reasons for the Aboh/Ogba war. All we are told is that Abohs usually came to Ali-Ogba and abducted Ogba first sons, i.e. enslavement of Ogbas. If that was the case, then Ogbas should have been the aggrieved party who should have attacked the Aboh offenders; not vice versa. It is significant that according to the oral historians, the Aboh warriors embarked for home immediately after the decapitation without any further destruction or pillage in Ali-Ogba. So, the Abohs may have come to teach their Okoya a lesson, not to fight against Ogbas.

There is certainly more to this decapitation story than meets the eye, which would require further intensive investigation. By their *Isiali* greeting of *Nwogbuehi*, it would appear that, whatever may have been the case, Ogbas have come to accept the Umuebe traditional rulership status. What is puzzling and incomprehensible is that it should be made to take precedence over the rulership status of Umuenyike (Nwadei) and Umuohali which have undisputed Ogba pedigree. A recent publication by Uche Dappa and Azu Idu "authorised by Chukwumela Obi" states (p.44):

> The achievements of the Oba were so majestic that Chief M.K.O. Abiola, at a conference on Apartheid in 1982, could not help calling him your Majesty. Hence the adoption of the title Royal Majesty.

We find it utterly absurd to say the least, that a joke by an honorary Yoruba Chief should be taken to mean conferment of a superior title on an Ogba traditional ruler. After the decapitation of Okoya, the Umuebe rulership position remained dormant for a long time. A later Umuebe ruler (Akwokwu) stated in evidence in the provincial court in 1928 that he could think of only "Olowu" being crowned an Umuebe "Eze Ogba" after the decapitation of Okoya. A new title "Oba of Oba (Ogba)" was introduced by Frank Akwokwu Dickay (sic). He himself a former court clerk, who was "crowned" in Omoku in 1928 introduced the title "Oba" as a rulership nomenclature in Ali-Ogba. It is noteworthy that none of the "kings" in the whole area east and south of Benin used the title "Oba". In Yoruba areas, the title "Oba" is commonly used to describe royalty. The title is obviously a Yoruba word which reached Benin from Ile-Ife through the Oraminyan connection. It may be that Akwokwu was trying to imitate the Yorubas by borrowing their word "Oba". If so, he did not succeed in borrowing correctly. As far as is known, the Yorubas have *Olowo* of *Owo* or *Olubadan* of *Ibadan* etc (notice the rhyming suffix), followed by "Oba XYZ" (name of a particular ruler). Even if they had a place called "Oba", I doubt if they would accept the tautological form "Oba" of "Oba" (or Ogba) as a title! South and east of Benin, "Kings" bear the title "Eze" or "Obi" (diminutive of Oba?) or Igwe. In "royal" *onuobdos*, it often happens that persons whose "re-incarnators" were called "Obi or "Eze" or "Igwe" are given such titles as their own names. This is obviously due to the traditional Ogba belief in reincarnation. Due to this belief, the children born within an extended family are given the names of their late ancestors. So many examples of the name "Obi" occur in the Umuebe *Onuobdo* (e.g. Obi nwa Chukwuma, Obi Nwigwe, Obi Ajie, Wokoma Silk Obi and Chukwumela Obi) that it would not be unreasonable to suppose that that *onuobdo's* "royal" title was "Obi".

It may be observed that the name Chukwumela which sounds Ogba (but was never used as a name by Ogbas) may have been deliberately coined in quest of authenticity and legitimacy. Similarly, the name "Eze" occurs so frequently in the Umuenyike *Onuobdo* (e.g. Eze Nwonyukwu, Isoma Eze, Oriogu Eze, Eze Ejeukwu, Eze Ocha, Eze Wudu) that to conclude that they enjoyed the "royal" title "Eze" would not be out of place. The Umuohalis (with the Ezeohali kingship) have the name "Igwe" (as in Igwe Olowu and Moses Igwe, the present Eze-Ohali) which is a recognised kingship title in many areas south and south-east of Benin.

After visiting and discussing with the members of all Ogba villages in 1930, Mr. W.F.H. Newington (Assistant District Officer) wrote in his Intelligence Report[4]:

> This title of Eze-Ogba [5] is something quite apart from Eze-ala... Omoku elected an Eze Ogba just before the above mentioned war (Aboh War) but apart from it and Obrikom a kindred in the same group none of the other kindreds have elected one... The Egis do not worry about this title,and they did not take part in the Aboh War. The Igburus in some cases assisted in the Aboh War, but they do not elect Eze-Ogbas in their

---
[4] W.F.H. Newington's Report written in 1930 is in the Public Library, Enugu.
[5] It is noteworthy that up to this stage, no mention is made of "Oba of Ogba" which was used subsequently by Akwokwu Dickav.

different kindreds. The remainder of the Usomini group all of whom assisted in the Aboh War do not recognise the Eze-Ogba of Omoku as their Eze-Ogba. From this it can be seen that Omoku is the only kindred to take this matter seriously, <u>and Obrikom sometimes elect one if they possess a man capable of filling the office...</u> (my underlining).

It is quite clear from Mr.Newington's account that the "Eze-Ogba" system was still comparatively new in Omoku, but it was no doubt an ancient practice in Ogba. The system certainly existed in Obrikom, as was confirmed by the evidence given to Mr. Newington. The Umuenyikes (i.e. the Nwadei *Onuobdos*) were and are the indisputable Usomini kingship groups with headquarters in Obrikom. But, Mr. Newington refers to Obrikom as a "kindred", which is incorrect.

Obi nwa Chukwuma versus Akwokwu Dike

In 1935, Mr. D.P. Stanfield[6] (Assistant District Officer), after a similar investigation and visit to all Ogba villages wrote, *inter alia*, in his own Intelligence Report submitted that year,:

> There is no doubt that in a village or quarter the Eze-ala is the nominal head. He is the priest of *Ala*, and undoubtedly, whatever the practice now, he was in the past invariably the senior of the senior family. In accordance with Ogba practice *Ala*, the land, could only be propitiated by the original owner of the land, and only that man's direct successors could inherit this office and privilege... The Eze-Ogba system is alleged to be superimposed on this basic "Eze-ala" system. The Ezeoba is supposed to be a king, who with his chosen councillors, over-rides quarter and village councils. In the Aboh clan such a system really does exist, though the title "Ezeoba" is unknown.[7] The Councillors (there are scores of them) have recognised titles some of which definitely derive from Benin. At Omoku similar titles are met with... There is no doubt that the title "Ezeoba" is an ancient one... In December 1928 Obi Chukwuma of Omoku brought the following suit in the Provincial Court against Akwokwu Dike (when the latter was "crowned".) "Declaration to Plaintiff's title of Ezeoba, an injunction to restrain Defendant from further claims to the title of Ezeoba..." The case was tried with great care, thirty pages of evidence being taken... All the witnesses seem to have come from Omoku, so that the opinion of the rest of the clan cannot be gauged, but there was no question at that time

---

[6] Stanfield's Report is in the public library at Enugu.
[7] The Abohs are not Ogbas, and could not therefore have Ezeogbas (Ezeobas) or "king of Ogbas". Obviously Mr. Stanfield did not have a thorough understanding of the Ogba or Aboh Dialect.

but that the title was recognised. Several conflicting accounts were given as to the origin of the title. In his evidence the Defendant stated... Okoya... (and)... Olowu... were the only two people I heard were really crowned; others were in name only... Warrant Chiefs were made from different places and the title lost its power... The finding is as follows, The Court Finds that the evidence on either side is so conflicting and vague that it is impossible to establish the claim. Case dismissed.

In a petition dated 5th March, 1935, addressed to the Resident, Owerri Province, Port Harcourt, "F.A. Dickay" (sic) accused the A.D.O. Mr. Stanfield of:

> Instigating or inciting the Omoku people and villagers (Ogba) to rebel against the Natural Ruler or F.A. Dickay "Eze-Ogba" alias Native King, by announcing publicly that the Oba-Ezeogba is not recognised by Government and will never be.

Mr. Stanfield continues (and repeats some points previously made by Newington):

> The Egis do not worry about this title... The Igbrus do not elect Ezeogbas in their different kindreds. The remainder of Osomini (sic) group... do not recognise the Ezeogba of Omoku.

In forwarding Mr. Stanfield's report to the Chief Secretary to the government, Mr. Kelly, the Secretary Southern Provinces stated *inter alia:*

> I am to add that in His Honour's (i.e. the Chief Commissioner's) opinion, Mr. Stanfield has made his enquiries with care and diligence and has written an interesting report.

Akwokwu Dike carried on as a traditional ruler unrecognised by government after the case brought against him by Obi nwa Chukwuma was dismissed. He was a bold and ambitious ruler. Apart from expanding his domain to Igburu, he founded the Seventh Day Native Church of God (SDNCG) in which he made himself Supreme Bishop. His rulership was fairly peaceful and he did not engage much in litigation or power tussle, except the celebrated case with Obi nwa Chukwuma in which he was the defendant. Akwokwu Dike was succeeded by Matthew Onwularu, the son of Onwularu the Younger, the son of Onwularu the elder, the son of Eluozo, the first son of Okoya. Matthew Onwularu's succession was disputed by Archibald, the son of Akwokwu Dike and after his death, by Ichokwu. Harassed by these disputes, Matthew Onwularu, a devout

Frank Dickay Akwokwu's House (First Oba of Ogbas)

Christian and man of few words and strong principles, abdicated the throne after seven years and concentrated on his religion.

Silk Nwokoma Obi, the son of Obi, the son of Chukwuma, the second "son" of Okoya, became "Oba" after Matthew Onwularu. He maintained very cordial relationship with Matthew Onwularu and indeed with practically the whole Ogba population. Silk died prematurely in 1970 after the Nigerian Civil War. The same year, his nephew (Chukwuemeka Obi, now Chukwumela Obi) the son of Silk's brother, Obuoha, was installed. Chukwuemela Obi's rulership started well initially, but soon it was alleged that he instigated Omoku Youths to destroy the house and properties of the Eze Ohali (Eze Moses Igwe) who retreated to his ancestral village, Amah. A criminal charge was brought against Chukwumela Obi. After a series of adjournments, the then Rivers Attorney-General, Chief C.D Orike, a son of Omoku, entered a *nolle prosequi* and the matter was discontinued.

The pamphlet entitled *His Royal Majesty* authorised by Chukwumela Obi and published by Uche Dappa and Azu P. Idu (1994) states that :

> notable among the Obas of Ogbaland are their Royal Highness Okoya Nwebe, Orkue Nwaogeri, Eleberi Nwaanesi, Ekne Nwaeze (aka Obi Nwaigwe), Nwaiwenya, Obi Ajie Wokoma, Silk Obi 1, and His Royal Majesty (Dr.) Chukumela Nnam Obi II.

It may be noted that this dynasty begins with Okoya, the decapitated Eze Ogba who was never called "Oba" (P.13). The name of Akwokwu Dike who introduced the title "Oba" into Ogba history has been carefully omitted. The same publication goes on to state that:

> The Oba of Ogbaland is a hereditary stool of the Royal family of Umu-Okoya (Umu-Eze Ogba) of Umuebe Community of Ogbaland; thus excluding the Egbru (i.e. Dike) branch of Umuebe which produced Akwokwu Dike, which is of course a travesty of history.

Umuohali oral historians (notably the Eze Ohali, Moses Igwe) recall the rulership of the first Eze Ohali (whose name was

Ohali) between 1400AD and 1500AD, claiming that his domain extended to the whole of Ali-Ogba prior to the Okoya tragedy. Ohali was succeeded by Akpudinkwu, who was succeeded by Ohaokpra, who was succeeded by Okaraeseoma, who was challenged by Egbelegbe Egi, "a warlike man who settled near Amah bush and indulged in killing the people of Ogba land."

A clear pattern of traditional rulership seems to have emerged in which the Umuohalis had jurisdiction over Egi territory, the Umuebes over Igbru territory and the Umuenyikes (Nwadeis) over Usomini territory. It seems eminently rational to accept that the three separate clans, with three distinct dialects and different traditional occupations and currencies should also have three leading traditional rulers, having regard to the general picture painted by the oral historians and the facts of archaeological and documentary evidence. Justice, fairplay and respect for historical truth demand that these three traditional rulerships be accorded equal status by the government and the Ogba community.

We may now examine more closely the position of the *Eze Ogba Nwadei Ogbuehi* rulership *onuobdo* with jurisdiction over Usomini group of towns and villages. The traditional headquarters of Usomini, Obrikom, is the highest populated town in Ogba, except Omoku. Practically half of Obrikom comprises the Umuenyike (Umudei) *Onuobdo*. The name "Enyike" (strong elephant) is obviously a nick-name as the founding ancestor was Ikpulada, the father of Yudara. The Umuenyikes are the only *onuobdo* in Ogba having the same political title "Nwa Ogbuehi" as the Umuebes. This title which denotes "kingship" status is preserved in the *Isiali* daily greeting. In addition, the Umuenyikes are also called "Nwadei in the *Isiali* greeting, a title by which they are connected with the Umudei (plural of Nwadei) "kingship" families in Onitsha, Aboh, Oguta and elsewhere. In Ekpeye, the Umuenyike are known as Isiokloko, which is the family (or *Onuobdo*) of the present Eze Ekpeye Logbo.

The Usomini "king" was known as "Eze-Ogba". The use of the identical title, Eze-Ogba, by Umuenyike and Umuebe must have become confusing in later days when the three practically independent groups met together in the new group "capital" Omoku, which is geographically within the Usomini area. Prior to that date, each of the three sub-groups must have regarded itself as "Ogba", to the exclusion of everyone else. Till this day, the Egis have a festival known as *"Egwu Ogba"*, but it takes place only within the Egi group. Therefore, the use of the word "Ogba" loosely in a descriptive sense appears to have been customary. Today, "chiefs" in Ali-Ogba call themselves by their chieftaincy titles followed by the suffix "of Ogba".eg. "Eze Ohuakia of Ogba". Grammatically, there is little or no difference between Eze Ogba and Eze "of Ogba". In any case, any title which requires the English preposition "of" to complete its meaning cannot be regarded as traditional because the British had not come to Ali-Ogba when our original traditional rulership titles were coined.

The rulership position of Umuenyike in Obrikom was confirmed by Newington and Stanfield in their Intelligence Reports cited above. Yudara, the leading ancestor of Umuenyike quickly established himself as a powerful ruler, because of the traditional position of the *nwa dei onuobdo*. He was particularly noted for his bravery and his victories in an age when evident might was right and rulership the price of strength and power. Yudara was nick-named *Enyike* (i.e. strong elephant) because of his power, and his *onuobdo* members were subsequently known as *Umu-enyike* (or sons of the strong elephant). Enyike's fighting spirit and his undaunted courage animated the whole *onuobdo* and earned them the praise name of *enyike ndogu* or *enyike* the warriors.

The position of Obrikom, their "capital" on high ground on the eastern bank of the Ebiam Creek which flows into the Orashi River ensured protection against water-borne attack from the open Orashi River. Secondly, the Orashi (and the Sombreiro flowing near it immediately to the east of Obrikom) provided an easy gateway to the Oru territory, the centre of the slave trade, which dominated economic life in the early days. Thirdly, the Onita Creek, flowing from the Niger and meeting the Orashi River about two miles south-west of Obrikom, provided the Enyike kingship group with a direct and vital connection with Aboh at a time when the Obi of Aboh was regarded as "king of the Ibos": (In his letter[8] to Crowther dated 22nd March, 1879 (C.M.S. CA3/04) John Withford laments,

> A long time ago (my underlining) the Abohs were regarded as the most powerful amongst their neighbours both for riches and strength, and as such were feared by all: but now such places as Onitsha and Alinso - once their slave grounds are lifting up their heads against them.

The factors which commended Obrikom as the best site for establishment of the capital of the Usomini group also contributed a century later towards the successful establishment of Omoku (only three miles due south of Obrikom and sheltered from the same Orashi River by the Omoku Creek) as the capital of all Ogba.

The Enyikes took appropriate traditional measures to make Obrikom secure. To the north, they consecrated a shrine known as *"egmo ka enyike"* [9] and invoked it to stop anyone pursuing them. *"Egmo"* means that which prevents or saves. *"Egmo ka enyike"* is therefore "saviour or protector of the enyikes". The *"Egmo"* was installed at a point through which all comers would have to pass. It was a dome-like structure based on two trees planted on opposite sides of the main access road and joined together with a crossbar at the top. Men of goodwill passed beneath unharmed; but evil men, it was believed, attempted to pass at their peril!

---

[8] Quoted in *A History of the Igbo People* by Elizabeth Isichei, Macmillan London 1976 (p.59).
[9] A well-known fetish object still remembered by the older generation of Ogbas today.

During this period, the Enyikes grew steadily in power and fame. No stranger or visitor to Ali-Ogba was left in any doubt as to where the political power lay. When the Aros came in the 17th Century, they recognised the kingship authority of the Umuenyike *Onuobdos* immediately and reached agreement with them on ways of mutual co-operation. The Aros called themselves "sons of God" *(Umuchukwu)* and were accepted everywhere as such.

Instead of appointing "Ambassadors" to Ali-Ogba, as they did in some neighbouring areas, the Aros appointed the Nwadei or Enyike people of Ogba as their agents[10] and partners and admitted them to the sacred title of "sons of God". In Ali-Ogba, the Enyikes became *"Umuchukwu oriogba ma yeriwo"* (i.e. sons of god which eat Ogbas except themselves) and acquired the sole right of conducting willing Ogbas and other interested neighbouring people to consult the Long Juju Oracle of Arochukwu.

Beginning from Yudara (alias Enyike), each Nwadei Ogbuehi handed over to his successor the following traditional symbols of kingship which have been preserved to this day: Staff of Office *(Akwruigwe)*, Elephant Tusk *(Odu)*, Bell *(Ukela)*, Traditional Symbol *(Ohuo)*.

When Enyike died, Eze Ogba Wudu was installed. Although he was not quite a terror like Enyike, he was noted for his courage, initiative and ability to influence people. In the early days when the different exogamous *onuobdos* occupied isolated spots in Ali-Ogba, it was necessary to control dowry payment and encourage inter-marriage among the *onuobdos*. Eze Wudu played a vital role in establishing what was known as *"Iwu-Ahiorie"* by which the maximum dowry was fixed at 50,000 cowries (equivalent of £25.00 or N50.00) throughout the

---

[10] Aro sources confirm that, in special circumstances, Aros appointed outstanding rulership groups as their agents or representatives. The appointment of Umuenyike to this position is upheld by many local oral historians and evidenced by the relevant Umuenyike praise names.

Usomini and Igburu areas. In the Egi area, an equivalent of that amount in manilla (which was the local currency in the Egi area) applied. As the name indicates, *Iwu Ahiorie* was located in a forest in *Ahiorie* square of present day Omoku, which was a spot most central for Ogbas. *Iwu Ahiorie* took the form of a terrible shrine to which all Ogbas paid obeisance until it was destroyed in 1916 in the wake of the evangelical activities known to history as the "Garrick Movement"[11]

Eze Odua, who succeeded Wudu was also a warrior king almost rivalling Enyike in bravery and courage. During his rule, one of the battles against Aboh occurred and he led the Enyikes to victory on all fronts. This particular battle which was fought early in the 15th Century should not be confused with the battle of early 19th century in which Okoya was beheaded due to betrayal by his bitch.

When Odua died, he was succeeded by Eze-Ocha. The latter was not a very warlike man like his predecessors but he possessed a charm and personality which made people come to him and do his will. His name translated as "white king" describes his person and his rule. In his time, there was general peace and friendship and through his charisma the villages of Obrikom and Egbeku which were a short distance apart merged together into one. The new Usomini capital was known either as Obrikom or Egbeku and has remained so to this day. In the course of time, some settlers from Odumelu, Obuloko, Ebocha and Ogu villages took up residence in the new capital to give Obrikom the highest population in Ali-Ogba at the time. (In 1935, Obrikom population was 1,600 which was the highest in Ali-Ogba after Omoku with a population of 6,200 [12]. Obrikom population of over 5,000 in 1963 was still the highest among Ogba communities except Omoku).

---

[11] See p.86 below for further discussion of the Garrick Movement.
[12] Intelligence Report by Mr. D.P. Stanfield, A.D.O. (p.6).

Isoma Eze who succeeded Eze Ocha carried his predecessor's peaceful traditions one step further. He prepared a charm known as *Odu-Ocha* (white elephant tusk) in order to protect Enyikes from war and to preserve peace. For *Odu-Ocha* to remain effective, it was believed that Enyikes must refrain from mushroom and *ona*. To this day, these food items are still forbidden in pagan Enyike homes.

When Odu Ellah succeeded Isoma Eze, his chief concern was the preservation of the dignity of traditional rulership. Before the end of his rule no commoner was permitted to appear in scarlet clothes on any occasion. Indeed, it became accepted that no ordinary citizen could dress in "kingly clothes" except in times of festivity. People born into other *onuobdos* by Enyike daughters were granted the privilege of wearing these special clothes on all occasions, provided they covered only one arm. Any breach of this custom was punished instantly by Enyikes by tearing the offending clothes forcibly from the back of the offender. The Enyikes became known as *"Umu-eze-awo"* (sons of the king of clothes) in addition to their other praise names and traditional titles[13]. The excessive powers of the Enyikes compared favourably with those exercised by their counterparts elsewhere in that unfortunate age when might was right.

Eze Ejeuku who succeeded Odu Ellah, suddenly moved to Obor to stay. Questioned why he should leave the rulership headquarters at Obrikom for the small village of Obor, he claimed that he merely went to farm whereas, in fact, he had observed the trend of approaching colonialism (from the activities of white men on the coast and explorers on the Niger) and felt that it was unsafe for royalty to remain exposed in the strategic centre of Obrikom.

---

13 There is no suggestion here that other Ogbas did not "dress up" in accordance with the prevailing standards. See the appropriate section in Chapter 4 for details.

Eze Ejeuku was succeeded by Eze Onyukwu who was soon killed through poisoning by his own relatives who had an eye on the kingship stool. He died in the *Ogboru* of the Umunwudu branch of the Umuenyike *Onuobdo* just across the Orashi River opposite Obrikom. In desperation, his sons, led by their eldest brother, Oriogu Eze, set fire to the whole *Ogboru* and burnt it down completely[14]. Although no soul was lost, the incident produced a shattering effect on the Umunwudu branch of the Enyike *Onuobdo*. Oriogu Eze and his brothers fled to their friends Oguezi, Ajuku and Awo of Ndoni (an Aboh town) who received them well and allocated land and fishing grounds to them at Utuku and Ogbo, roughly two miles from Ndoni on the Eastern bank of the Niger. Oriogu and his brothers built roads in these areas and made them their *Ogboru*, and they have remained so till this day. Here Oriogu met Ekoji the son of Odu, who was the son of Eke of Ikaka, a neighbouring *Ogboru*. The Ekojis were members of Umuebe *Onuobdo* who were already settled in Omoku. Oriogu's son (Ellah) eventually married Adah Owre, a daughter of Ekoji.

It is significant to note here that a grandson of Odu *nwa* Eke, Frank Akwokwu Dike (or Dickay) (i.e. a third cousin of Ada nwa Owre) was destined to became the first "Oba" of Ogba. It is also significant to note that the marriage of Ada nwa Owre and Ellah would have been impossible, if the Umuenyike's and Umuebes were at all related as is sometimes incorrectly claimed by the latter. The marriage relationship eventually drew Oriogu and his family towards their in-laws who were already resident in Omoku as well as in Ikaka *Ogboru* rather than to Obrikom, where the enmity created by the murder of Eze Onyuku and the arson which followed it had not been forgotten.

Oriogu and his followers consequently came to Omoku in the company of their in-laws, the Odu *nwa* Ekes of Umuebe. Omoku had already become a capital to which all Ogbas flocked.

---

[14] The ruins can still be seen.

John Wokocha Ellah - *12th Eze Ogba Nwadei Ogbuehi (Jan., 1900 - March, 1993).*

However, there was pressure from Obrikom for Oriogu's return as the different sides of the Umunwudu branch of the Enyike *Onuobdo* there had begun to make peace. On the return of Oriogu Eze to Obrikom, he was made the *Eze Ogba Nwadei Ogbuehi*, especially due to his "travels" and experience in Aboh territory which was regarded as the centre of civilization. The children of Oriogu viz: Ellah and Eluozo remained in Omoku with their close relatives - the Oseres, the Oduas and the Ogus (all descendants of Eze Nwonyukwu).

After Oriogu Eze's death, no one succeeded him immediately. The colonial authorities were then busily engaged in putting down the slave trade and the traditional rulers who had supported it. The most active "kings" had to lie low. In particular, the *Umuchukwu oriogba maya eriwo* (i.e. the

Umuenyikes or Umudeis) had to lie very low when the *chukwu* which they "shared" with the Aros was destroyed by the colonial authorities in 1902. In 1931, Ellah Oriogu became a "low key" Nwadei Ogbuehi. He made it quite clear that he did not have to return to Obrikom since Omoku was within the Usomini area. He pointed out that other kingship stools traditionally based in Ikiri and Ohalielu had been "transferred" to the new Ali-Ogba Capital, Omoku, which is part of Usomini.

Ellah Oriogu died in 1954 and his son John Wokocha Ellah occupied the Nwadei stool from 1959. Following the chieftaincy enquiries by the Rivers State Government in 1975 and 1976, he was recognised in his position in regard to the Usomini area of Ogba along with two other "kings" of Ali-Ogba. Eze Ogba Nwadei Ogbuehi, Chief John Wokocha Ellah, a Christian (Catholic) helped in the establishment of schools, colleges and a hospital in Ali-Ogba.

Iyasra (Prime Minister) - Umuogidi and Umuagbda

The position of *Iyasra* (Prime Minister) which ranked next to the "king" was apparently derived from the Benin *Iyase* (*Iyasra* in Oguta, Aboh and Onitsha). "*Iyasra* acts in the absence of the king". *Iyasra* does not remove his cap when greeting the king"[15] "*Iyasra* sits next to the king in the palace".

Umuogidi and Umuagbda *Onuobdos* are the *Iyasra Onuobdos,* a title which is traditionally preserved for them in the daily *isiali* salutation. Nweze, the father of Agbda was the brother of Ogidi but it is not clear whether it is this particular Ogidi that was the ancestor of Umuogidi.

Umuogidi earned their high *Iyasra* position because of their victories against the Abohs and their heroic exploits across the rivers and lakes. *Ogidi-oji-madu-esi-eje; eje-rima-madu-wre-azu-kwugwo*[16] Their choice of the leopard as their totem animal must have instilled fear into their enemies and enhanced their

---

[15] As narrated by Chief Ebenezer Osima, the *Iyasra* of Umuogidi and Johnson Ogidi of Umuogidi, on 14th March 1980.

[16] The Ogidis use human beings to create a dam; the dam "eats" the human beings and pays back with fish.

prestige among their friends, under the "watchful eyes" of their terrible *Odu-ka-Ogidi* shrine.

Nweze, the ancestor of Umuagbda was reputed for stubbornness and courage by his refusal to surrender his son to Aboh slave raiders. Eventually Umuagbdas made a name when they defeated Aboh slave raiders in a battle on the Sombreiro River. Whether this victory was due to the activity of real or "human" crocodiles remains to be proved beyond doubt. After this victory, Umuagbda became *Umu-omela ekiri!*[17] To cap their achievements, Umuagbda learnt blacksmithery and introduced iron works to Ali-Ogba. They became *Agbda-lu-uzu*.[18] All these achievements combined to gain for Umuagbda the high position of *Iyasra*.

Isoma and *"Igbazu-keze"* - Ihiukwu and Umuorodu

The Ihiukwu *Onuobdo* were among the early emigrants from Obigwe to Omoku. The story is that a few years after the Ihiukwus (followers of Ebelechi) had settled down in Obrikom, the Aboh-Ogba war occurred. Naturally, the brave Ihiukwu people were called upon to produce a "War canoe". They quickly produced a magnificent war canoe which was placed under the command of Isoma, one of the sons of Ebelechi. Ebelechi's other sons were Dike and Okiriekwota.

Isoma had, among the warriors in his war canoe, a brave young man named Osoh, one of his nephews (or *nwoyigmos*). At a critical stage in the war, Osoh was the first to shoot down a warrior in an Aboh canoe. Isoma boarded the Aboh canoe and cut off the victim's head as well as his seat *(nga)*, thereby earning for Ihiukwu the praise name, *Umu-Ogbu-ebri-nga*[19] which is still current today. The sword believed to have been used by Isoma has been preserved to this day.

Subsequently, credit for the gallant act was disputed between Isoma (of Ihiukwu) and Osoh (of Umuorodu) and it was wisely decided by the elders that credit for any act done from a war

---

17 Sons of those whose strength lies in eddies.
18 Agbda the blacksmith.
19 Those who kill and cut off the seat.

canoe should first go to the Commander of the war canoe. Consequently, Ihiukwus were given a greater honour than Umuorodus for the gallantry of Isoma and Osoh. In the *Ogudu* (or big *Okgu)* ceremony, the lead is always taken by Ihiukwu, followed by Umuorodu and others. When a cow is to be killed in a public ceremony, it is the descendants of Isoma (i.e. Ihiukwu) who are entitled to cut off its head as they had cut off the enemy's head in the Aboh war.

On account of his gallantry, Isoma (or Ihiukwu) was given a special pre-eminent position in the traditional cabinet, next in rank to *Iyasra*. Cases were sent to him for hearing. Under Isoma's general guidance, the oldest member of Ihiukwu *Onuobdo* was recognised as "the keeper of festival records" for all "Ogba". He divided the year into sections according to custom and declared when Ogba festivals such as *Egwuji - onube, ebiam* or *nchaka* should begin and end. No other authority was permitted to interfere with or alter the dates declared for each festival.

On their part, Umuorodus confirm they did not produce a war canoe and that Osoh (an Umuorodu son) had shot an Aboh warrior while he was fighting as a member of Isoma's war canoe. But there is some conflict in regard to the issue of cutting off the Aboh warrior's head which Umuorodu and Ihiukwu have each claimed for Osoh and Isoma respectively. Since Ihiukwu are satisfied with the title *Umu-Ogbu-ebri-nga*[20] while Umuorodu answer *Umuogbu-ebrisi*[21] the Umuorodu claim appears more genuine.

Today, in the *Nchaka* or *Ogudu* celebration, Umuorodu must fire the first shot (in commemoration of Osoh's shot) before anyone else. The Ihiukwu have a right to lead every *Ogudu* procession in Omoku, followed by Umuorodu and others in a traditional order of precedence. Traditionally, Ogba "kings" do not join in *Ogudu* or *Nchaka* procession. Umuorodu bear the political title *Igbazu-ke-eze*[22] or chief adviser to the king.

---

[20] Those who kill and cut off the seat.
[21] Those who kill and cut off the head.
[22] Chief adviser to the king.

Owerre (Guard, Commander) - Umueke

Eke, the ancestor of Umueke, was the junior brother of Orodu, the ancestor of Umuorodu. As early arrivals in Ali-Ogba, Umueke occupy the powerful position of "*Owerre*" [23] in the Court of the Eze-Ogba. According to V. Osi, S. Okroma and T. Ezegbrika,[24] "Every gift intended for Eze-Ogba must be inspected by the "Owerre". When Eze-Ogba wants a new wife, it is the *Owerre* that must select one for him and he dare not reject the *Owerre's* choice. No dowry is paid on the wife of the Eze-Ogba. The *Owerre* is the only Chief that has automatic right to enter the Royal bedroom. He alone has the right also of entering the Royal kitchen to inspect whatever the Eze-Ogba may eat. At any time of day or night, when the *Owerre* knocks at the Royal doors, they must be opened for him to enter. When the Eze-Ogba sits in Council, the *Owerre* sits beside him".

The rights and privileges of the *Owerre* appear to me to be somewhat exaggerated. There is no doubt that as a superior Guard or Commander, he had considerable power and influence at Court or in the royal palace, but it is unbelievable that the Eze-Ogba could not reject a wife selected for him by the *Owerre* or that the *Owerre* was entitled to enter the Royal kitchen or the Royal bedroom at any time of day or night! Such privileges would reduce the Eze-Ogba to the state of a prisoner or servant of the *Owerre*, rather than vice-versa.

Eke served creditably as the *Owerre* until his death when Osu Nwa Igwe became the next *Owerre*. The latter was a strong and brave man whose efforts could be compared to those of Eke. He was particularly good at settling disputes -he believed that a dispute should be justly settled so that the parties may not resort to *erisi?*[25] Osu Nwa Igwe had only one wife who gave birth to three sons: Osoh, Okroma and Okirie-Ukwu. However, at his death, he was succeeded as *Owerre* by Osi, not by one of his

---

[23] Guard Commander.
[24] V.Osi, S. Okroma and T. Ezegbrika, were interviewed in Omoku on 21st and 24th November 1979.
[25] Fetish or juju.

sons, as the title is hereditary within the *onuobdo* but not within an individual family in the *onuobdo*.

Osi became the *Owerre* at an advanced age - some said he was almost nearing the grave; but nevertheless he was not a weak *Owerre*. He declared a number of inter-*onuobdo* "wars" in which he performed creditably. He married up to four wives and had many children.

When Osi died, he was succeeded by Isidor. At that time, the influence of modern civilisation had begun to be felt, so Isidor did not declare inter-*onuobdo* wars, but loved peace and harmony. He had one wife, Awayu, and two children. He died from natural causes during the Biafran War.

The present *Owerre*, Victor Eke Osi, succeeded Isidor in 1970. He believes in peaceful relationship and a well-ordered family life. He also believes in the maintenance of the customs and traditions of the Umueke *Onuobdo*. In *Isiali*, members of the Umueke *Onuobdo* are greeted *Nwa-eze-ngwo* (i.e. adepts at preparing fish dishes) in recognition of their discovery of many Creeks and Rivers and because of their unsurpassed fishing talents.

Ojoka (Hawk) - (Obosi *Onuobdo*)

This title is enjoyed by the Obosi *Onuobdo*. The title was earned when they sighted the Aboh war-canoe and warned other *onuobdos* of the impending danger. They also had the distinction of killing an Aboh war leader, hence the terrible title that depicts courage and determination against fearful odds.

Onocha, a son of Obosi, had migrated from Obigwe to Omoku at the earliest period and settled near the Omoku River water-front to the north. This gave him or his descendants the privilege of being the first to sight the Aboh war canoe. As has been narrated before, on an earlier expedition on the Omoku River, Onocha had encountered Eke, the ancestor of Umueke, who had challenged Onocha's right to fish in the river. The elders heard the case and found that Eke of Umueke *Onuobdo* and Onocha of Obosi had discovered the creek independently. They decided therefore that each should have a right to fish in the --

Omoku Creek, and that each should use a different fishing equipment. To this day, Obosis have the sole right to use the *enuma ogudu*[26] for fishing in the Omoku Creek while Umuekes have the exclusive right to use the *eri ogbasi*.[27]

Ochioha (Leader of all) - (Umuekedi, Umuodogwu Onuobdos)

The Umuekedi ancestors discovered many lands on the west bank of the Orashi River opposite Kreigani. At that time, the Abohs were very active slave raiders in this area. Umuekedi became inevitably involved in many battles against the Abohs. Two Umuekedi and Umuodogwu warriors deserve special mention.They are known to history by their praise names. The Umuekedi warrior was called *Nwahurogwu ju iri*[28] while the Umuodogwu warrior was named *Isikraka wakude atu*."[29] Both warriors were supposed to have relied on a charm called *epripa*, which had the effect of deflecting any weapon aimed at them so that it would injure someone else on the side of the opponent! Thus Umuekedi won so many victories that they were awarded the title *Ochioha* (Leader of all).

A son of Ekedi (Uchenwechi of Ikiri) introduced two special societies to Omoku: *Ukuali* (land society) and *Ukuprimam* (silent society). *Ukuali* was supposed to be responsible for passing judgment in criminal and civil matters whereas *Ukuprimam* was an "action" society which undertook to carry out the decision of *Ukuali* - Persons disobeying *Ukuprimam* were sometimes beaten to death "silently". It may be observed that the two societies do not appear to have had any legitimate traditional standing.

Prominent Umuekedi leaders (Okiye Ali)[30] were Onyige nwa Onyeowu, who was succeeded by Onyije nwa Onyije,who was succeeded by Nwata nwa Ochu, who was succeeded by

---

26 Fishing screen.
27 Rectangular fishing net.
28 The one who saw war and refused food.
29 The tough head that challenges the buffalo.
30 Head of the land.

Ekuku nwa Ozuroke,who was succeeded by Elemchukwu nwa Onyige, who was succeeded by David nwa Onyige.

Ajie - ike - Oha (Uriem, Umuimegi (alias Umuolota) and Umuokrocha *Onuobdos*)

Umuimegi and Umuolota are all members of the larger Uriem *Onuobdo*. When Uriems had settled in Obigwe, the tragedy occurred in which Eyio killed his wife because she ate the food that he himself had prepared. *Ito-Abo-Ohuo* or dissolution of the unity shrine which bound all Uriems together resulted and Uriems were separated into Umuolota, Okposi-Obodo, Uriem - Ahia - Orie and others.

During an Aboh - Ogba war, a seven-foot tall, brave and fearless *Okparionyohia*[31] a son of Uriem *Onuobdo* (from Umuokrocha branch?) challenged the Abohs and won several victories against them. He was a huge, hairy, terror-striking man with a frightful, cracked voice. When the Aboh war-canoes were sighted, he beat his loud gong and urged the people to stand firm and fight the enemy. He succeeded in rallying many lesser warriors together, a feat which helped much in destroying the Aboh invaders. At the end of the "war", Uriem (with Umuimegi and Umuokrocha) were given the title *Ajie-Ike-Oha* [32] (or Commander) - which they enjoy to this day.

Akogu (Loyal Leader) - Umunkaru

During the "Aboh - Ogba war [33], each *onuobdo* had a specific assignment. Briefly, the story is that Aboh warriors invaded Ali-Ogba via Onita Creek and the Omoku River. Everyone fled from Omoku on the approach of the Abohs except the Umuebe traditional ruler who had become an Eze Ogba in Omoku. He hid himself in a bunker underground but was betrayed to the Abohs by a bitch which kept barking near his hiding place. On suspicion, the Abohs excavated the site and found and beheaded

---

[31] Warrior at large.
[32] Ajie, who has the strength of a multitude.
[33] This "war" was most probably the best remembered one among many such "wars" between the two groups.

the ruler. Having done this, the Abohs assumed they had won complete victory. So, guarding their "trophy" jealously, they embarked for home.

But on their way out through the Omoku River, the *Umunkaru Onuobdo* felled a tree at *Edebu* near *Onu Omoku* and sank the Abor war canoe with its crew, warriors, trophies and all. According to the original war plans, the Umunkarus were supposed to fell that tree to check the Aboh *entry* into Omoku River. But it is believed they were unaware when the Abohs first passed. But they may have altered the strategy deliberately on their own initiative. To this day, Umunkarus are called *Umu Odilura Kebo Gahwreri* (the sons of those asleep when the Abohs passed).

Even if it is accepted that they may not have been sufficiently alert when the Abohs entered, we must acknowledge that the prompt initiative, tactful calculation and instant courage exhibited by them which utterly destroyed the Aboh war engine deserves commendation. Umunkarus call themselves *Umu okapre mu enya* (those pretending to sleep but are wide awake). It is generally believed that on certain days, a man rowing past *Edebu* may be fortunate to see the Aboh canoe rise almost to the surface of the Omoku River, untarnished by age! I have never seen the canoe myself, and it is not for want of trying.

During the Aboh war, as a result of Umunkarus' performance, Eke-nwa-oji of Umunkaru *Onuobdo* was given the title *Oka-okwu* (i.e. he that plans and speaks). Later, *Oka-okwu* was shortened to *Akogu* and embellished with the epithet *Onyogu* i.e. the "Warrior".

Eke nwa Oji died soon after the Aboh war and his son, Ogbowu, became the next *Akogu*. Ogbowu was fearless and impartial and was well loved by Umunkarus. At his death, his junior brother, Ahia, was chosen to be the next *Akogu*. Ahia was an energetic and enterprising man. His greatest legacy was the number of fish ponds he created. These are all communally harvested by his descendants to this day.

When Ahia died, his son, Ossia, became the next *Akogu*. Ossia was very war-like and prosperous. He is also reputed to

have been very generous. At his death the first of his four sons (Adah) was the next *Akogu*. Adah had more than eight wives, thirty children, forty slaves. He was the wealthiest man in Ali-Ogba in his day and was reputed for his courage and industry. He was appointed a warrant chief when colonial administration came. He built the first permanent storeyed building in Ali-Ogba. (See photograph of building in the next page).
In 1907, Chief Adah Ossiah gave automatic scholarship to all pupils who agreed to attend the new government primary school established in Omoku. In 1917, he was behind what was known as "the Garrick (religious) Movement" in Ogba. Garrick was an Evangelist of the Salvation Army Church whom Chief Adah brought from Kalabari area where he traded to Omoku. Chief Adah allocated a room in his storeyed building to Garrick, and when the latter had a bath upstairs, many followers waited downstairs directly below his bathroom so that the bath-water might touch them and cure them and make them holy. In 1923, Chief Adah had trouble with the colonial government possibly connected with an allegation that he had continued to deal in slaves which led to the withdrawal of his warrant as a Chief. In 1927, when taxation was introduced in Ogba, Chief Adah opposed it on the ground that Ogbas were no slaves who should pay "a ransom for their heads." He died in October the same year.

    The next *Akogu* was Ajie. Although he was unable to reach the standards set by his predecessor, he was a brave and just man. Ajie was succeeded by Edward Ogbowu Ossia. During the latter's term as *Akogu,* local governments were introduced into Ali-Ogba and the elders met and nominated him to represent the Umunkaru *Onuobdo* as Local Councillor as well. At the same time, the youths of Umunkaru met together and nominated one of his (i.e. Edward's) cousins, Nwabriegu Ukwosa Ossia, to be the Councillor. These conflicting nominations caused a dispute which led to the establishment of a new *onuobdo* known as Umuchi or sons of Chi, the father of Nkaru. The new *onuobdo* which was formed by a dissident group from Umunkaru is the smallest *onuobdo* in Ogba today.

First Permanent Building in Omok.. (Owned by Ada Nwa Osia famous Warrant Chief)

When Edward Ogbowu the *Akogu* died, he was succeeded by Benedict Ossiagor in 1959.

Oyro- Umuoyro

The title, *Oyro*, is enjoyed by the Umuoyro *Onuobdo*. That *onuobdo* is closely related to the Umunkaru *Onuobdo* through their common ancestor "Chi". Like Umunkaru, Umuoyro were also involved in the tree felling at Onu-Omoku which destroyed the Aboh invaders. The duty of the *Oyro* in traditional government is to act as one of the advisers of the Eze-Ogba.

Ewo (peace-maker) - Umualinwa

Umualinwa was among the *onuobdos* that came to Ali-Ogba from a westerly direction through an Aboh town (Ogwu-Aniocha). Apparently, they were among the latest to arrive at Ali-Ogba. Umunkaru and Umuoyro must have arrived before them.

Consequently, unlike Umunkaru and Umuoyro, they refused to fight against the Abohs. They were therefore not admitted as members of the prestigious *"Igbu"* society (or Club of "killers"). To this day, the *Ogudu* [34] procession does not pass through Obakata quarter where the Umualinwas live in Omoku. At the end of the Aboh war, they were awarded the title of *"Ewo"* or peace-maker. As they hold this title in common with the Umuohali *Onuobdo*, it may be safe to assume that the latter did not participate in the Aboh war, though apparently for the different reason that they (the Umuohalis) were mainly based in Ohalielu and Ama when the war occurred in Omoku.

Omodi or *Onueze* (mouth-piece of the "king") - Umuossia

Ossia, the ancestor of Umuossia, was a son of Ebe, the ancestor of Umuebe. Ebe nwa Alia had five sons altogether - Egburu, Okoya, Ossia, Akoluka and Enyasi. Okoya, one of Ossia's brothers, was the Eze-Ogba who was beheaded when the Aboh slave raiders invaded Omoku. His predecessor was a member of

---

[34] Great mourning.

the Umuenyasi branch. At the demise of the Umuenyasi ruler, Okoya's mother succeeded in making her own son (Okoya) the Eze Ogba by helping him smuggle away the royal regalia as has been narrated. Okoya paid the supreme price for his mother's trickery.

Okoya migrated from Obigwe to Ikiri in the company of his father, and thence to Okiye Obi between Omoku and Aligu. He was there when the Aboh-Ogba war in question occurred and he was hidden in a bunker. It appears he was unable to leave Okiye Obi for Ikiri or elswhere for fear of reprisals from his own relatives who considered themselves the rightful heirs.

In the palace of the Eze-Ogba, Umuossia are represented by the Omodi or Onueze ;

> who is always responsible every morning for checking whether there is any trouble in the (Eze's) family... they also take care of visitors... and run some errands for (the Eze-Ogba).

"Kingmakers"

Umueriehi are the traditional "kingmakers" entitled to crown the *Eze- Ogba Nwadei Ogbuehi*. It appears the Umuebes are traditionally crowned by the Umuohalis. This has certainly happened on one occasion witnessed by this writer in Omoku. On the other hand, the Umuohalis emphasise that as "kings" themselves, their duty does not include or end with crowning other "kings".

Probable Existence of an earlier Political Order

A careful examination of the structure described above tends to show almost conclusively that it must have been "superimposed on (this) basic *eze-ala* system", to borrow the expression used by D.P. Stanfield in his "Intelligence Report" of 1935.

In the first place, the title and special traditional respects accorded the "Umuezeali (i.e. "kings of land") *Onuobdo* show that that *onuobdo*, probably arrived at Ali-Ogba long before the others and that the members adopted the political systems of their neighbours. They probably occupied a position similar to that of *"Ceremonial" ezes* in the neighbourhood of Ali-Ogba today. That their political stature became subsequently diminished was most probably due to the "superimposition" of the new kingship system of *Eze Ogba* by later "immigrants".

The name of the Ogba political unit, "Onuobdo" is itself very significant. *Onuobdo* means literally "mouth of the city". Below that level, Ogbas distinguish only *imogba* or *etesi* (i.e. compound) and *umudidi* (sons of one great grandfather). Ogbas do not have the eight political levels or categories ably described by Elechukwu Njaka in his *Igbo Political Culture* [35] viz; *Ama, Ngwuru, Numara, Umunna, Mkpuru, Ogbe, Ebe,* and *Obodo* (except the last one *Obodo* which survives in the term *onuobdo*). It appears that these categories may have existed in the pre-Ali-Ogba days in the distant past before the arrival of Ogbas but were extinguished or reduced in number on the emergence of a superior "kingship" order.

Concluding his comments on Bini and Igbo political systems Elechukwu Njaka states:[36]

> Fundamentally, there is no radical difference between the Bini political system and the Igbo political organisation, except that in Bini, the Obi or Eze ("Oba" in Bini) is a ruling king, not merely a constitutional, ritual and ceremonial one, as among the Igbo. Consequently, the Oba appoints officers, advisers, judicial members, executive and legislative councils, and war lords, and confers on them their honorific titles, a method characteristically un-Igbo... The structure of these Obiships in riverine Igbo states vary, as each state has its own adaptation. Thus in some states, like Onicha, only particular *Ebe* can provide candidate for the Obi (position), while others rotate their Obi among the *Ebe* that constitute the state. However, they all have their prime ministers... In all the riverine Igbo states, titles are recognised and institutionalised. Each holder has specific duties to perform.

In Ali-Ogba, political "titles" were recognised and institutionalised. But over the past few years, there has been a proliferation of titles without responsibilities, which is by no means traditional and which may destabilise or destroy the traditional system in course of time.

---

[35] Elechukwu Njaka, *Igbo Political Culture*, Northwestern University Pres Evanston , 1974 p.26
[36] *Op.cit*. p. 138.

Law and Custom

Supported by their traditional courtiers each of the traditional rulers of Ogba took judicial decisions within his domain. Apparently, the rulers concerned themselves mainly with re-enactment of existing customs or "laws", which were based on fundamental principles adopted from Benin or from the different groups encountered by Ogbas during the course of their migrations. Law and custom were maintained at several levels viz: extended family, *onuobdo*, traditional ruler, village or town assembly. The oldest members presided over extended family "Courts" and *onuobdo* "Courts" and the ruler" presided over his own "Court" and the village or town assembly.

Ogba "laws" and the unwritten moral code dealt with such matters as marriage, births, deaths and burials. In regard to marriage, exogamy within each *onuobdo* was strictly observed. Polygamy was practised and a uniform bride price was fixed and revised from time to time. An elaborate marriage ceremony was instituted in which bridesmaids and bridal trains featured. Definite conditions were laid down for divorce.

A birth was welcomed as the return of an ancestor, except that twins were believed to be the handiwork of evil spirits. A female child born at night when *Okrosu* was being performed was named *Nnowu* and given special privileges and "right of passage". Other children were named after their "re-incarnators" after verification by *Dibia* through "divination".

The death of a young person was a tragic and sad occasion, but a mature or elderly person's death was an occasion for elaborate rituals involving eating, drinking and dancing by *Okrosu* and the members of the traditional societies (ie.g. *Igbu*). Ogbas looked upon a deceased elder as a forerunner in the world beyond, who continued to take keen interest in the affairs of the living.

A customary "code" prescribed the traditional law in such matters as murder, adultery, theft, debt, inheritance. In regard to murder, the penalty was an eye for an eye - if a member of one *onuobdo* killed a member of another *onuobdo*, the members of the former *onuobdo* were made to produce someone of comparable standing(e.g. of the same sex and age-grade) who would walk courageously to his death by public hanging. Killing in self-defence or warfare was recognised as an act of bravery and a qualification for entry into the prestigious *Igbu* society. Adultery involving one of the king's wives incurred capital punishment. A man who spoke to a married woman frivolously would be compelled to pay penalties. If she was sitting down with her feet outstretched, any male who stepped across her feet knowingly or unknowingly, was considered guilty of an offence attracting substantial penalties - so high were the standards of morality and propriety!

Theft rarely occurred because all property were perpetually under the watchful eyes of *erisi*.[37] Debts arose mainly as a result of unpaid or partly paid bride price. In the slave trade era, the relatives of a bride were apparently entitled to sell their *nwoyigmo* (that is their sister's offspring) in *oru* country in order to recover any bride price in arrears. Today, a common joke is for *nwadialis* to "threaten" to sell their *nwoyigmos* if the latter are insubordinate. In regard to inheritance, the patrilineal tradition recognised strict adherence to primogeniture.

Judicial Hierarchy

A judicial hierarchy existed from the family level upwards. Minor cases were heard within the extended family headed by the oldest member. Important cases were heard by a council of the elders of the *onuobdo* concerned, headed by the oldest member. More serious cases went to the king's cabinet. The most serious cases, such as murder, were heard by an Assembly of all the people in a Town centre which was established in every Town or Village.

Traditional judiciary at the family, *onuobdo*, cabinet or Assembly level made scanty use of rules of evidence or jurisprudence. Although, it was customary to call and hear witnesses, the veracity of statements or evidence was usually tested by reference to *erisi* [38] not by cross-examination.

---

[37] i.e. the gods.
[38] Traditional deity or god.

Consequently, *erisi* formed part and parcel of the judicial process from the lowest to the highest level. In fact, the formality of judicial processes was frequently discarded by some aggrieved parties who would go straight and complain to *erisi* about any injury they suffered, calling upon *erisi* to ensure that the culprits paid the ultimate penalty. The complainant would carry away substantial quantities of earth from the soil of the *erisi* and "scatter" it (*ziza ziza*) through the area inhabited by the suspects and their relations praying the erisi to "clean out" the whole area, leaving no one alive if it found any member of the family guilty. Frequently, the unknown criminals would step forward and confess their guilt (real or imaginary) for fear of the wrath of the *erisi* and the safety of other members of their families. In this way, individuals were known to have confessed to wizardry and witchcraft.

But the principal function of *erisi,* it would appear, was to serve as a Court of Appeal for cases heard at any level. It was only occasionally that a case would go up gradually from the lowest to the highest court before appeal was made to *erisi*. Frequently, appeal was made from each and every court to *erisi*, whose decision (supposed to involve the death of the guilty party) was final. The procedure was for the accused to appear before the designated *erisi* and swear before it that they were innocent of the accusations brought against them, adding that if the *erisi* found them guilty of the charges, it should kill them. Sometimes, they would drink some substance from the *erisi* site. The accused were given up to one year (or more) after which they were declared innocent of the charges, if they were still alive.

In practice, minor courts appealed to minor *erisi* (diety) and major courts to major *erisi*. Some hardened criminals could, it was believed, "immunise" themselves against death by *erisi* through *igbuchiehu*. Major *erisi* reputed for cruel efficiency were not affected by *igbuchiehu*. Therefore, in the most serious cases, it was customary to patronize the most deadly *erisi*, no matter the distance, or who the owners were, or the cost to the parties.

The most serious cases were referred to the greatest *erisi* of all in the form of the *chukwu* (high god) of Arochukwu known to people elsewhere as long juju or *Ibinu Ukpabi*. In Ali-Ogba it was simply known as *chukwu abiama*.[39]

In some parts of Nigeria, the Aros sent ambassadors who were also "priests" of *chukwu* responsible for conducting litigants to Arochukwu. These ambassadors usually lived closely to the local population but did not intermingle with them. The old Aro outposts have survived in areas outside Ali-Ogba as distinct villages bearing the names of the neighbouring villages prefixed with the word *"Aro"*. But no such Aro villages exists in Ali-Ogba because, as has already been explained, the Aros appointed the Umuenyike *Onuobdo,* viz: Nwadei people, to be their agents and representatives and eyes and ears on the spot. In Ali-Ogba, the Umuenyikes were the "priest" who conducted litigants to Arochukwu. The Aros extended to the Umuenyikes the priestly titles of *"Umuchukwu oriogba maya eriwo"* (sons of god which ate Ogbas except themselves).

Before conducting any accused persons to Arochukwu, Umueyikes studied the merits of each case carefully and briefed the Aros accordingly. Consequently, most innocent people were "vindicated" by *chukwu*. In this way, confidence in the wisdom of *chukwu* increased and more and more cases were appealed to it. Apparently, the Aros did not disclose to Umuenyikes the details of the trickery and manipulation whereby those declared by Aros to have been "eaten" by *chukwu* were secretly sold into slavery.

After the Aro economic cum religious cum political exploitative machine had been dismantled by emergent colonialism, Ogbas resorted to another oracle, the *Igwekali* of Umunoha, noted for its talkativeness. To be as talkative as *Igwekali* became a customary expression in late 19th century Ogba diction.

The Executive

Execution of judicial or legislative decisions was achieved through family or *onuobdo* elders, or through social pressure; or the ubiquitous *erisi,* or the age-grades. Ogba society was largely gerentocratic. ("A younger person has to bow to an older

---

[39] 'Abiama' is probably a corruption of the word 'Obioma' which means 'love or kindness'. Thus 'Chukwu Abiama' could mean 'god of love'.

person, other things being equal") The oldest male in an extended family has always been the head of the extended family. The oldest male in an *onuobdo* is the Head of the *onuobdo*. Where a new priest is required by an *erisi*, the oldest male member of an *onuobdo* is usually appointed. Consequently, enforcement of a law, custom or decision was usually carried out by the different *onuobdos* under the direction of their elders.

Sometimes, implementation was achieved through ostracism or social pressure. A person guilty of an abomination was avoided like plague, for fear of infection with the calamity that was destined to befall the transgressor. The consequence of losing the goodwill of their associates must have operated as a strong deterrent to some intending criminals. Sometimes, the names of guilty individuals or notorious suspects were mentioned in songs purposely composed to expose the offenders to ridicule or compel them to make restitution. Sometimes, it was the ubiquitous *erisi* that was invoked to kill someone who failed to do as was expected of him. In all cases where a specific public service was to be done, or where hardwork or sacrifice of time and energy was called for, or where there was risk to life and limb, the youth age-grades provided an ever-ready agency for executive action.

General Observations

From the praise names of the various *onuobdos* in Ali-Ogba today, we may be able to understand the political organisation of the traditional society. These praise names or titles have been carefully preserved in the *Isiali* ceremony which is still prevalent as the normal form of greeting in Ali-Ogba.

Cursory examination of the praise names or titles reveals a political hierarchy with meaningful responsibilities attached to the various levels depicted. Beneath this elaborate "royal" structure, there is a republican structure in which oldest members of extended families (especially in the villages) operate as *ezealas* as is the case among the more remote neighbours of Ali-Ogba.

Traditional jurisprudence rested partly with the traditional rulers, partly with the peoples assembly and partly with *erisi* or various gods. Indeed, final appeal was always made to the gods of which the long juju was the most terrible. In Ali-Ogba, the

Umuenyike (Nwadei) family were the *Umuchukwu Oriogba maya eri wo* responsible for conducting litigants to Aro. After the destruction of the long juju by the British, Ogbas turned to *Igwe ka ali* of Umunoha but this patronage was shortlived as the latter shrine was soon destroyed by colonial officials.

Thereafter, some Ogbas depended on the local gods but a good number accepted the modern jurisprudence introduced by the British authorities.

In regard to executive action, the age-grades of Ali-Ogba played a useful role. Since everyone belonged to an age-grade, it wasn't very difficult to mobilize the people for concerted action when the need arose.

Ogba traditional rulers enjoyed high respect from young and old, undoubtedly because of the veneration in which rulership was held in Benin and elsewhere to which Ogbas trace their origin. It is true that Ogbas do not prostrate flat on the ground (as in some areas west of the Niger) to greet their traditional rulers, but neither do they "stand erect" to greet "royalty", unless they come from *onuobdos* traditionally entitled to do so. Since independence, indigenous Nigerian governments have sought to accord appropriate recognition to traditional rulers. But these governments (military and civilian) have allowed traditional rulers much less power than the latter enjoyed under colonial "indirect rule". Today, the older rulerships are growing more glamorous and artificial ones are springing up, especially in the eastern parts of the country. At the same time, the "power" of traditional rulership is waning as we march awkwardly towards "democracy".

On the whole, Ogba society had a solid base in which everyone played his or her clearly defined role with pride and dignity in the general interest. A combination of such societies able to adapt themselves wisely to changing times and circumstances, should produce a great nation.

Chapter 4

Social And Economic Organisation

The unique political pattern in Ali-Ogba produced a distinct social and economic organisation. The "hybrid" political structure which was monarchical and republican at the same time, in turn produced citizens who were egocentric and arrogant, yet industrious, adventurous, self-conscious and conservative.

We shall appreciate the full impact which the peculiar Ogba political structure had on the Ogba people as we examine below how Ogbas lived, what they wore, what they ate, how they worked and worshipped, and how they danced and wept for the dead.

Ogba Houses and Towns

According to Newington (1930 paras.43-45),:

> Omoku is easily the second largest town in the (Ahoada) Division next to Port Harcourt... All the kindreds outside Omoku have constructed their villages in a very suitable manner. All the towns have a clean open space in the middle about the size of a small parade ground, the houses are roomy and usually in good condition and there is no sign of sanitary refuse. Omoku is the only one of these kindreds fit to be called a town and it possesses almost one third of the entire population of Okoba (i.e. Ogba). The total population of Ogba was estimated at 20, 292 in 1927 comprising 5,479 adult males, 6,203 adult females, 4,419 boys and 4,191 girls. The population of Ali-Ogba today may be estimated at 100,000 souls, or .1% of the entire population of the Federal Republic of Nigeria[1].

Over the years, Ogbas established roughly forty towns in *aliulo* i.e. "home land", as distinct from *Ogboru* or "work place". The number of towns varied slightly from time to time as a few old sites were abandoned and new ones were established.

---

[1] These are rough estimates made by me personally through long experience and protracted interaction with my people.

Originally, Ogba buildings were built of characteristic mud and wattle and roof thatched with raffia palms. The plan was somewhat rectangular in shape and the sizes rather substantial. Sometimes, walls were made solely of mud with only a few hardwood structures to serve as pillars *(Okwa)*.

In the early days, these buildings were uninhabited for more than half of the year when the inmates were in *Ogboru*. During the farming season, the town became quite untidy. Even the town or village square would suffer from neglect, pending the return from *Ogboru (ilo Liguiji)* at the start of the dry season in late October, when the houses would be repaired, the roads cleared and the squares bustling with dances and wrestlers and age-grade celebrations. But the period of intensified activity in the towns is the period of inactivity in *Ogboru*. When the towns were bustling, *Ogboru* was deserted, and vice versa. As a result of this mode of life, the average self-employed Ogba person today tends to love long holidays. Judged by the modern standard of eight working hours a day, the average self-employed male Ogba is on vacation half of the year. Female Ogbas seem more industrious. To a greater or lesser extent, this male "indolence" applies to most Nigerian traditional societies, except that the "traditional" societies are no longer in existence as such anywhere.

Food, Drink and Health

The oldest Ogba staple food appears to have been yam which was frequently roasted, or boiled or "pounded". The pounded yam was eaten with a gravy or "soup" prepared with fish or "bush" meat and vegetables and much pepper and salt. In the 17th Century, cassava displaced yam as the standard staple food for the common folk and pounded yam became the diet for festive occasions or the staple food for successful, elderly men.

Because of their love of song and dance, Ogbas also loved drinking. The chief arena for drinking were the age-grade meetings and burial ceremonies *(Okgu)*. Some amount of drinking also took place during traditional dances such as *oru-orie*. In the early days, the principal drink was palm wine of which the *Igbrus* were specialist producers. From the 16th Century onwards, alcoholic drinks were imported in substantial quantities. Old containers of these drinks (labelled "Long John") have been excavated at Obrikom and Omoku. Side by side with imported alcohol, Ogbas manufactured and drank an alcoholic drink from fermented palm wine. This drink, known popularly as *kaikai* (abuse word in Hausa language presumably used frequently by persons who are drunk?), was termed "illicit drink" and forbidden by law in colonial times, but the law was honoured more in the breach rather than the observance. And yet alcoholism appears to have been rare in Ali-Ogba. This may be attributed to the abstemious or miserly drinking custom of the Ogbas. In the early days, only elders were expected to drink alcohol. As a rule, every elder owned his own drinking "horn" which he carried with him on every outing when he was likely to encounter drink. The wisdom in this custom was to avoid poisoning by enemies. Poisoning by "wizards" must have been quite common. The incident in which Eze Nwa-Onyuku was poisoned at Obrikom is an outstanding example. It appears that secret poisoning was frequently adopted in doing away with people when the gods (or *erisi*) proved too slow.

When imported alcoholic drinks were introduced, they were served in tiny glass containers (demi-Johns). The drinks were so highly valued and expensive that they were even used as currency. Apparently, many Ogbas could not afford to own more than one or two demi-Johns, so it became customary for a house-full of people to drink in turns from a single tiny "demi-John". This custom ensured that only small quantities of alcohol reached each drinker on any given occasion. However, the unhygienic custom of serving several drinkers with one cup does not appear to have done too much harm. Perhaps the alcohol itself sterilized the "demi-Johns" thereby preventing infection. Despite the dangers of alcoholism, many Ogbas were blessed with long life - a good number of them lived to see their children's children's children i.e. three or four generations. Hence, Ogba have words for *nwa* (immediate offspring), *nwanwa* (grandchild), *nwanwa nwanwa* (great grand child); *nwanwrara* (great, great grandchild).

Ogba Cultural Development

Ogba culture seems to have undergone considerable change over the years as a result of contact with other cultures. The most obvious changes occurred in speech, dress and religion which are considered below in turn.

Speech

It has already been shown that Ogba speech was probably adapted from the speech of the earliest inhabitants who lived in Ali-Ogba about 5,000 years ago. The identity of the early inhabitants has not been fixed but it appears they were people from the same stock as the present Ogba neighbours. With the language of those pioneers forming the basic structure, the dialect bears marks of influence from Ogba immigrants of all generations from Benin, Aboh, Oguta, Egbema, Ekpeye, Ikwerre, - to name only a few. Egi and Ekpeye dialects have more Edo accent than Usomini and Igburu dialects, but the peculiarity of all of them remains unique.

Ogba Dress

Until half a century ago, male Ogba elders could still be seen in heavy white, or black and white, cotton cloths (*arigidi*) passed under the right armpit, tied above the shoulder and covering it, and flowing from there right unto both ankles - more or less in the form of a Roman *toga* or an Edo nobleman's dress. A cap (red cap for rulership *Onuobdos*) usually adorned the head. Anklets were often worn by titled persons. Elderly women of repute wore the same cloth tied to their chests and reaching down to the calf, with appropriate headgear, and beads around their necks. The very well-to-do women also wore very heavy elephant's tusks, polished and shaped like massive rings, around their ankles. This made ordinary locomotion almost impossible, thereby reducing the wearers to a state of respectable immobility. Girls below marriageable age wore mainly beads.

These dress items were most probably inherited from Benin. In his work *Esmeraldo* written in 1506, Pacheco Pereira mentions trade in cloth in the Forcados River. Fernandez bought 1,816 cloths which he described as 'muslim'. According to Father Francesco da Monteleone (1692) quoted by Alan Ryder in his *Benin and the Europeans,*:[2]

> ... this commerce, which consists in slaves, ivory and various kinds of cotton cloth (my underlining), is very slow: the cloths are not found ready made, but they take goods on credit, and with these goods they have the cloths made in five or, at the most, six months....

Alan Ryder goes on to show that ;

> "the Portuguese quickly discovered that certain varieties of stone beads available in Benin and the Forcados River could be exchanged for gold on the Costa da Mina.... Most of the beads were fashioned from a blue stone veined with red: the Portuguese called them *coris*... All these beads must have reached Benin and the rivers through trade with the interior, and possibly from a source which also had links with Costa da Mina for it seems likely that they were known there prior to the Portuguese period.

Ogba Traditional Religion

> On the whole, the religion strongly resembles that of ancient Egyptians, who combined a belief in the existence of an Omnipotent Supreme God... with that in multitudes of sub-ordinate deities, mostly personifications of natural phenomena.[3]

This observation by P.A Talbot in his *Peoples of Southern Nigeria* applies to Ogba people. Sir Alan Burns makes a similar point in his *History of Nigeria*[4] when he says:

> It is important to realise that the existence of a Supreme Being is appreciated practically throughout the country... however,.... more attention is paid to minor deities, good and evil, who are considered to have a greater interest in human affairs. But even these are held to be spirits, and the images which the people venerate are but the representation of the spirits, not the gods themselves. In most cases, there is a tribal god, a lesser god for each village of the tribe, a household god for every family in the village, and a personal god for

---

2   Ryder A.F.C, *Benin and the Europeans 1485-1897*, London 1969 p. 37
3   P.A. Talbot *The Peoples of Southern Nigeria*, Oxford University Press 1927 (re-issued 1969) p.iv quoting a report of 1816.
4   Alan Burns, *History of Nigeria*, George Allan & Unwin, London 1972 edition)

every member of the family. Add to these, a god or devil for every striking object of nature, for every river or stream, for every hill or grove and for every large or remarkable tree, and it will be understood how remarkable is the African's mythology

Alan Burns goes on to say that;

> Many tribes have their totems, and there is a widespread belief in the power of certain men and women to change themselves at will into animal. In some districts, it is believed that the killing of a wild animals will result in the death of the person whose soul is occupying either temporarily or permanently the body of the beast.

He quotes C.K. Meek (Government Anthropologist) as saying that ;

> the belief in the ability of individuals to turn into animals is universal among the general mass of Muslims.

In his *Dual Mandate,* Lord Lugard says;

> I recollect the surprise of a Chief Justice new to Africa when an accused man pleaded guilty to having turned himself into a hyena by night and devoured children, because there was a consensus of village opinion that he had done so.

Let us consider some of the traditional Ogba beliefs:

Transmigration

One of the most curious phenomena in Ogba traditional religion is the belief that the members of of the different *onuobdo*s can transmigrate into various lower animals such as python, leopard, elephant, crocodile, ants and beetle. This is obviously an extension of the universal totemic culture characteristic of many indigenous groups, which is still depicted today in their various "coats of arms". But Ogbas treat their totems with extreme respect, almost raising them to the level of humanity in a most peculiar association whose details we shall try to unfold later.

Frequently, the members of an Ogba *Onuobdo* have to abstain from certain food items because of their transmigration animal or totem. Offenders have to propitiate certain gods which appear to have been created purposely for that reason. The following instances speak for themselves:

Totems of Transmigration

Python

Umuezeali, Umueke, Umuorodu, Umuohali, Umunkaru and Umuoyro claim ability to transmigrate into python. Every Umuezeali male person has a corresponding python which will die when he himself dies. This power was acquired by Umuezealis through a charm prepared for them by the Arochukwu people or the Awka people or a people of no fixed address known as *Umuodilamo* (sons of those in the land of the dead).[5]

> Umueke people have power to change from human form into the form of the python. They acquired this power during the Aboh war and it helped them escape from the enemy. Every male member of the Umueke *Onuobdo* has one python which he uses for protection. When the man dies from natural or other causes, the python dies also.[6]

> Umuohalis transmigrate into the python. Every Umuohali member has his opposite python. When he dies, the python dies, and vice versa. The python visits his "patron's" home unseen.[7]

> Umunkarus can transmigrate into the python. Every Umunkaru member has a python as his opposite number in the animal world. When a person dies, his python dies also. Recently, when Isaiah Nwa Ossia died, his python was creeping around the house helpless until it was taken up and buried with its owner ... Ordinarily, it is impossible to kill a python belonging to an Umunkaru as an *anu ezi* (transmigration animal) even with machine gun; but if an *anu ezi* misbehaves by killing an innocent person for instance, then it can be killed even with bare hands.[8]

> *Orji Aligu (Aligu* Iroko) is the habitat of many pythons which are sacred to Umunkaru and Umuoyro. If a python enters an Umuoyro or Umunkaru house, it must be treated with reverence and returned to the bush from whence it came. Umuoyros can transmigrate into pythons.

---

5 As narrated by Chief Mark Ogwe, the oldest member and Head of Umuezeali *Onuobdo*, at his residence in Obigwe on 10th January 1080.

6 As narrated by Chief Victor Eke Osi, the *Owerre* of Umueke, in his palace in Usomini on 10th November, 1979.

7 As narrated by *Osi nwa Orji* of Obakata, the oldest member and Head of Umuohali *Onuobdo*, and Gilbert Nwajari, leading member of Umuezeali *Onuobdo*, 13th December, 1979.

8 As narrated by Nwokogu Adah, head of Umunkaru *Onuobdo* Benedict Osiagu, the Akogu, and Pius Adah, on 26th September, 1979.

When the python into which an Umuoyro has transmigrated is injured, the Umuoyro transmigrator is injured also. In the presence of an Umuoyro, a gun aimed at a python or *Abba* will not fire. But it is hard to see a transmigration python. Whenever it appears, it is regarded as a bad omen. When Umuoyros are in danger, they go to *Orji aligu* and seek the help of its pythons.[9]

Leopard

Ihiukwu, Umuogidi, Umuokrocha, Uriem and Umuimegi claim that their members migrate into leopard.

Ihiukwus have power to transmigrate into *Anu-akpor* (leopard). An Ihiukwu leopard cannot be killed even with a bomb except when it commits an offence. Ihiukwus do not eat leopard meat because if they do, they may be eating one of their own people without knowing. Ihiukwus also refrain from eating anything killed by a leopard or any food of which the leopard is fond of such as *ede* (coco-yam) or *okro*. [10]

Umuogidis can transmigrate into *Anu-akpor* (leopard). Before an Umuogidi transmigrates, he must go to *Odu-ka-Ogidi* (the ivory of Ogidi - a shrine) at Osiakpu and sacrifice a fowl. The oldest member of Umuogidi is the high priest of *Odu-ka-Ogidi* at Osiakpu. The present high priest is called *Akio*. The *anu-ezi* (i.e totem or transmigration animal) is usually sent to eat the goats of an enemy. Every Umuogidi member should abstain from eating *okro*. If an Umuogidi should knowingly or unknowingly eat *okro*, he will suffer from serious infection which will produce spots on his skin resembling a leopard's spots. The remedy is to go to the high priest at Osiakpu with a fowl for *Odu-ka-Ogidi*. But there is no remedy for the *okro* itself - If it was standing in the field and touched an Umuogidi - that *okro* will never bear fruit any more.[11]

Uriems have the power to change from human form to that of *anu-akpor* (leopard). Every Uriem has his corresponding leopard but not all Uriems can change into the form of leopard. When a child is born, it will be known if he will be able to change through his heart beat. If the child has a heavy heart beat, the elders know at once that he will be able to change into leopard when he becomes an adult. Whenever he cries, he

---

[9] As narrated by Chief Godfrey Owugbonu, oldest member and Head of Umuoyro *Onuobdo*, at his residence in Usomini quarters of Omoku on 6th March ,1980.

[10] As narrated by Chief David Ojadi, the *Isoma* of Ihiukwu, Albert Nwoko second oldest member of the *onuobdo*, Jeremiah Eleba, oldest member and Head of Ihiukwu *Onuobdo*, Wilson Onyige and Bathwell Ibra, prominent Ihiukwu elders, in Omoku on 22nd November, 1979.

[11] As narrated by Chief Ebenezer Osima, the *Iyasra* of Umuogidi and Johnson Ogidi of Umuogidi, at their residence in Omoku on 14th March ,1980.

would be made to lie on *Agbahi* grass and after that he will be taken to the elders who will "lay hands" on him to "cool" him. When that child becomes an adult, he will send his leopard to fight against his enemies and destroy their crops. A king of the Abohs known as Obonwa grew tired of the troubles of Uriem leopards;so he prepared a charm which had the effect of neutralizing the ability of Uriems to transmigrate into their leopards. Uriems abstain from leopard, as well as from squirrel, frog, *ubelebe* and *mma-ekwu* because they all look like leopard. Any Uriem eating any of these things must sacrifice to the shrine on *Eke* night. He should paint his whole body with white chalk and appear before the *Mkpitima* shrine. If *Mkpitima* wants a goat from an Uriem, it may afflict him with leprosy until the goat has been presented.[12]

Although Umuokrocha have become a separate *onuobdo* from Uriem, they still share many of the characteristics of all Uriems. Their *anu-ezi* (transmigration animal or totem) is still the leopard. When an Umuokrocha member dies and is about to be laid to rest in his grave, all male in Umuokrocha will start growling like leopards... when a person dies, his transmigration animal dies also, and its fellows in the bush will give it a befitting burial so that no one will see its body and take it home as meat. Umuokrochas have to abstain from *okro* and *mmaegwu* palm fruit. They also abstain from leopard meat to avoid eating their totem by mistake, which would be tantamount to cannibalism.[13]

Umuimegi abstain from *okro* because the seeds of the *okro* are like the spots of a leopard, their transmigration animal.[14]

Elephant

Only Umualinwas claim the ability to transmigrate into elephant.

An Umualinwa member is capable of transmigrating into an elephant for the purpose of fighting his private or public enemy. When an Umualinwa elephant attacks an enemy, it goes to the yam plantation of the enemy and destroys all the crops; then it gathers the yam stakes together in one neat heap like an intelligent being just to prove to the farmer that the destruction was done by an Umualinwa elephant, not by an ordinary wild elephant. The following items associated with the elephant are taboo to Umualinwas: mushroom, *ona* and *uga*.

---

[12] As narrated by Jumbo Nwaogbaligwe of Ekwelamini Basilugbo Age Grade, a leading member of Uriem *Onuobdo*, at his residence in Okposi on 20th January, 1980.

[13] As narrated by Chief Ibra Nwaegburi, oldest member and family head of Umuokrocha *Onuobdo*, at his residence in Usomini quarters on the 15th of March, 1980.

[14] As narrated by Chief Lawyer Eluozo, the *Ajie* of Umuimegi and Chief Johnson Ake of Otu German, the *Okie Obudo* (head) of Umuimegi *Onuobdo*, in their house in Omoku on 20th January ,1980.

Transgressors are infected with leprosy and must go at once to *Odu-ka-Ajie* shrine with one white goat, three yams and as many kolanuts as possible. After the priest of *Odu-ka-Ajie* has performed the necessary ceremonies and eaten the offerings (assisted by male worshippers only), the leper will begin to recover rapidly. *Odu-ka-Ajie* commands the confidence of Umualinwas, so much so that in time of danger an Umualinwa would normally exclaim *Odu-ka-Ajie bianim'* (*Odu-ka-Ajie* come to my aid).[15]

Crocodile

Umuagbda members are the only Ogbas who claim to have the ability to transmigrate into crocodile.

Umuagbdas have to refrain from eating crocodile because they have the power to change into crocodile in order to frighten or harm their enemies.[16]

Ijere (Ants)

Umuenyikes claim to be able to transmigrate into *Ijere* (ants). This probably reflects their strong military organisation in the past. They refrain from *ona* and *eru* (mushroom).[17]

Ede(Beetle)

Umuebes (Edihurus) and their relatives Umuossia transmigrate into beetle (called *ebe* in Ogba) and abstain from *eru* (mushroom).[18]

Ogba belief in transmigration was by no means a wholly original idea in that some of the totems had some ancient religious significance as in Greek pythonism and Hindu Ganesha. On the other hand, the choice of such totems as the ant and the beetle, which have a distinctive scientific and philosophical significance, must be recognised as a mark of rare ingenuity and uncanny knowledge on the part of early Ogbas.

---

[15] As narrated by Chief Will Orike, second oldest and next leading member of Umualinwa *Onuobdo*, in his residence on 19th November ,1979.

[16] As narrated by Chief Sunday Onyeocha Amadike, the *Iyasra* of Umuagbda, in Omoku on 24th October, 1979.

[17] As narrated by *Eze Ogba Nwadei Ogbuehi*, John Wokocha Ellah, and *Okie Onuobdo* Lazarus Ezi Osere, at the Nwadei Palace in Omoku, on 26th September, 1979.

[18] As narrated by Chief Mark Obiohuru (*Otu Akpo agi*), the *Emodi* of Edihuru, at his residence in Omoku on 9th March, 1980.

The "Skills" of Transmigration

Professor Elizabeth Isichei[19] has said:

> I think it is possible that Igboland's *dibia* were developing real skills - or sciences - in the sphere of what we would now call extra-sensory perception. The imposition of colonial rule has basically put an end to those skills, and deflected Igbo intellectual energies into such "modern" spheres as medicine or physics. It is possible that in doing so it cut off a real and original advance of the human knowledge.

It is not clear whether transmigration into various beasts was among the "skills" contemplated by Prof. Isichei. It is practically impossible to verify the true position regarding these transmigration totems because of the very nature of the claims associated with them: According to Umuoyro;

> it is hard to see a transmigration python. Whenever it appears, it is regarded as a bad omen. And when it does appear, we are told that it is impossible to kill a python belonging to an Umunkaru as an *anu-ezi* even with a machine gun. An Ihiukwu leopard cannot be killed even with a bomb.

> And if we should succeed in killing a totem in order to examine it, we cannot take it away because, according to Umuokrocha;

> when a person dies his transmigration animal (totem) dies also, and its fellows in the bush will give it a befitting burial so that no one will see its body (my underlining) and take it home as meat.

Superficially, the case of Isaiah nwa Ossia whose python was creeping around helpless until it was taken and buried with its owner may appear credible. But in an environment where pythons have been allowed to flourish unperturbed for generations, where they have been treated with respect and have never been threatened or frightened, it is not unthinkable that the appearance of a python near a household could coincide with the fatal illness of one of the inmates in an era of limited life expectancy and constant deaths.

Another "evidence" is that when a dead Umuokrocha member is about to be laid to rest, all male Umuokrochas will start growling like leopards. But it is obvious that any group of persons could easily "growl like leopards" if they stand to gain any advantage by such behaviour.

---

[19] *Op. cit.* p.124.

The most revealing claim appears to be that an Umualinwa elephant "gathers the yam stakes together in one neat heap like an intelligent being". One strongly suspects that "intelligent beings" were somehow physically behind the alleged behaviour of most, if not all, the totems.

Finally, we are given a most unsatisfactory reason why these transmigrations cannot happen today. According to the Uriems,:

> A king of Aboh known as Obonwa grew tired of the troubles of Uriem leopards; so he prepared a charm which has the effect of neutralizing the ability of Uriems to transmigrate into their leopards.

People able to make charms to enable them transmigrate into animals should be able to make charms for the protection of such terrible powers.

The indications are that these totems were adopted by the different *onuobdos* during the earliest period of their arrival in Ali-Ogba when Ali-Ogba was mostly an "animal kingdom" inhabited mainly by beasts which frequently attacked and killed some of the few human "intruders". The fact that the chief occupation of the human "intruders" was "hunting" (e.g. the sons of Ezeali, Agburu and Okpraeme were great hunters) provoked revenge and thereby aggravated the situation.

It is significant that only a few animals were adopted by Ogbas as totem out of the obviously large variety of animals then in existence in the area. Each animal, it would appear, was adopted for a specific reason that struck terror into outside *onuobdo*s, thereby enhancing the prestige of the devotees.

The python, which is patronised by at least six of the *onuobdo*s is the most popular. The python is noted as a monster which kills its prey by the strange method of constriction. Greek mythology and the religions of various communities throughout the world acknowledged Pythonism in which persons supposed to be possessed by pythonic spirits became the "mouth-pieces" of such spirits and uttered the messages of such spirits prophetically. A woman possessed by such a spirit was known as a "pythonness" or witch. Although Ogbas believed in witches, they associated their own witches with a drowsy, ugly, *bird* commonly known as the witch bird, not with pythons.

Ogba witchcraft beliefs are comparable to those of Abohs and Ogbarus.

The next most popular totem, patronised by up to five Ogba *onuobdos* is the leopard which is noted for its belligerency. The leopard (*panthera pardus*) belongs to the order *Carnivora* and the family *Felidae* and is closely related to other flesh eating cats such as the lion and the tiger. Leopards in Ali-Ogba were fond of eating helpless baboons which appear to have abounded in Ali-Ogba in the early days; hence they were particularly hostile to human beings at first sight.

Only one Ogba *onuobdo*, Umualinwa, with Aboh connections, have the elephant as their totem,. It appears that the African bush elephant (*Loxodonta africana*), which occurs over much of Africa south of the Sahara, was common in early Ali-Ogba. This kind of elephant may have been among the types domesticated by the ancient Carthaginians and used in wars with the Romans. Elephants are depicted on medals of Faustina and of *Lucius Septimius Severus*. As late as World War II, elephants were of considerable value in military movements over the mud-clogged roads of south-east Asia. Elephants can also be a menace to cultivation. Wild herds that break into a plantation may destroy acres of produce in a single night. The association between men and elephants goes far back into mythology - The elephant faced god, *Ganesha*, plays a part in hinduism as a remover of obstacles.

The Umuagbda *Onuobdo* claim the crocodile (family-*crocodylidae;* order *crocodilia;*) as their totem. To a group that lived and worked on the banks of the Sombreiro River, the swimming ability and feeding habits of the crocodile must have appeared most impressive and worthy of emulation. In the floating position, a crocodile waits for a potential prey, usually a small mammal, to come to the waters edge to drink. When it sees the prey, the crocodile submerges, almost without a ripple, and cautiously swims towards the animal till it is only about twenty feet. away; then the crocodile abandons caution and with one or two powerful beats of its tail is upon the startled quarry. The prey, seized between the crocodile's gaping jaws, is pulled into the water, drowned and swallowed whole or in bits. Some species are known to attack and eat men.

Only the Umuenyike *Onuobdo* (i.e the Nwadei group) have the ant (family, *formicidae*) as their totem. From the nick-name *Enyike* (which means "as strong as the elephant"), they might have been expected to choose an elephant totem, but the wisdom of the ancients sometimes passes understanding. The greatest diversity of genera and specie of ants is found in the tropics. Of all earthly creatures (including man), ants have probably the best organised establishments ("Colonies") complete with "queens" and "workers" engaged in uniform productive activities which the Umuenyike kingship group most probably aspired to emulate.

Umuebe are the only *onuobdo* having the beetle (order-*coleoptera*) as their totem. In the animal kingdom, beetles form by far the largest major group or order. At least 250,000 kinds are known, which constitutes more than one quarter of all known animal species. It is apparently for this reason that they were chosen as totem by Umuebe, a kingship group. Many beetles are injurious either as larvae or adults. The carnivorous habit of seeking and devouring living prey occurs in the ground beetles, tiger beetles, lady beetles or ladybirds and in predaceous diving beetles. Among those which attack farm crops, the wireworm is important.

In all the oral traditions obtained by this writer and in the accounts recorded in the Intelligence Reports by Messers Newington and Stanford, there is no single instance in which "human elephants" or "human leopards" or "crocodiles" or other transmigration animals featured in warfare. But there are stories of isolated attacks and killing of individuals by one totem animal or the other.

In the early days, when practically all Ali-Ogba was a natural animal habitat or an animal kingdom, attack of human beings by wild animals must have occurred frequently. In such a state of affairs, crafty individuals able to convince their contemporaries that they were responsible for at least some of the attacks could easily boost up their prestige in a superstitious community.

Occasionally today, an Ogba may be seen growling like a lion and jumping across the house tops swiftly, and vigorously like a cat. They say such a man's leopard is fighting in the bush. But the same amount of energy and dexterity could be displayed by a drunken or drugged man. It is interesting to note that the "kingship" *onuobdos* which exercised the greatest political powers have the least frightful totems (viz; ants and beetle and python)! Perharps, they had the least need to boost up their already high prestige. That the colonial intruders armed with a few muskets were eventually able to win the day in Ali-Ogba, after little or no fighting at all, in spite of the "human elephants" and leopards and "extra-sensory perceptions", indicates the grave futility of these "skills", especially those supposed to make men "bullet proof" or "matchet proof". It appears, on the whole, that these mysterious "powers" raise the hopes of simple villagers in small matters only to "betray them in deeds of greatest consequence."

A typical example is narrated by Lily Nwabudike who visited Ugbodu village (Bendel State) "where men can turn to lions ... to settle a score'. In an account given in the *Observer* of 22nd July, 1989, she writes;

> the Obi (of Ogbodu) said that a concoction of a leaf, called *Ozuireti*, (It's not possible for one to see one's ears) seven seeds of alligator pepper and a little quantity of native chalk if taken, protects one from cutlass or any sharp object cuts.
>
> He said the medicine is effective for one day but if one takes it every day, one is automatically immuned from matchet cuts. When asked to demonstrate how they commune with leaves, the Obi went into his room and brought a very peculiar type of calabash which he called *Onunu*. It was wrapped in red cloth with two cowries.
>
> He told the *Onunu* to stay on its window buglary proof, and it did. He also told it not to stay and it equally obeyed. At this juncture, I asked him if there was magnet in it. He said "no" I then asked him if I could try it. He said I could, and I was instructed what to tell the *Onunu*. These are; *Duo* (stand) and *ma duo* (don't stand) when I told it to stand, it did, but when I said *ma duo* it refused to fall.
>
> At this point, he commanded it to fall and it did, when I asked him why the *Onunu* refused to obey me, he said; "It belongs to me. On the use of the *Onunu* he said it's for protection and detection of thieves.

When he was asked to demonstrate how they commune with the leaves, he picked up *Akpakaemuren*, a type of leaf and said;

Uwoyi ewe, Osebua, no kpe ni, eneyi fohin inowun igbona, amohan di tutu". This means; "you leaf, God creates you, this person says her stomach in hot, make it cool". He said if after talking to the leaf, it remains dormant, it means there 'll be no cure for the ailing person. But if the leaf responds then it would perform the healing.

However, whether or not Ogba *onuobdos* were actually able to achieve their intended purposes is of less importance than the fact that they believed the purposes to be achievable through the means they adopted. According to Umuezeali, the power (to change into the python) was acquired "through a charm prepared (for Umuezealis) by the Arochukwu people or the Akwa people or a people of no fixed address known as "Umuodilamo". Umueke acquired the power "during the Aboh war and it helped them escape from the enemy". We know that the Aros believed in taking people to their great *chukwu* in Arochukwu, not in preparing lesser deities or charms for anyone. In any case, the Aros did not reach Ali-Ogba until the late 17th Century.

A common feature of the totems or transmigration animals is that they enjoin abstinence on the members of the *onuobdos* concerned. Ihiukwus do not eat leopard meat because if they do, they may be eating one of their own people without knowing. They also refrain from eating anything killed by a leopard or any food of which the leopard is fond such as *ede* (cocoyam) or *okro*.

Uriems abstain from leopard, as well as from squirrel, frog, *Ubelebe, mma-ekwu* because they all look like leopard. Umualinwas abstain from mushroom, *ona*, and *uga*, Umuenyikes from *ona* and mushroom; and Umuebes from mushroom.

Now, every law (including traditional laws of abstinence) must have a sanction otherwise it will be frequently breached. We know that Ogba traditions of abstinence were most strictly observed by the members of the different *onuobdos*. Even today persons who do not believe in the traditional religion avoid the taboos of their *onuobdos* more or less as a social etiquette.

Shrines

Ogba *onuobdos* have various penalties for offenders against the different "laws" of abstinence:

> If an Umuogidi should knowingly or unknowingly eat *okro*, he will suffer from serious infection which will produce spots on his skin resembling a leopard's spots. The remedy is to go to the high priest at Osiakpu with a fowl for *Odu-ka-Ogidi*.
>
> Any Uriem eating any of these things (which are taboos) must sacrifice to the shrine (*Mkpitima*) on *Eke* night. If *Mkpitima* wants a goat from an Uriem, it may afflict him with leprosy until the goat has been presented.
>
> Transgressors (Umualinwas) are infected with leprosy and must go at once to *Odu-ka-Ajie* with one white goat, three yams and as many kolanuts as possible[20].

Thus, every transgressor can make amends for his offence by presenting certain items (usually of food) to a designated shrine. Consequently, each *onuobdo*, which has its own transmigration animal and taboos, also has its own shrine e.g. Umuogidis have *Odu-ka-Ogidi*, Uriems have *Mkpitima*, Umualinwas have *Odu-ka-Ajie*, Umuenyikes have *Odu-ocha*, Umuebes have *Odu-ocha*.

In addition, Ogbas had (and still have) numerous other "shrines" such as *Ndeze, Abohuo, Erisi* Omoku, *Egbamini, Odu-ka-Ogidi, Otu-Ohali, Awiya ocha, Akpu eze, Utu Aligu, Orji Aligu, Mkpitima, Odu-ka-Ajie, ezumezu Ema-ka-Dike*.. We shall examine the social or religious significance of some of these shrines or deities very briefly:

Ndeze (Kings)

These "kings" were carved images representing the immediate ancestors of the extended family. They were highly honoured as the guardian spirits of the family who continued to take an interest in the affairs of the living. The head of each extended family (i.e. the oldest member) is the priest and curator of *Ndeze* responsible for worshipping them and giving them their share of

---

[20] *Ema-ka-dike* is also referred to *Egbu-akwra-akkru* or that which kills and carries off the goods of the victim. The "alias" arose from the practice of surrendering half of the property of the victim to the shrine to prevent it

food and drinks as occasion may demand. An elder of the family would not eat his meal or take his drink without first throwing a small part on the ground for the ancestors to eat or drink. At traditional festivals, the images of the ancestors are displayed and showered with food and drinks. When an elder of the family dies, he is counted among the *Ndeze*, after the apropriate funeral ceremonies shall have been performed. In time, new children born to the family are named after the late elder (their re-incarnator), as may be directed by the soothsayer, assuming the elder had led a good, exemplary life.

Abohuo (basket of traditional symbol of authority)
This "basket" which contained the *ohuo* of each family was usually kept under the custody of the oldest member of the *onuobdo*. It represented a bond or union of all branches of an *onuobdo*. A serious dispute leading to disruption of family ties within an *onuobdo* (as happened in Uriem after the murder of Eyio's wife) would cause the dissolution of *Abohuo* and the disintegration of the *onuobdo*. Elechukwu Njaka defined *ofo* (or *ohuo* without the basket or *abo*) as:

> A symbol of authority,[21] the link between the dead, the living and the unborn, God and man; a symbol of truth and justice, trust and confidence. The *ofo* has both religious and political significance, and without it no religious ceremony can be fittingly performed.

Ohuo or *ofo* is usually made of wood or iron. It is often conical in shape, ancient in appearance and convenient in size so that an elder can punctuate his pronouncements by raising and striking it on the ground at will.

Erisi Omoku (Omoku Shrine)
> Umueke are the custodians of *Erisi* Omoku. They are always entitled to produce a priest for the *erisi*. The post is not hereditary in any one Umueke family but when a priest dies, a soothsayer is consulted who must announce the next Umueke son selected by the *Erisi* to be her priest. *Erisi* Omoku is worshipped by all Omoku sons and daughters, except Christians. *Erisi* Omoku does not permit an Omoku son or daughter to get drowned in the Omoku River. When things go wrong, diviners must find out why *Erisi* Omoku is angry and endeavour to

---

[21] Elechukwu Njaka, *Igbo Political Culture*, Northwest University Press Evanston 1971, p. 156.

appease her. In approaching the *erisi*, they must take a white goat, a white fowl and white clothes to offer to her because she does not accept anything off colour. *Erisi* Omoku is worshipped only on *Eke Ukwu* day.²²

Egbamini (boundary waters)

Before an Umuorodu goes to war, he must first visit the *onuobdo* shrine known as *egbamini* to ask for protection, taking with him one white goat, one white hen or cock, four white pieces of cloth and an eagle's feather. Umuorodu sons and daughters seeking for more children, more wealth, happiness or other benefits, may also visit *egbamini*, provided that they take along with them the enumerated items. *Egbamini* is unlike many other shrines in that it cannot be invoked to kill an enemy or harm anyone or do any evil. It is solely concerned with doing good. Its demands from those that worship it are identical with the demands made by *Erisi* Omoku from her own adherents: except that additionally Umuorodus have to refrain from eating certain species of fish namely *ukawu, ogbor, nnebruhie*.²³

Odu-ka-Ogidi (The elephant tusk of Ogidis)

Before an Umuogidi transmigrates, he must go to *Odu-ka-Ogidi* at Osiakpu and sacrifice a fowl. The oldest member of Umuogidi is usually the high priest of *Odu-ka-Ogidi*. The present high priest is called *Akio*.²⁴

Otu-Ohali (Ohali group) and Uzor Oru (Oru way)

The *Otu-Ohali* shrine in Ohalielu is worshipped in common by all Umuohalis. The oldest member of Umuohali is its high priest and any Umuohali found guilty of *Isoruhu* (i.e. desecration of Umuohali totem) must appease the gods through the intermediary of the high priest. Apart from *Otu-Ohali*, Umuohalis are also the owners of *Uzor Oru* which is regarded as the protector of Umuohalis wherever they may be. The oldest Umuohali member is automatically the high priest of *Uzor Oru*.²⁵

---

22 As narrated by Victor Eke, *Owerre* of Umueke, in his palace at Usomini quarters in Omoku on 10th November, 1979.

23 As narrated by Chief S. Okoroma (*Otu Awusa*), oldest member and head of Umuorodu *Onuobdo*, and Thompson Ezegbrika (*Otu Akpo Agi*), second oldest member of onuobdo, at their house in Omoku on 21st November, 1979.

24 As narrated by Ebenezer Osima, the *Iyasra* of Umuogidi and Johnson Ogidi of Umuogidi.

25 As narrated by Osi Nwa Orji, oldest member and head of Umuohali and Gilbert Nwajari, leading member of Umuohali.

Awiya Ocha (white eddy) Akpu eze (king's cotton tree) and Utu Aligu (Aligu stream)

> Umunkarus worship *Awiya Ocha, Akpu eze* and *Utu Aligu*. These gods do not kill anyone, but they bring good and keep away evil. The high priest of each of the shrines is chosen by a soothsayer after consulting his oracle.[26]

Orji Aligu (Aligu Iroko)

> *Orji Aligu* is the habitat of many pythons which are sacred to Umunkaru and Umuoyro... When Umuoyoros are in danger, they go to *Orji Aligu* and seek the intervention of its pythons.

Mkpitima

> Any Uriem eating any of these things (viz: frog, *ubelebe* and *mmaekwu* which are taboo to Uriems) must sacrifice to *Mkpitima* shrine on *Eke* night. He should paint his whole body with white chalk and appear before the shrine (*Mkpitima*).

Ezumezu

An *ezumezu* shrine is usually located in a conspicuous position within the premises where the principal devotee resides. It often comprises a small hut containing several "action" images moulded in mud. The devotee and his family have to worship it night and day with frequent beating of loud drums and much energetic dancing near it. The *ezumezu* "cult" was most probably adopted from the Isoko or Urobo clan of former Bendel State.

Adult Ogba males had (have) *Ihe joku* or the yam god supposed to reside in a small pot *(udu or nchaka)* which is placed in the home of every prosperous yam farmer.

Male Ogba traders had *Ikenga* or *Inyama* which is a carved stick supposed to help them prosper in their trade.

Females had *nnemulo* (Abo word) or *whimuno* which is a shapeless wooden object covered with clay supposed to help with fertility.

---

[26] As narrated by Nwokogu Adah, oldest member and head of Umunkaru *Onuobdo* and Benedict Osiago, the *Akogu* of Umunkaru and Pius Adah.

The Place Of The Supreme Deity In Ogba Traditional Religion

Ogba traditional religion, although based on an ultimate belief in an Omnipotent Supreme God (*Chukwu Abiama*), involves belief in transmigration and worship of numerous subordinate deities collectively called *erisi* comprising all manner of natural phenomena, especially marshes, lands, creeks, highways, images representing ancestors, elephant tusks, trees (especially cotton and iroko). *Chi* is symbolised by a wooden plate. Only women have *chi* in Ali-Ogba. But in other areas outside Ogba, men also have *chi*. According to Njaka (p.33),

> Every adult male, upon having a house of his own, has a shrine for his *chi*. An Igbo woman who takes a husband builds a shrine for her own *chi*.

Njaka describes chi as *chukwu's* manifestation in all created things. In man the *chi* is his spiritual double. A chi is the manifestation of the individual ego in the spirit of life. It is that being which links its house, man, to the one soul *(chukwu)* ...A *chi* is the sustaining essence of a living man but not the man who dies. The *chi* leaves the man at death - in fact , its leaving is death, because the *chi* is likened to the breath of life ... the *chi* is the man's double, linking him to *chukwu,* his ancestors, and the unborn, guarding, guiding, and protecting him... *chi* is omniscient, can foresee danger, and is concerned only with (one individual) with whom it remains through one life time... The Igbo negotiates with *Chukwu* through the *arusi*, but he deals directly with his *chi,* his ancestors, other men".

Obviously, *chi* cannot mean so much to the Ogba if it is relegated to a deity fit to be worshipped by women only. To the Ogba, *chi* appears to be more "a goddess of luck" than anything else.

Njaka goes on to describe *chukwu:*

> *chukwu* is a name given to the Supreme Being, but not in the way the West conceptualizes the Supreme Being...To the Igbo, *chukwu* is an unknown wonderous creator and the origin of all things; nothing exists or can exist without him... He has everything and does not need or demand anything from man... To the Igbo, *chukwu* does not need any worship... Man can build no shrine to satisfy *chukwu.*

On the contrary, an Ogba traditional family head builds a shrine called *Ihi chukwu* (or the "face of *chukwu*") with wooden "stumps" on either side. Sacrifices are offered to Ihi *chukwu* whenever a diviner or soothsayer calls for them.

Ogbas also had (have) an *Ihi Osa* or the "face" of *Osa* which comprises the foot of the central pillar in the living room of the "family" head's house. Around this pillar, carved sticks said to represent every dead ancestor (called *egu* or re-incarnator) are heaped. Every *Nchaka* day, the *egus* are washed and feasted. A diviner or soothsayer may call for the feasting of an *egu* or group of *egus* at any time.

Re-incarnation

The belief in *egu (or re-incarnation)* is a cardinal point in Ogba traditional religion. The good man returns to earth as often as he wishes within his agnatic group. A woman returns within the agnatic group of her husband. A female may return as a male or a female, but a male never returns as a female. A bad man, or woman dies deepest death *(imida)* and never returns to earth in any form.

The belief by Ogbas and other traditional societies in *egu* or re-incarnation may be based on strange experiences such as the one reported by Sebastain Ofurum in *The Guardian* of 8th August 1987, which was culled from *The Guardian* of 1st March 1986, which was culled from the *Weekly World News* published in the United States of America. According to that story:

> six witnesses including medical doctors were stunned because at birth a child spoke clearly in English for twenty minutes. The child was no sooner stabilized after birth than she began to cry out for her husband and children and demanded to know where she was... The baby was spoken to in answer to her question and she reportedly replied "No. No. It's May 1841. Please don't scare me". As seconds ticked away, the baby's words became slurred and were broken by infantile whimpers and cries. The child dozed off and was not to speak in that fashion since then.

There is another story of how a boy who was born in the eastern states of America travelled to a house in Los Angeles at the age of twelve years and calling his supposed children one by one by name, showed them a treasure he had buried somewhere in the premises in his previous life.

A few curious incidents have also occurred in Nigeria. In the Umuahia area, a man's corpse turned out to be taller than the coffin prepared for him. So, to save the costs involved in making another coffin, his legs were broken at the ankles and forced into the undersized coffin. When his wife, who was pregnant at his death, delivered a child, the baby (which was claimed to be a re-incarnation of the deceased,) was naturally endowed with broken ankles and walks on his insteps till this day.

In Akabuka, one of the Odus who was supposed to be a re-incarnation of his grand mother, was born with marks of the Ivory bangles(?) worn by his late grand mother on his wrists and ankles.

In his *Philosophy and Practice of Yoga* (C.N. Fowler Romford 1978 p.108), James McCartney says:

> It is a fact that practically all the eastern races believe in rebirth. Indeed, in terms of numbers, more than half the world's population have accepted the premise of rebirth and Karmic Law, but the Western World with its scientific approach, has found it hard to accept something which cannot be proved, and Christianity, the religion of the West, denies it. But now there is hope for evidence is coming to light by all quarters, of people who have conscious memory of previous lives.

We would contend that no amount of superficial or apparent "evidence" can supersede scientific truth. It is the Western World which believes in scientific truth that has brought the world to where it is today in terms of technological development which has changed and improved man's standard of living throughout the world; not the Eastern world that has accepted rebirth and Karmic Law. The amount of technological development that has occurred so far in the East has been based on Western Science. But there is the consolation that what the world knows of truth today is only an infinitesminal fraction of existing truth. The Eastern World should do its best to prove and propagate its theories and beliefs in a manner that will be acceptable and beneficial to all mankind.

Economic Pursuits

It is significant that the natural objects or phenomena which Ogbas deified were the most valuable economically, religiously or aesthetically, given the prevailing conditions in their immediate environment and their traditional occupations. Creeks and marshes determined the daily fortunes of a predominantly fishing community; lands produced the farmer's crops and protected the ancestors; the Iroko tree provided the strongest wood for construction; the highways led to forests, farms and markets; elephant tusk was a prized possession widely recongnised as the highest of all royal insignia. In contrast, the taboos were usually inconsequential objects e.g. *Okro*, from which Umuogidi refrain, is a gummy ingredient which is naturally distasteful to some people. *Ede* (cocoyam) which is avoided by Ihiukwus is inferior to the ordinary yam. *Ona* from which Umuenyikes abstain is also an inferior yam. The mushroom (another object of abstention by Umuenyikes) is used in place of fish by less affluent families when fish is not available. Umueke abstain from *Oku-egbe* and *nnebruhie* "which are the dirtiest fishes in the water". In the Ogba world, religious and economic pursuits, social organisation and even political organisation were closely associated, leading to a certain stability, peace and orderly traditional government.

Under the shadow of their pervasive traditional religion, Ogbas engaged themselves sparingly in various economic pursuits. In general, living was comparatively easy because of scanty population and consequent limited economic competition.

Economic pursuits in Ali-Ogba were carefully regulated by customs, tradition and religion among the three distinct groups of Usomini, Igburu and Egi. In each group, there was a clear division of labour between the men and women. The Usomini people were mainly farmers and fishermen, but certain fishing and farming operations were reserved for women. In Igburu, where there is abundance of palm wine trees,[27] the men were

---

27 Because of the swampy terrain. The leaves of the palm wine trees serve as the raw material for mat weaving.

mainly palm wine tappers, while the women were mat weavers. Similarly, in Egi, with abundant oil palm trees, the men climbed palm trees and cut down the palm fruits, while the women prepared oil from the palm fruits.

The above structure should not imply that a few Igburu's or Egis did not adopt fishing or that Usomini women did not undertake occasional mat weaving. What existed were very broad divisions of labour which must have been imposed on the different groups by environmental constraints. An occupation in which Ogbas participated irrespective of their group of origin was farming, although the Egis and Igburus tended to engage more in farming since there was less fishing to distract their attention in their areas. Because of limited land in *Aliulo* (i.e. the high ground east of the Orashi), most of the fishing and farming took place at *Ogboru* during the months of February to October every year. Through the agency of the priests and diviners, one of the four days of the 'week' (especially *Eke*) is held sacred to each farmland deity. On such a day, no work at all is permitted on such a land.

Yam and Cassava

The oldest and most important crop planted was the yam, (*Dioscorea rotundata and Dioscorea cayenensis*), which is indigenous to West Africa. Ogbas were already familiar with the art of yam cultivation when they arrived in Ali-Ogba. The practices and methods adopted at that time have hardly been varied to this day. Towards the end of the dry season, the men clear the forests and prepare the yam seedlings. As Ogbas became somewhat affluent (due to the slave trade and the palm produce trade) they started avoiding the more tedious farming operations. Instead of clearing the bush for farming, most Ogbas would simply wear their best clothes and go to the *Orie* market square. There they would find migrant laborers known as *Isu* (they probably came from the over-crowded area near *Isu Njaba*). At a modest fee, an Ogba would hire a number of *isus* for the day. Apart from the fee, an *isu's* contract was usually loaded with perquisites: free food, free shelter, free entertainment. Consequently, an *isu* was able to save practically all his wages. Some *isus* built large houses in their villages after a single sojourn at Ali-Ogba. Some bought slaves and engaged in large-scale agriculture or trading.

And yet, Ogbas derived very little benefit from the physical contributions made by the *isus*. In the first place, *isu* efforts were usually very feeble. Their attitude was to do the least work for the highest pay. They would arrive late at the farm and leave early. And they were noted for their ability to feign illness at the slightest opportunity, hence the Ogba expression *Oria ka umu isu* [28] When referring to someone who pretends to bę sick. Thus, the bulk of the farm work was still left for Ogbas to do when the *Isus* were gone.

The arrogant practice of employing *isus* to do manual work must have grown out of semi-capitalist tendencies on the part of Ogbas who had surplus land (due to the low population density) and were able to provide farm inputs out of the surplus proceeds from their fishing exploits. The location of much of Ali-Ogba on navigable waterways (the most notable means of communication during the period) meant that most Ogbas were exposed to the beneficial influences of civilization immediately the colonial powers began their policy of penetrating into Nigeria through the waterways. These influences affected the cleansing, adornment and decoration of the human person. Consequently, the disparity between the riverine and the hinterland peoples in their styles of dress or "undress" was quite conspicuous, especially in the different "common markets" they attended. It is this disparity that led to a vain and idle feeling of superiority by one group, which the other group was clever enough to exploit to their own advantage in the inevitable economic rat race among the groups. Even today that no distinctions exist, except perhaps in the opposite direction, some local maniacs still cling to the meaningless anachronisims.

After the first or second rain of the year, a man's wives and children help him plant seed yams in the cleared area. A small seed yam weighing about one kilo is planted whole.

---

28 Translated as "isu illness".

Alternatively, it may be split into two and each part is planted separately. Each planted seed yam is covered in a circular mound about twelve inches high and eighteen inches in diameter. After about three months, the women clear the weeds in the farm and the men install wooden poles to support the tendrils of yam plants. At suitable intervals, the women repeat their work of farm clearing and the men supervise the growth of the yam plant and ensure that the tendrils are carefully twisted around the poles provided. Roughly nine months after planting, the yam is harvested by the whole family-men, women and children - and everyone is ready for the *Nchaka* Festival.

Another major crop which became a staple food for Ogbas is the cassava which was introduced by the Portuguese late in the 15th Century. Although the Portuguese made early contact with Benin, it appears that cassava reached Ali-Ogba only in the 17th Century from other sources. Cassava does not feature in any of the traditional religious or social ceremonies established when Ogbas first settled in Ali-Ogba. Apparently, cassava reached Ali-Ogba from the Delta (*oru*). According to Elizabeth Isichei, "Cassava was well established in the Delta by the late 17th Century".

Probably because *yam* was the only major crop known in the earliest periods, men and women were permitted by custom to combine their efforts in its cultivation. A superior position is accorded to yam in all traditional festivals. On such occasions, only pounded yam may be eaten. As a custom, the most respectable family elders (males) are expected to eat pounded yam daily, in season and out of season. Every respectable adult male should have his yam barn (*Oba*) fully stocked every harvest season, sufficient to last him through the season of scarcity (*Ukwuya*) until the next harvest season.

Cassava has always been regarded as a woman's crop. By the time it was introduced in the 17th century, it appears that men were so pre-occupied with yam farming and with fishing that they left its cultivation wholly and solely to women. Furthermore, the fact that cassava is cultivated in less fertile land (secondary or tertiary rain forest), which can be cleared and maintained with minimum physical strain, may have influenced its consignment to the realm of women's activities.

Maize, Tomatoes, Bananas, Cocoyams and Plantains, etc.

Maize , which was introduced into Ali-Ogba around the same time when cassava was introduced (17th Century) is cultivated more or less indiscriminately by men and women. It is usually inter-planted among the yams, harvested within three to four months, and eaten between meals.

Other crops which were introduced through contacts with the Portuguese include chili peppers and tomatoes from America and Cocoyams, bananas and plantains from Asia. Most of these were "women's crops". Any male cultivating them in the traditional society were considered mean or vulgar. Tomatoes were not used until recent times, but bananas were regarded as delicacies. Other delicacy crops included sugarcane and ground-nuts cultivated in limited quantities on the alluvial soil on the banks of the River Niger and its distributaries.

Plantains, which were cultivated almost as a hobby by men and women, featured in occasional dishes. Vegetables (especially *Okro*) were women's crops. *Okro* in particular and cocoyam were frequently taboos to some *onuobdos*. Kola-nut and coco-nut trees were men's crops; but only a few trees were ever planted by any individual in his life-time. These crops were often inherited by one generation after another. Kolanut is still regarded as sacred. "*Onye wiyeri oji wiyeri ndu*". [29] It was always brought to a visitor to assure him that he was welcome. Kolanut is not served in the night (*uchi zukabala oji*), [30] apparently for reasons of security. [31a] Whenever kolanut is served according to Ogba tradition, it must first be offered to the ancestors (their share is always thrown to them on the ground), then to all males in turn beginning from the oldest, then to women. The Ogba kolanut culture, with its emphasis on reverence to *Chukwu Abiama* (Almighty God) and individual

---

[29] He that brings kola-nut brings life.
[30] Night has hidden kola-nut.
[31a] Anyone eating kola in poor light at night may eat poison unknowingly.

ancestors, is very similar to the *igmo and* Aboh culture; unlike *oru* culture in which strong drinks (e.g. gin) are poured as libation to water gods and the great God (*Tamuno*).

Fishing, Hunting, Arts and Crafts

> *Fishing:* This chiefly concerns the OSOMINI (sic) group. The general methods employed are either casting a net from the bow of a canoe, or the stationery method of bamboo stockade which are felled during high water. The net is the most popular. Besides these two, there are ponds which occur wherever there are small creeks.[31b]

Throughout the year, even during the clearing of yam farms, men had to provide the protein required for food in the family. Usomini men concentrated on fishing, while their Igburu and Egi counterparts concentrated on hunting. Agburu and Okpraome who are said to have discovered Omoku were believed to have done so during the course of a hunting expedition undertaken from Obigwe, an Igburu village. The hunting practices of Ogbas are among the most outstanding customs and traditions which depict Ogbas as their brothers' keepers. Reference has already been made to the custom of *Whekanu* in which a young *Nwoyigmo* takes the whole of the first animal he kills to his *Nwadiali* for monetary and other presents and "blessing". Thereafter, any sizeable animal killed by an Ogba is traditionally shared among the extended family in such a way that everyone gets a share; but the sharing must conform strictly to tradition in every detail. The killer of the animal is given one "hand" (extending from shoulder to fingers) and one "leg" (i.e. from waist to toes); plus half of the neck and the whole tail (*okpasi anu*). The other "half-neck" is given to the "carriers" of the animal from the "bush" to the "house". The head of the animal goes to a member of the "family" (*imogba*) immediately *next* in seniority to the animal killer. In return, he marks the killer's hand with the sign of white chalk, which may be accompanied with monetary or material donation. The oldest member of the *imogba* gets *okpu anu* (sometimes called *egwu anu*) (comprising the lungs and all around it). He also marks the

---

[31b] (Newington's Intelligence Report 1931 page 40).

hand of the killer with the sign of white chalk plus or minus monetary or other material donation. The next oldest person in the *imogba* gets an upper arm *(Nkwoji anu)*. The mother of the animal killer gets the top of the abdomen around the *okpu anu* (i.e. *ehuanu*). The remainder of the animal (mainly entrails, liver etc minus the bile of leopards) is cut into small sizes and prepared in such a way (as *awuya*) that every member of the *imogba* has a share. Sharing of *awuya* begins from the eldest (regardless of the share already taken) and extends to the very youngest member of the *imogba*. Consequently, the killing of an animal by a member of the extended family was an occasion for rejoicing by all members of the extended family; just as a misfortune affecting a member was lamented by all - a culture of traditional "communism" or "communalism", which could be usefully incorporated into some aspects of modern rural development plans for Ali-Ogba and other Nigerian traditional areas.

Usomini men prepared and installed fish baskets at favorite fishing spots and inspected them regularly. In *Ibegwre* (February to April), Usomini, Ogbas and a few Egis and Igburus would fish communally in large lakes or ponds. These ponds vary in size from thirty acres of water surface to half an acre. When the Niger and Orashi over-flowed their banks, the ponds were completely submerged. When the flood receded, the ponds reappeared with considerable fish life left behind by the flood waters. These practices continue today with little, if any, modification.

By custom, Ogbas harvested their fish ponds communally. When the date for the communal harvesting of a pond was announced, the whole community assembled on the appointed day at the appointed time determined by the position of the sun in the sky. The owner of the pond was entitled to one-third of the fish caught by each person. The traditional procedure was for the fishermen to construct *eje* (dam) and bail the water across it in rhythm with *egwu ekwo* (bailing song). When the pond was almost dry, they fished with nets, baskets, spears and bare hands. Men and women did not bail the same ponds together.

Women bailed smaller ponds by themselves without any help from men.

In season, men would migrate to "distant lands" on the Niger or Nun River and engage in fishing with *ojoglo, eri, ukpo* and *agdagu* [32]. Some *onuobdos* (e.g. Ihiukwu or Agwo olo) excelled in fishing and earned for themselves the distinctive praise name and isiali title of *nwangwo* (or adepts at preparing fish dishes). Umuogidi relatives of Ihiukwu, were adepts at bailing ponds. They were also ruthless warriors, hence the saying *Umuogidi ojimadu esi eje; eje rima madu were azu kwu ugwo*. [33]

Ogbas could not have become successful fishermen without adequate means of transportation on water. Some men with a creative bent specialised in boat building. The average male was expected to build his own *ugbakiri* out of the *ukpo* tree; but only really talented professionals were able to build large canoes capable of carrying fifty men and arms. Ogba craftsmen also produced various wooden utensils such as *Mkpru* (mortar for preparing food), *Ojosi* (large spoon), and *Okwa* (wooden plates). More gifted artists produced masks for certain companies of *Okrosu*..Ogbas also produced wooden clubs *(akube)* which could disarm a man armed with *Omrenyi* (elephant's doom). [34]

Iron-Working (Agbda-Luzu)

Fire-arms may have reached Ali-Ogba through Benin sources or through Umuagbda. In regard to other iron tools generally, Ogbas relied on the Umuagbda *Onuobdo* whose efforts were supplemented by the work of itinerant black-smiths from Awka. It would seem that some Awkas actually remained behind in Ali-Ogba and were afterwards absorbed by the Umuagbda *Onuobdo*. It was obviously the high importance attached to these

---

32 *Ojoglo, eri* and *agdagu* are different types of nets made from thread.
33 Umuogidi used human beings to create a dam; the dam ate the human beings and paid back with fish.
34 A descriptive name given to a sharp heavy cutlass used principally in warfare.

tools that earned the Umuagbda *Onuobdo* the high political position of *Iyasra* [35] and the "economic" title of *Agbda-lu-zu*. [36] Excavations at Obrikom/Obieh indicate that some ancient people skilled in the working of iron and in tools manufacture were living in Obrikom/Obieh in C.235 B.C. Human habitation in that area dates from C.3000 B.C. (Dr. Nwanna Nzewunwah excavations). The exact relationship between the latter generation Umuagbda and the early iron workers whom they succeeded appears uncertain. The early settlers or iron workers may have been absorbed, eliminated or displaced by their successors.

In any case, Ogba hunters and warriors appear to have been quite familiar with fire-arms from the early 17th Century when the latter became available, hence the Umuenyike were able to undertake long distance journeys to Arochukwu. Their Aro associates were also in a position to give them fire-arms and other weapons obtained from Apas or Abams, Ohafias and Eddas. Furthermore, Ogbas were in a position to obtain firearms through their contacts with Oru (Delta) traders who got them from Europeans during the course of the slave trade.

Until very recent times, practically every adult male of the Umuenyike *Onuobdo* was an adept in the use of fire-arms. To a certain extent, similar claims could be made by other *onuobdos*. This "king" of weapons displaced other weapons in Ali-Ogba immediately its use became popularised. It became indispensable as a means of defence, aggression, and hunting. Older methods of hunting, such as the use of *Nkughru* and *uta* were relegated to the world of child's play, immediately fire-arms became available to Ogbas.

Markets

The crops and fish produced by the Usominis, the palm wine and mats from Igburus, and the palm oil, yams and cocoyams produced by the Egis were inter-changed at various markets in

---

[35] The *Isoma*, *Iyasra* and *Nwadei* (plural Umudei) titles appear to be the only ones which Ogbas have in common with the Oguta, Aboh and Onitsha with whom they share a common history of Benin origin.

[36] "Agbda - the black-smith".

Ali-Ogba. Close neighbours of Ogbas attended the famous *Nkwo* and *Orie* Markets in Omoku, especially Abohs, Ndonis, Ogutas, Awaras, (Ohaji), Ekpeyes and Orus (Ijaw).*Ndoni* Market was attended by Abohs,Ogbas, Onitshas and Ijaws. *Ase (Imonita)* Market was attended by Abohs, Ijaws,Osasamaris, Onitshas and Ogutas. *Emegi (Biseni)* Market was attended by Ogbas, Engenis, Ekpeyes, Abohs and Kalabaris. *Eke Ibocha* market was attended by Ogutas, Abohs, Awaras, and Egbemas. *Okirikiri* Market near Egwukwu Ogboru was attended by Ogutas, Abohs and Ogbas.

Most of these markets appear to have been established between C.1600 and C.1700 when the population of Ali-Ogba had become fairly substantial. Needless to add that these markets were attended mainly by Ogba women while the men (especially Usomini men) were engaged in fishing. A man could visit a market occasionally to purchase one item or the other or to help in selling yams, but in Ali-Ogba (until modern times), trade was left almost exclusively to women. It appears that the fear of slave raiders contributed in preventing men from attending markets because Aboh slave raiders in particular preferred to hunt for "sons". Ogbas do not appear to have engaged much in long distance trading as did the Aros and Nkwerres; but their traditional links with Aros must have led to exchange of goods. Consequently, it is true to say that, apart from the mingling of peoples as a result of constant migrations in the early days the various central markets also provided frequent meeting points for indegenes (especially women) to meet with their neighbours from Omoku, Ndoni, Oguta, Awara, Ekpeye, Onitsha, Ijaw, Ossamari, Emegi (Biseni), Kalabari and Egbema. From these market meetings, traders learnt new fashions, new songs and dances and new ideas, giving rise, in course of time, to a distinct"Ogbaru" culture, which is still discernible today.

Money

Trade in Ogba markets could not have flourished without the use of currency. Although some degree of trade by barter was carried on, the use of cowries (from the Indian Ocean) in the Usomini and Igbru areas was as old as the arrival of Ogbas in

Ali-Ogba. According to Elizabeth Isichei, "Cowries were used in Benin before Europeans came there".[37] Apparently, Ogbas brought these cowries with them from Benin or they obtained them from their neighbours (Oguta, Aboh), who obtained them from Benin. In the Egi area, manillas were used instead of cowries. These may have been obtained from Igbo Ukwu (excavations by Prof. Shaw revealed objects resembling manillas) or from other sources. The use of different currencies in different parts of Ali-Ogba indicates the different outside groups with which various Ogba groups came into contact.

There was also another type of currency in circulation mentioned by Elizabeth Isichei:

> A Seventeenth Century visitor to the Delta described the sting-ray shaped currency, the size of the palm of the hand, made by the *Southern Igbo of Moko* .

In his book *The Trading States of the Oil Rivers*, G.I. Jones comments on the position of *Moko* and states:

> John Barbot's general description is mainly a paraphrase of Dapper with suitable amendments... The territory of *Crike (Okrika?)* is placed some leagues north, north-west of Rio Real, and borders towards the south on that of Moko, which lies near the sea.... John Barbot is clearly not very happy about the site of *Moko* and the identity of *Bany* and *Culebo*....

It has been suggested elsewhere that *Moko* refers to an *Ibibio* group visited by early European traders and explorers, which merely complicates the issue because an *Ibibio* group is not a *Southern Igbo town* as contained in Dapper's and John Barbot's descriptions.

Names of towns within the Igbo area resembling *Moko* are *Okomoko* in Etche and Omoku in Ogba. For some unknown reasons, all Nigerian maps made before 1940 designate "Omoku" as *Omoko*. It may be that the "Sting-ray currency" was actually made near *Omoku* (e.g. in Obrikom) where iron was worked in 235 A.D. [38]

In addition to cowries and manillas, Ogbas speak of "iron rods" which were used side by side with cowries in the Usomini

---

[37] Elizabeth Isichei, *A History of the Igbo People*, Macmillan London 1976 p.33.
[38] Excavations by Dr. Nwanna Nzewunwa 1984.

and Igbru areas and side by side with manillas in the Egi area. It may be that these "iron rods" were also made into a sting-ray shaped currency by Awka or Umuagbda blacksmiths; or they may have been produced in Obrikom.

Social Organisation

Ogbas (especially the Usomini group) spent a good part of the year on economic pursuits, mainly fishing and farming, which are seasonal. During this period (February to October), they lived mainly in *Ogboru*. In the off-season (October to February), when there was little to do, they returned to *Aliulo* (the mainland east of the Orashi). The weather during this time of the year was usually cool and dry (harmattan), and thus conducive to out-door life. As Ogba houses were usually frail and insubstantial (chiefly mud and wattle until recent times), out-door life in the dry season suited Ogbas very well. Consequently, Ogbas tended to reserve all their traditional ceremonies till they returned home to *Aliulo* in the best season of the year. The Ogba custom of living cheek by jowl in their towns and villages encouraged social interaction, unlike the isolated compounds (*ama*) of the more interior clans which bred individualism.

Marriages

It was mostly when Ogbas from different *onuobdo*s and different *Ogboru*s returned to *Aliulo* that engagements took place.

The Ogba young man or woman began his own separate family life at an early stage in life . The women could get betrothed as early as the age of four or five years. At the age of roughly fifteen years , they began to live with their husbands who would themselves be about eighteen years of age.

As the men were usually entitled to as many wives as they could afford to marry, the first wives were usually chosen by the parents, but they usually took their own decisions on the subsequent wives.

A marriage usually established a bond between two extended families (*onuobdos*). Marriage between two members of the same *onuobdo* is strictly prohibited, even though some *onuobdo*s now have over seven thousand persons and have spread through ten or more separate villages and many generations.

The traditional wedding ceremony itself was comparatively simple: Usually, in *Ibegwre* [39] each year, intending couples prepared for their wedding. The family of the bride had to buy presents for the bride and the bridegroom had to pay a dowry on the bride. A wedding ceremony usually took place late in the evening in the home of the bride, with the parents and relations of the bride and bridegroom present or properly represented. Thereafter, the bride was led to her matrimonial home loaded with gifts from her own family comprising household utensils and clothes which may be worth even more than the dowry paid by the bridegroom. These articles were conveyed on the heads of six to twelve bridesmaids aged between five and fifteen years who would remain with the bride for four market days attending to all her necessities.

A unique marriage custom occurred in the case of a "king" who was entitled to marry any unmarried woman that caught his fancy simply by fixing an *iche* (Parrot's) feather on her head, either personally or through an emissary. To have attracted the king's parrot's feather was regarded as a mark of great honour and pride. When a person died, his next of kin who inherited his personal effects also "took over" (*Okwugasi*) his wives and looked after his children.

Births

Much premium was placed on the birth of as many children as possible (especially males) to swell the work and fighting force of the family. Daughters were referred to as *Okpokragba"*(empty vessels) and accepted with resignation. A few women acquired the art of traditional midwifery from their parents or relations and were usually in high demand in *Aliulo* or *Ogboru*, in season and out of season. Twins were forbidden and daughters born during *Okgu* when *Okrosu* was performing, automatically acquired the title *Nnowu* after a traditional visit by an *Okro*su company.

---

[39] November to February.

Nnowus were accorded certain rights and privileges in *Okro*su societies which were denied to other women and uninitiated males (*okpokisi*).

The first problem that had to be solved after the birth of a new child was to find out who it was that had returned to his kindred from hades. To tackle this problem, a *dibia* was consulted. *Dibias* were soothsayers as well as physicians and priests of the numerous *erisi*. The profession was usually handed over to one's progeny after a complicated system of prolonged initiation and practical training. In spite of the taboos with which the profession was hedged about, the practitioners seem to have had some knowledge of the properties of various herbs. It appears also that they knew some metaphysics.

Dibias usually came up with a name for every child, after studying the lie of their divination kolanuts or cowries on the ground. Of course, the *dibias* were well acqainted with the immediate past generation in every family. When a dibia announced that a particular ancestor was the re-incarnator of a particular child that declaration was usually accepted without challenge. My father is supposed to be a re-incarnation of Eze Nwonyukwu, the "king" who was poisoned in Obrikom. I am supposed to be a re-incarnation of Ajie Olowu, a renowned *dibia*, who frequently turned himself into a woman to avoid harassment by tax gatherers as women did not pay tax in his time. The story is that my father (John Wokocha) who had become a Christian insisted that no *dibia* should be consulted to find out who was my re-incarnator, assuring the family that he had the greatest of all *dibias* in his possession. Then, he brought out his Catholic missal and observed that I was born on the day of the feast of St. Francis of Assissi. So, he declared that my name was Francis, to the consternation of his pagan relations. Then, my grand father (Ellah) observed three scars on the instep of my left foot. He immediately burst into laughter, pointing out that I bore the scars of Ajie Olowu Nwokpra Nweke and there was indeed no need to consult any soothsayer or diviner. Until his death, he always called me Ajie Olowu and addressed me as if I was an old respectable relation of his, which I found embarrassing as a child. Some weeks before the controversial "naming ceremony", my maternal grand father (Ada nwa Osia) had told my mother during the advanced stage of her pregnancy that a "great spirit" was coming to her, a fact which went to confirm my grandfather Ellah's observation and pronouncement. Incidentally, I have never had the courage or conviction to practise as a *dibia*. The art of turning oneself temporarily into a woman would have been such great fun!

The belief in re-incarnation made it very difficult for outsiders to be absorbed into Ogba *onuobdos*. Children born to non-*onuobdo* members who may have been residing as neighbours of Ogba *onuobdo* were occasionally given the names of the late members of such *onuobdos*, if the relationship had been very cordial, but this very rarely happened. Outsiders who settled successfully in new areas in Ali-Ogba were usually fellow emigrants, with an identifiable Ogba ancestry, whose late members re-incarnated within their own extended family groups. Such groups eventually became individual *onuobdos* in their own right. The fact that the number of *onuobdos* has increased very slowly indicates the high degrees of stability in Ogba society.

A very different state of affairs arose in the days of domestic slavery following the abolition of the slave trade. As is well known, the Aros continued with the slave trade long after the abolition leading to the destruction of the Long Juju in 1902 by the Colonial Administration. Even after that date, domestic slavery continued "surreptitiously" for which a few prominent Ogbas were penalised by the Colonial Authorities.

In the days of domestic slavery, well-to-do Ogbas bought slaves to do their farm work and their trading for them. Like the slaves of the Efiks, Ogba slaves were kept in *Ogboru* and were hardly ever allowed to visit *Aliulo*. They could only inter-marry among themselves and the names of their offspring were determined by their owners without the intervention of *dibia*. It was apparently assumed that they could not have re-incarnators. Owners usually gave their slaves' children *(Omrululo)* non-Ogba names invented by themselves or encountered by them outside

Ali-Ogba during the course of their business travels. Such slaves remained socially differentiated by such names and discriminated against from generation to generation. Happily, the discriminations have since reduced or disappeared due to colonial intervention. But such usages as *Nwoyigmo* and *Nwadiali* , apparently derived from slave dealing, have persisted as additions to Ogba vocabulary.

Age Grades

As soon as the child was old enough to associate with others, he combined with children of his own age to form a new age-grade.

The names of the known age-grades and their various years of foundation are given in the Appendix. The names of the age-grades appear significant as they seem frequently to reflect the most topical issues at the time when particular age-grades came of age (i.e. when the members were fifteen years of age). [40] At that age, most age-grades took a permanent name. The following examples may clarify this point: The *Osukwu* (highest grade oil palm) age-grades members (born about 1868) were about fifteen years old in 1883 when legitimate trade in palm oil was most probably at its peak. *Ogbomdi* (cannon) age-grade members (born 1888) were fourteen years old in 1902 when the "expeditionary forces" used cannon to subdue different parts of Southern Nigeria (e.g. Arochukwu expedition for the destruction of the long juju or *chukwu* took place in 1902). The Abaam age-grade born about 1890 were fifteen years old in 1905 when many of the battles of resistance against colonial conquest were fought. (The Abaam people near Ohafia and Arochukwu were the recognised professional mercenaries hired by the Aro and others in their resistance efforts). The "German" age-grade youths were fifteen years old in 1901. (Around this time, German control of the neighbouring Cameroon territory may have been topical). *Okpamma* (armed men) age-grade suggests violence and insecurity around 1905. *Awusa* (i.e. Hausa) age-grade youths were fourteen years old in 1914 when Northern Nigeria (locally known as Hausaland) was amalgamated with

---

[40] Young people apparently married at the age of 15 years.

Southern Nigeria by Lord Lugard and Hausas began to travel freely in large numbers to settle in Southern Nigeria. Zik age-grade born about 1944 were about fifteen years of age in 1960 when Dr. Nnamdi Azikiwe (Alias Zik) became the Governor-General of Independent Nigeria. Ghana age-grade were fifteen years old in 1965 when the international fame of Ghana reached its peak. The 'Rivers State age-grade were about fifteen years old in 1970 when the Nigerian Civil War ended and former combatants came to acknowledge the Rivers State for the first time.

New age-grades were formed every two or three years. An age-grade had a "President" and other officials and was organised to levy fines and dues and enforce discipline. This pattern was apparently borrowed from Oru through the contacts made since the late 18th century. Every *Nkwukwu* or sixteenth day, members of the male age-grades hold traditional meetings at which they drink and dance *asawa* and sing in the Kalabari (Ijaw or Oru) tongue (*egwu asawa*), although only an occasional member may understand that language[41a]. All age-grades have their female counterparts but these are more or less "notional" associations. On great occasions, women attend the male age-grade meetings in company of their husbands.

Wrestling

Elsewhere in the world, wrestling matches might be arranged by weight of contenders; but in Ali-Ogba, it was people of the same age-grade that challenged themselves irrespective of weight. In Omoku, teams from the three quarters (Usomini, Obieti and Obakata) into which the capital was divided challenged one another; the other fourty towns and villages organised "home" and "away" matches against one another. Every wrestling match took place in the great arena or "parade ground", usually located in the most conspicuous central point in the town or village.

[41a] The "Indian" age grade (my age grade) began to sing Asawa songs in the Ogba dialect some years ago (on my personal intervention). All other age grades have followed suit. The drumming and dancing styles remain unchanged.

The outlay of the villages is on the whole fairly good. They are compact and much is included in a small space, but they always possess a wide and airy town or village meeting place in the centre.[41b]

The different age-grades wrestled in turn and the match ended when the oldest wrestling age-grade (those aged about twenty-five) had performed their part. When it was the turn of an age-grade to wrestle, the challengers and defenders in their colourful outfits danced round the arena to the sound of the *agbadi* whose deep vibrations made the very soil itself quiver. Then the wrestlers would take their positions at opposite ends of the arena. Usually, the weakest members of the opposing team were often invited first to wrestle. A reputed great wrestler might find that no one was bold enough to invite him. And if he took the initiative, everyone invited by him might decline wrestling. It was considered more honourable to decline than to be thrown by an opponent.

As many matches as possible could go on simultaneously in the same arena, provided that all wrestlers were of the same age-grade. Among the older age-grades, only a few pairs wrestled simultaneously. No wrestler was permitted to take the obvious action of pulling down an opponent by holding his legs. You must adopt sophisticated manouvres such as *Ogblo* (summersault) in accordance with the traditional wrestling etiquette. If you can lift your opponent up from the ground so that his two feet are dangling in space, then to all intents and purposes, he is regarded as "thrown". If any part of his body, even his small finger, touches the ground, he is considered thrown - No need to push a man about until he lies flat on his back in utter indignity! Besides, only a few contests are actually allowed to reach conclusion as the relatives or friends of each contestant are always at hand ready to intervene and stop the contest at the slightest sign that their idol might be thrown.

Whenever, in spite of every precaution, a person is eventually thrown, the victor is carried shoulder-high, with his mouth wide open, his tongue outstretched, his eye-brows raised, and the skin below each eye pulled down with the fore-finger, as if to say to the defeated wrestler - "you had been warned". The whole arena is at once taken over by the crowd of spectators,

---

41b (Intelligence Report by W.H. Newington 1931 page 39).

each in his colourful outfit dancing *iza* (the wrestling dance) to the deep sounds of the massive *agbadi* wrestling drum - the delight of champions and the dread of cowards. Ogba wrestling (like Ekpeye wrestling) is very different from the styles adopted in the immediate neighbourhood in which opponents can practically roll on the ground without being thrown until perhaps the "small" of their back touches the ground!

Professor Bolaji Idowu indicates one source of this unique Ogba wrestling etiquette in his *African Traditional Religion* (1973 - p.113):

> In Yorubaland for instance, wrestling is an art implying artistic movements and beauty of strategy; and when once any part of a contestant's body (apart from the feet) has touched the ground, be it no more than the tip of a finger, that contestant has been defeated and the contest is over.

It would appear that the Yorubas learnt their wrestling art from Benin (or vice-versa) which is obviously the source of the peculiar style adopted by Ogbas; or it may be that the Yorubas and Binis acquired this art from a common source. Nevertheless, this is one of the most revealing customs that Ogbas have retained to this day, which confirms their Benin origin and their traditional relationship with the Ekpeyes.

Every wrestling performance in Ali-Ogba was watched by a large team of friends, relations and fans, practically the whole population of an Ogba town or village turned out at the arena when there was a wrestling match. Everything else seemed to stop for many miles around when the *Agbadi* was heard. It was probably the greatest social occasion in the old days.

Dancing

Ogbas are great lovers of rhythmic music and dancing. In Ogba music, the *ukela* as well as drums made of wood and animal skins play a prominent role. But, generally, it is the *ukela* which plays the most prominent role, because it is always available and can be played solo in the absence of other instruments.

The *Ukela* is a conical metal piece used for keeping time and maintaining rhythm in traditional Ogba dance. The word 'ukela' is itself peculiar to the Ogba **tongue; but** there is a stringed instrument used for the same purpose in Hawaian Islands (capital Honolulu) situated in the centre of the North Pacific Ocean called *Ukulele*. The similarity between *Ukela* and *Ukulele* is very striking, especially as they represent musical instruments used for similar purposes in two widely different parts of the world.

The *Ukulele* was not native to Hawai but was developed from a small guitar brought there by Portuguese laborers around 1895. The steel guitar was invented in those islands in that year. The Hawaian census of 1890 does not indicate the presence of any negro at all but the one of 1910 indicated 695 negroes. Subsequently, some negroes most probably arrived with the Portuguese laborers in 1895 bringing an Ukela with them which was later corrupted to Ukulele. It is quite possible that an Ogba person or someone who had come in contact with Ogba ancestors, played an important role in that episode.

Apart from its use as a musical instrument, the *Ukela* was also used in traditional Ogba society to summon people together to hear a public announcement of general interest. It may be said that in traditional Ali-Ogba, the *Ukela* alone served the purpose which are today served by the newspaper, the radio, telephone, telegram, television and other electronic and print media.

We may consider a few Ogba dances so as to gain an idea of their peculiarity and variety:

Oru-orie (work on *Orie* day) - The leader wore *awuruawu* dress and other members sang a chorus and clapped their hands in unison with a rhythmic *ukela* sound in the background. Dancers bent themselves fully at the waist bringing their trunks at right angles with their feet. Each dancer stepped along rhythmically moving his weight from one foot to the other so as to give the back a tantalizing, wriggling, effect.

Orabrochi (drinking till dawn) - Another traditional dance in which older folk predominated. The dancing appeared less vigorous but there was more singing and eulogy. The steps were slow and dignified. The dancer remained almost in a standing position, waving his horse-tail and fan in different directions and balancing and swaying himself from side to side as the music dictated. The dress worn was the traditional *arigidi* cloth (of Benin origin) tied at the waist and reaching down to the ankles.

Ekworu (the cry of work) - This is mainly a ballad in which the singer played the most important role. A man or woman could perform *ekworu* solo and derive maximum satisfaction. The singer could vary and improvise a rhythm to suit his temperament and the tempo of his work. It was a kind of "music while you work". *Ekworu, Oruorie* and *Orabrochie* will feature again in the funeral ceremonies which will be narrated later. Other purely social dances included *Egwu Oji* (black or African dance) copied from the Aboh country (the singers speak Aboh dialect during the dance). Each *Oji* club had an emblem or coat of arms comprising an elaborate carving depicting some local phenomenon. *Egwu-elende* (the "proud" dance), *Egwu ayamba*, (a peculiar dance which attempted to modernise traditional music) introduced by the *America* age-grade; *Egwu Oregbu* in which a wooden xylophone was used, obviously introduced from Ikwerre land where it is still frequently performed on great occasions. *Obiemeni*, an Ekpeye dance in which very young girls (about eight to nine years old) were made to perform fantastic acrobatic feats - it was claimed that the dancers came from the spirit world and the manner in which they tossed their heads restlessly from side to side, blinking their eye-lids as if blinded by the common light, appeared to support that claim. *Egwu Alikiri* was another introduction from Ekpeye (?). *Egwu Abana* came from the Abos like *egwu-oji*. *Egwu Awudu* was an original Ogba invention which represented an attempt to improve on the more ancient Ogba dances and songs using peculiar Ogba rhythm. *Egwu Asawa* is sung by all age-grades at their periodic meetings. Singers and dancers spoke the Kalabari (Ijaw) dialect often imperfectly. The drums and rhythm have been retained but the words are fast becoming "ogbanised" by the new generation. Then there are the purely functional songs and dances such as *egwu mgba* or *egwu agbadi* (wrestling dance). The *Agbadi* provided the rhythm and the background and the wrestlers were the dancers. Initially, wrestlers "bluff" their way around the arena assuming various traditional postures but the climax was reached at *ihinkwa* (front of the drum) when they would perform acrobatically like Atilogu (hinterland Ibo dance) dancers. There was *Egwu Amra* (paddling song) which was sung mainly by women paddling large canoes to and from the distant markets. *Egwu Dibia* (native doctor's dance) used only by the *dibia* while invoking spirits to help him in his art. The songs and tunes were usually bizarre and frightful. *Ezumezu* drumming frequently resembled *egwu dibia* drumming. *Egwu Ogwu* (war dance) - usually brisk and monotonous, calling for vengeance or calling for blood and recalling offences.

An unusual function of traditional songs was that they were often used to check misdemeanor. The facts of an accusation were summarised in verse giving clear though cautious indication of the persons involved. Few, if any, remedies for slander existed; but allegations had to be substantially true and evident to achieve widespread condemnation of the accused.

The functional dances and songs featured as the occasion arose but the "Club" dances occurred mainly during *Ibegwre* and periodically at *Nkwukwu* and special feasts. The major Ogba feasts were: *Nkwukwu Ikpochi Ali* (Locking up the land); *Ebiam,* when everyone ate pounded yam; *engwuji onube; Nchaka* (or *ejanka*) the greatest of them all, celebrating the end of year when all evil forces, sickness, poverty, witchcraft, wizadry, must be swept away and a peaceful life ensured until old age.

Nchaka or new yam celebration may be regarded as the open sesame to a half-year of festivity and merry-making. *Nchaka* marks the end of the farming season. The first part of the celebration is known as the "female" *Nchaka* which occurs on an *Ahuo* day proclaimed by the traditional authorities. At the setting of the sun, all married women (other than widows), once the signal is given, proceed in groups, carrying fire brands and "Olive" branches, to the river bank chanting in unison:

Ajama biapu
Ejagbra biapu [42]

---

[42] Evil spirit be gone; Wicked ghost be gone"

Standing beside the river, they throw the fire-brands and "Olive" branches into the river and turn round making for home and shouting at the top of their voice *Uruo, Uruo, Uruo* [43] - All doors are thrown open for the celebrants to enter.

The next *Ahuo* day is the "male" *Nchaka*, when the whole community turn out at the crack of dawn, all clad in ceremonial attire. The different groups are led by the various *onuobdo* elders, many celebrants carrying weapons, fans and walking sticks in their hands. All celebrants assemble on the eastern bank of the Omoku River. Two elderly chief celebrants take their position at some distance in front of the crowd and communicate with the latter through two messengers. Then the great prayer rises as from one man:

Cha - cha - cha, cha - a - a - a -! (thrice)
We - we - we, we - e - e - e -! (thrice)

The *chaa* and *wee* invocations are in fact a ritual anticipation of the refrain that follows. *Chaa* is obviously from *Nchaka* and wee from the verb *wre* which follows it in the response *Nchaka wre onye...* As soon as the ritual incantations are spoken and the traditional sign is given, the guns boom and the festival cry rises

Leaders: *tua njoli!*
Response: *Nchaka wre onye mgbasi.*
Leaders: *tua njoli!*
Response: *Nchaka wre onye amisu.*
All: *tua njoli!* [44]

Nchaka, the traditional god of the harvest is obviously seen as a just god that will punish evil and reward good. The two chief celebrants return to their houses, without looking back. The worst calamity is feared, if either of them should look back before reaching home. All celebrants dance along as they return

---

[43] "Profit, profit, profit".
[44] Leaders: "Hei, evil be gone!
Response: *Nchaka* take the wizard.
Leaders: Hei, evil be gone!
Response: *Nchaka* take the witch.
All: Hei, evil be gone!".

home where merriment and festivity continue for the rest of the day.

Death and Burial Ceremonies

Death ceremonies and rituals in Ali-Ogba were very elaborate. Immediately the death of a member was announced, the *Okrosu* were alerted and the *Ukgu Okrosu* (*Okrosu* societies) came in turn to perform their ritual. *Okrosu* featured mainly in the ceremonies of the dead and has little or no connection with Ogba traditional religion, except that it (*Okrosu*) is supposed to come from the spirit world.

The heart and soul of *Okrosu* is supposed to reside in the *echina* which according to Umuzeali was carved for them by "Umuodilammo".[45] *Okrosu* speaks *nkaba*[46] with a death-like accent. In fact, *Okrosu* (sic) has been traced to Umunguma in the Ohaji area of Imo State where it still exists today. There is no indication from where Umunguma adopted their *Okrosu* tradition which appears to ante-date the coming of Ogbas. Ogba persons of means belonged to at least one *Okrosu* company among others e.g.: *Otuikpra, Owanunu* and *Ukundoche*.[47] The last named (*Ukundoche* or society of elders) as the name implies was the most influencial and respectable. Some companies such as *owanunu* are noted for their exquisite dancing; whereas *Otuikpra* and similar companies specialise in pursuing at sight and scourging women and the uninitiated (*Okpokisi*). Other *Okrosu* "companies" include *Ogalugwu,* those that walk on stilts, *Ayiro* (migratory birds), *Awoh-Okwa* (mask head), *Nklobi* (the king of birds), *Onye dibia* (the witch doctor), *onye uko* (the suitor), *Atu* (buffalo), *Mkpi* (goat), *Eze-uku-Lobobo* (His Royal Highness), *Onyoriamama* (the invalid), *Nwanyinma* (beauty queen), etc. All *Okrosu* companies are secret societies not open to women or the uninitiated (*Okpokisi).* They play their major role in traditional funeral rites. If no person of repute (deserving

---

45 Most probably medicine men from Nri who Adiele Afigbo calls "Ojenamo" *ibid* p.64).
46 *Nkaba* is another word for *Igmo* or Igbo.
47 See full list of Okrosu companies in the Appendix.

Okgu by *Okrosu*) dies and the members of *Okrosu* are anxious to perform, they would persuade someone to celebrate the burial of a notable who died ages ago. The *Otuikpra* group came to the residence of the dead by daylight. At night time, the *Ukgu Ndochi* came first to enquire (*ijuaju*) and later to perform other secret rites such as *Igbaji Mgbra*. In the case of women or uninitiated men (*Okpokisi*), the traditional rites may involve such curious activities as *Igbu ewu obu* in which a goat is killed and the heart taken out and placed on the chest of the deceased. If the deceased belonged to the prestigious *Igbu* [48] society, he was made to lie in state sitting upright propped up against a chair.

After the preliminary rituals of the *Ukgu Okrosu*, the deceased was buried after midnight in his house [49] by his closest extended family relations. To oversee the delicate proceedings, a "master of ceremonies" was usually appointed to receive the parting presentation made to the deceased by various relations. Each presentation(usually cloth) was placed on the coffin and some liquor was poured on it by the "master of ceremonies". Thereafter, prayers followed asking the spirit of the deceased to guide, protect and preserve the individual donors whose full names were clearly announced. The details of each donor's relationship to the deceased were also carefully repeated for emphasis. When the prayers ended, an expert *Ebowu* singer was invited. The singer praised and eulogised the deceased in *Ebowu* style and everyone joined in the chorus, clapping hands vigorously. Thereafter, the grave was filled with earth, amidst wailing and weeping for the departed. At the crack of dawn all mourners parade (*Igoha*) the whole town (Usomini, Obieti and Obakata) in a body, singing and drumming.

Burial obsequies in the form of *Okgu* (minor mourning) or *Ogudu* (great mourning) were announced soon afterwards or at a later date depending on the financial readiness of the next of kin

---

[48] *Igbu* is an adjective derived from the verb "to kill" and describes those who "have killed" "public enemies" in fact or in theory.

[49] Assuming that he was of good traditional standing and did not die of any "shameful" (i.e. infectious) disease.

of the deceased. A small mourning *(Okgu)* lasted eight days, while a great mourning *(Ogudu)* lasted longer. The cost of *Okgu* was within the reach of an upper class Ogba while that of *Ogudu* could only be paid by "aristocrats". Both the *Okgu* and the *Ogudu* involved prolonged performances by various *Okrosu Ukgus* which danced and feasted to their hearts' content, while bemoaning the passing away of the deceased by songs and various traditional gestures. Thereafter, the deceased is counted among the ancestors, to be invoked and honoured on traditional religious occasions; and to be mentioned by *dibia* as the re-incarnator of new born members of his extended family, if he had lived an exemplary life.

Observations

The above accounts indicate the lifestyle of an Ogba indigene before colonial times. Having been declared by *dibia* to be a definite re-incarnated ancestor, an Ogba child was immediately accepted by his extended family and accorded the respect and protection due his revered re-incarnator. As he grew up, he was taught the traditions and culture of the group by the elders. He learnt about the supreme deity *(Chukwu abiama)* and about innumerable deities to be found in trees, swamps, creeks, and highways. Consequently, he feared every unusual natural phenomenon and surrounded himself with charms and "gods" for protection against witches and wizards (*amisu* and *mgbasi*).

He respected his traditional ruler and the elders and became a valuable member of a young, dynamic, age-grade. He spoke his mind freely in the age-grade meetings and in the extended family meetings and enjoyed considerable freedom, subject to the fiats of the traditional ruler and the *dibia* and the *erisi*. His was a life of "despotic republicanism" which was peculiar in the contemporary society of his day. He worked hard on his farm and in the fishing ports but he also enjoyed prolonged relaxation at *Nchaka, eguji onube, Nkwukwu abekwu, Nkwukwu Ikpochi ali* and numerous other traditional festivals. He participated intensively in wrestling, *okrosu* and traditional dances. He usually lived to a good old age, sometimes seeing his *nwanwa*

nwanwa nwanwrara (great great grand children). More often than not, he lived at peace with his immediate neighbours who were mostly considered as his relations. All Ogbas were sons of Ogba and therefore "brothers" and "sisters" to one another. He did not know sophistication and technological development but he shared that lot with many of his contemporaries world-wide.

Many Ogbas who have accepted Christianity have abandoned all traditional and cultural practices, calling them fetish and devilish temptations. On the other hand, a few Ogba Christians have adopted these cultural practices along with the associated fetish and pagan rites, which is like serving God and Mammon. Admittedly, there would be no Ogba without Ogba culture which comprises the dialects, the dance and masquerades, the peculiar customs and traditions. At the same time, we cannot continue to worship carved wooden objects and natural phenomena. The solution lies somewhere between the two extremes. Christians and non-Christians should see the wisdom of preserving the cultural practices without idolatory. It should be possible to enjoy *Okro*su dances without the *echina* and *ewu obu*. Ogbas, Christians and non-Christians alike should get together and work out a *modus vivendi* which would ensure the preservation and protection of our noble culture without detriment to our religious beliefs and practices.

Chapter 5

The Colonial Experience

The life of comparative affluence and superstitious contentment lived by the average Ogba person was soon jolted by events of a completely different order, which came subsequently to be known as "colonialism".

In the view of contemporary Ogbas, colonialism occurred mainly in "distant" lands, but, eventually, it had the most profound effect on Ogbas, as on other Nigerians.

The colonial influences which affected Ogbas came from Benin (their "legendary" ancestral home), Arochukwu (the Long Juju Headquarters), the sea coast (where the Europeans first landed) and Aboh (occupying the most strategic point on the Niger Delta). We shall examine each of these influences very briefly to see how they affected Ali-Ogba.

Benin Influence

In 1481, John II who ascended the throne of Portugal immediately embarked upon measures to exploit to the full his monopoly of European trade in this part of the world under the Papal bull of demarcation. He planned to lay firm foundations of a Portuguese Empire by means of sea-borne and overland exploration which might lead to the discovery of the long-sought Christian King, Prester John (the Oba of Benin?) who might be able to assist Portugal in her age-old wars against the Moors. In pursuit of these objectives, King John II constructed the fortress of Sao Jorge Da Mina, assumed the title of Lord of Guinea, commissioned the voyages of Diogo Casto to the Congo and Angola, colonised Sao Tome, despatched envoys to the rulers of the Congo and Western Sudan and entrusted to Joa d'Aveiro the duty of *visiting the hinterland of the "Slave River" (in the Bight of Benin) in 1486.*

Joa d'Aveiro went to *Ughoton* and over land to Benin City where he met Oba Ozolua. The *Oghene* of Ughoton accompanied the visitors (as an "Ambassador") to Lisbon and was described by the Royal Chronicler, Ruy de Pina, as "a man of good speech and natural wisdom". From d'Aveiro"s reports, it was assumed that the *Oghene* (or *Ogane*.)" must be Prester John" Subsequently, the Dutch, French and the British came into contact with Benin. Catholic Mission delegations sent mainly from Portugal (e.g. the Capuchins) did not take root; so Benin dealings with Europeans were kept principally at the commercial and diplomatic level. Eventually, British influence displaced other European influences in Benin especially after the Berlin West Africa Conference of 1884/85. Ogbas who left Benin in various "waves" most probably from the 14th century onwards gained much from these contacts e.g. gun powder, arms, cloth, geographical knowledge, etc which helped them in their quest for a new habitation.

Deposition and Banishment of the Oba of Benin

During the era of the abolition of the slave trade in West Africa and the growth of "peaceful" trading in products other than slaves, the British found their relationship with Benin very "unprofitable" and took immediate steps to "amend" the situation.

In November, 1896, Acting Consul-General J.R. Philips, in a letter to Lord Salisbury, asked "His Lordship's permission to visit Benin City in February next, to depose and remove the King of Benin (Overanmi).

I wish to take a sufficient armed force consisting of 250 troops.[1]

To prove his point, Philips attached a letter in which James Brownridge of Miller Brothers complained that;

> So long as the King of Benin is allowed to carry on as he is doing at present, it means simply losses to merchants, native Itsekiri trade as also the Protectorate.

Permission was duly granted to Philip to visit Benin but his party was ambushed at 4.pm on 4th January 1897 between

---

[1] F.O. 2/102 Philips to Lord Salisbury 24th Nov., 1896.

Gwato and Benin and only two officials (Captain Boisragon and Locke) escaped. All efforts made by Oba Ovonramwen to prevent some chiefs from attacking the party failed. Boisragon's book, *The Benin Massacre* tells a part of the story.

The Consul-General Ralph Moor returned speedily from his home leave and retaliatory military preparations against Benin were set in motion. The only defensive military post encountered on the way to Benin was at Gwato. Benin fell as easily before the British troops. The Oba fled on two occasions but was captured and tried and banished to Calabar where he eventually died in exile. According to Egharevba (p.61), his last words in Benin were:

> Oh Benin, Merciless and Wicked! [2]
> Farewell, Farewell.

The Consul-General Ralph Moor declared his Benin policy in the following words:

> Now this is the whiteman's country. There is only one king in the country and that is the whiteman...Overanmi is no longer the king of this country.

Late emigrants must have carried Ralph Moor's words to Ali-Ogba where they sounded like fable and sacrilege to those who feared and revered "Oba Odudu". It was as if their world had been turned upside down, as they wondered in complete amazement and utter disbelief that such events could happen. The conquest of Benin was indeed an indirect conquest of areas associated with Benin historically or by legend, such as Ali-Ogba as it weakend the natural spirit of resistance in Ogbas well in advance.

The Aro Influence

Aro influence, which was felt throughout the eastern parts of Nigeria and beyond, had considerable political, economic and

---

[2] Egharevba, *A Short History* Cap. XXV.

religious effects on Ogba society. Dr. K.O. Dike has described the operations of the Aros in detail:[3]

> Two types of trading organisations operated in the hinterland. The first, centred upon the Aros, obtained mainly in the period of the slave trade. Their influence was based on the *Aro Chukwu* Oracle which was universally respected and feared throughout Iboland, and in fact by every tribe in Eastern Nigeria. This Oracle was supposed to reside in the territory of the Aros, a section of the Ibo tribe. In 1854 Baikie wrote of the noted City of Aro where there is the celebrated shrine of *Tshuku* (God), to which pilgrimages are made, not only from all parts of Igbo proper, but from Old Calabar, and from the tribes along the coast, and from Oru and Nembe. The town is always mentioned with great respect, almost, at times, with a degree of veneration, and the people say *Tshuku ab yama* or God lives there. Aro people (whom the Ibos call *Umu Chukwu* - the children of God) exploited this belief in their oracle in many ways, principally in order to dominate the life of the region economically, and they made themselves the sole middlemen of the hinterland trade. This they did by establishing Aro colonies along the trade routes of the interior - like the Greeks, the course of whose colonizing expeditions was largely directed by the priests of the Delphic Oracle. In its wake they organised a trading system which had its ramifications throughout practically the whole of the country between the Niger and the Eastern side of the Cross River. Every quarter of Aro Town had its "sphere of influence" in matters of trade... Acting as mediators between God and the clans and assuming themselves to be the spokesmen of the Almighty, they held a privileged position throughout the land, erecting what amounted to a theocratic state over Eastern Nigeria. Aro colonies became the divinely ordained trade centres in the interior; Aro middlemen, the economic dictators of the hinterland. During the time of the trade and in the period of legitimate commerce they acquired immense wealth through a monopoly all believed to be divinely appointed, and with wealth, came great political influence[4].

Wherever Aro Ambassadors went, they established a separate colony some distance from the local village and maintained a calculated aloofness in keeping with their claim to be the chosen people, a race set apart as the representatives of God on earth. There were up to one hundred and fifty Aro "colonies" altogether including Aro Egwe (near Oguta) and Aro Ikwerre.[5] To this day, their descendants still maintain a separate identity and a close association with the Aro homeland.

---

3   *Trade and Politics in the Niger Delta* Oxford 1956 (pp. 37/38).

4   The sites of Aro colonies still exist today though they are no longer trade routes, nor is any special significance attached to them; but they are still inhabited by Aro descendants.

5   *The Aro of South Eastern Nigeria 1650 - 1980* by Onwuka Dike and Felicia Ekejiuba, University Press Ltd. Ibadan 1990.

According to Aro strategy, the Ambassador was a priest, doctor, diplomat, soldier, teacher and merchant - the wise philosopher who knew all the answers to life's problems. Whatever he did not understand could easily be communicated to him by *Chukwu* himself, who was fixed to a spot in Aro-Chukwu, who alone knew all things, past, present and to come. No wonder in all cases in which the modern world would seek enlightenment through jurisprudence, the people flocked to *Chukwu* or *Ibinukpabi* (as the Efiks and Ibibios called it), under the personal conduct, direction and leadership of the Aro "Ambassadors". Many went to consult the Long Juju but few returned. We now know that many of those reputedly "eaten" by the Long Juju lived again in the New World.

Professor A.E. Afigbo adds more details (*op. cit.* p.24).

> The Aro organised their business differently... In central, southern and eastern Igbo areas as in Ibibio land, where they were most active, they established permanent settlements at strategic points to serve as collecting and distributing centres for the wares in which they traded. <u>Furthermore, they established enduring links with various well organised local groups and where necessary operated through these.</u> (my underlining).

In Ali-Ogba, the Aros established no settlements whatsoever. No trace of an Aro settlement can be found in Ali-Ogba today; whereas they are commonly found in many neighbouring areas. Instead, Aros established "enduring links" with the Umuenyike *Onuobodo* (i.e. the Nwadei Kingship group) and appointed them to be their agents. To merit this agency, Umuenyikes must have impressed the Aros as the strongest power in Ali-Ogba, capable of carrying out efficiently and effectively the great responsibilities usually entrusted to fellow Aros elsewhere.

In their recently published work, *The Aro of South-Eastern Nigeria 1650 - 1980* (University Press Ibadan 1990), Dr.K.O. Dike and Felicia Ekejiuba explain in detail how the Aros created "powerful alliances" and made "treaties of friendship" whenever they found it expedient to do so -

> By using the system of *Igbandu*, the Aro were able to create powerful alliances between themselves and local chiefs in the area of their trade. These treaties of friendship were often ratified and cemented with blood - that is, the blood of the contracting parties or of livestock or goat. The

blood pacts were a peaceful and a diplomatic means of gaining entry into new territories where a frontal attack or forcible entry would generate resistance or hostility and disrupt trade. These treaties of friendship and alliance implied no acceptance of Aro sovereignty or economic and political overlordship. (p.119). Just as there were individual clients so there were client villages, who, though autonomous in many ways, paid tributes, provided manpower for trade and warfare for the Aro patron-village in exchange for protection and such patronage resources has assured access to Aro oracle and trade goods (p.275).

In pursuance of the agency granted to the Umuenyikes, the Aros conferred on the Umuenyikes their own awesome title, *Umu Chukwu* (children of God), which Ogbas elaborated into *Umuchukwu oriogba maya eriwo* (sons of God which eat Ogbas except themselves) because Umuenyikes always returned safe and sound from their frequent trips to Arochukwu and were never "eaten" by *Chukwu*.

Before Umuenyikes conducted any litigant to Arochukwu, they charged an all-inclusive fee which was fixed at the equivalent of £5 which was paid in the form of 160,000 cowries (making up eight loads). One half (i.e. 80,000 cowries) was spent en route as travelling expenses. The other half (i.e. 80,000 cowries) was retained by Umuenyikes and shared among the component groups of the *onuobdo*. Superficially, the Aros gained nothing at all from the transaction; whereas in fact they gained tremendously by abducting the "guilty" parties and selling them into slavery.

As a result of the association between the Aros and the Umuenyikes, the latter gained considerable material benefits from the Aro oracle which was outwardly the highest appeal court but in reality a terrible engine for prosecution of the slave trade. Under the prevailing social and economic conditions, it was the slave trade that helped promote and support the institution of traditional kingship in Ali-Ogba as it did elsewhere during the period.

Umuenyikes conducted litigants to Arochukwu through the Aro trade routes with which they were familiar. It appears that a favourite route crossed the Imo River (probably near Umuahia), then passed through Bende (which had a famous slave market), and thence to Arochukwu in a south-easterly direction. Journeys to and from Arochukwu usually started from, and ended at Obrikom, the Umuenyike headquarters. Those "eaten" by *Chukwu* (i.e. those declared "guilty" by the Aros who would later be sold secretly into slavery) were announced by the Umuanyikes as having been "eaten by *Imo*". Imo River which all who "go to *Chukwu*" must cross was thus represented as a lesser deity than the high *Chukwu* of Aro.

It may be that some attempt was made on the part of Umuenyikes to conceal the "abduction" by the Aros of certain litigants, or that Umuenyikes were not taken into confidence by the Aros and were not aware of the secret of the long juju which was a clever manipulation devised to promote the Aro slave trade. Authentic accounts show that more than half of those enslaved and sold to European traders came from the highly populated hinterland areas and that more than fifty percent of all the slaves passed through the long juju. A great number of slaves who passed through Arochukwu came from the riverine areas. The reputation and influence of the oracle were most pervasive . This was another peculiar instance in which Ali-Ogba served as a veritable half-way house between freedom and slavery.

Afigbo has stated that:

> an Aro does not tell another Aro that the long juju has asked of him.

In other words, the long juju was an open secret to all Aros. It may be that it was also an open secret to other groups such as the Umuenyikes who had special links with the Aros but this fact has not been confirmed by oral evidence. Perhaps all non-Aros were made to believe in the long juju as the true high god.

Demolition of chukwu of the Aros

> From the standpoint of the British Administration of the protectorate, the Aros were a thorn in the flesh[6] . (Anene page 224)....

It became the practice of the protectorate to ascribe every disturbance in the divisions of the protectorate to the baneful

---

[6] J. C. Anene, *Southern Nigeria in Transition*, Cambridge University press 1966.

influence of the Aros. On a visit to the central division, Sir Ralph was "reliably" informed that owing to pernicious Aro influence, the trade in oil at Oguta (thirty miles North of Omoku) had fallen from 250 to 100 puncheons. (Anene page 226)[7]. Sir Ralph Moor urged continually that "it is only by going to the heart of the matter at once and breaking up the power of the Aros that the country can be opened up and pacified". The last straw was the report transmitted to the Acting High Commissioner, Leslie Probyn, forwarding a letter sent to him by a native political agent to the effect that the Aros had recently carried off many hundreds of Ibibios and sold them as slaves... Sir Ralph Moor, who was in England, saw the report and convinced the colonial office that the raid might "be regarded *as the technical justification* for the expedition against the Aros... already decided to be necessary on more general grounds. (Anene p3. 272)[8].

The head chiefs of Arochukwu, the seat of the Long Juju and the home of the Aro, were unaware that the Government of Southern Nigeria had decided on a colossal war against them[9].

Since the Aros were believed to be almost everywhere, the scope of the proposed British expedition was extensive. Three areas were specifically marked out. The first theatre of military operation was to embrace the Cross River and the hinterland or New Calabar, Bonny and Opobo. The second was the neighbourhood of Oguta. Both the first and second theatres includes Ali-Ogba. The third territory comprised the territory between Onitsha and the Westernmost fringe of the Cross River.

The Military expedition was little more than a farce. The ... opposition to the passage of British troops was haphazard and was encountered mainly in towns and villages where the inhabitants were unwilling to surrender their guns, as demanded by the British. ... All four military columns involved in the expedition converged and assembled in Arochukwu on 28th December, 1901... The Supreme Commander, Lt. Col. Montanaro set up a military commission which sentenced and

---

7   Anene, *Op. cit* p. 226.
8   J.C. Anene *Op. cit* p. 272.
9   J C. Anene, *Op. cit* p. 228.

hanged those Aro Chiefs believed to be the "ring-leaders". The long juju shrine was set on fire which Montanaro believed destroyed "all traces of the oracle". After destruction of the oracle, the troops were sent out in detachments to operate in several directions. The area involved in the Aro expedition was estimated to cover six thousand square miles; Twenty-five thousand war guns accumulated by the natives had been confiscated (Anene p. 233).[10] At the end of March 1902, Sir, Ralph made his way to Arochukwu. Arochukwu was made a sub-district headquarter, and the political officers left here and at Bende were instructed to form "<u>Native Courts</u>" (my underlining) for the settlement of individual and inter-tribal disputes (Anene p. 234).[11] Sir Ralph requested for substantial increase in the civil establishment because "<u>he had had to do away with practically all the system of the natives</u>" (my underlining).

News of the defeat of the Aro and the destruction of the long juju spread like wildfire throughout the Niger area and beyond. These events affected the Ogbas tremendously, especially in the light of the Aro Association with the Nwadei *Onuobdo*. News about the terrible destruction of Benin and the banishment of the Oba which occurred three or four years earlier was still "current". If Aros" the sons of God" could be crushed and *Chukwu* their high God and last Court of Appeal destroyed, what then was real, dependable and indestructible? Who or what exactly were these iconoclasts and how far would they go?

Influences From The Atlantic Coast

Portuguese efforts in the Bight of Benin and their contacts with Benin City in the late 15th century had not produced much lasting effect when developments of far reaching consequences began to occur on the Atlantic coast. That coast (which is less than fifty kilometres south of Ali-Ogba) stretches from the Benin River in the West to the Cross River in the East, covering a distance of about two hundred and seventy miles in length and

---

[10] J. C. Anene, *Op. cit* p. 233.
[11] J. C. Anene, *Op. cit*. p. 234.

one hundred and twenty miles in width or depth. About this area (the Niger Delta), Mary Kingsley[12] has written;

> the great swamp region of the Bight of Biafra is the greatest in the world, and in its immensity and gloom, it has a grandeur equal to that of the Himalayas.

Dr. Dike[13] has said that the area was "practically uninhabited by the tribes of the Nigerian interior before the Portuguese adventure to the Guinea Coast began." He goes on to show that "many of the most southerly Delta tribes (i.e. the Ijaws) trace their origin to Benin. Major Leonard collected and used Ijaw traditions to trace the Benin origin of some of the Ijaw towns. The migrations from Benin were, however, pre-fifteenth century, and took place possibly centuries before the advent of the Portuguese.

Dr. Nwanna Nzewunwah (op.cit) has shown that Obrikom in Ali-Ogba (3015 BC) was settled or occupied before Ke (2000 BC) which is the oldest of the saltwater sites. Consequently, it is speculated that the saltwater areas must have been originally occupied after the healthier mainland areas were occupied. But this earlier occupation must not be confused with the subsequent or later migrations in which people from the present mid-western area or Benin City and its environs moved southwards and re-occupied such places as Ali-Ogba and the southern Ijaw areas. As Dr. K.O. Dike states;

> the most important movement of populations occurred between 1450 and 1800... This second wave of migration followed the development of slave trade and involved all the tribes to the delta hinterland...[14] With further migrations to the coast barred by the rise of the City-States (on the Atlantic sea-board), the lure of the great commercial highway of the Niger valley itself stimulated another migration within the hinterland,and the hardy and adventurous people from the Benin area once again established themselves at places on the river bank favourable to trade... This third migratory wave is generally accepted to have taken place about the middle of the seventheth century, at a time when the Atlantic middlemen having fortified their privileged position on the

---

12 *Travels in West Africa*, (1898) C.F.A.C.C. Hastings, *The Voyage of the Day spring*, (London 1857) pp.73-74.
13 *Op. cit* p. 19.
14 K.O.Dike *Op. cit.*p. 24.

Atlantic Coast brooked no rivals. According to an Onitsha writer, the date of their arrival at the present site was about 1630. The traditions of these seventeenth Century migrants, which are closely related to that of Benin shows that although they are Ibo speaking, they were not originally Ibos. Moreover, whereas the Ibos east of the Niger have no kings - an Ibo proverb has it, - *Ndi Igbo Echi Eze*, i.e. "The Ibos make no kings". Yet these Ibo speaking riverine towns... have a society patterned after the semi-divine kingship of Benin[15].

It has been shown how Ogba society is "patterned after the semi-divine kingship of Benin" like the riverine Igbos of Aboh and Onitsha. Although Ogba legends of origin indicate that Ogbas first arrived at their present home in the early 14th century[16] it would appear that their kingship institutions were not fully developed until the 16th and 17th centuries. The Ogba migrations from Benin must have followed closely on those of Ijaws. In other words, most probably, they constituted Dike's second "wave" of emigrants. The geographical location of Ali-Ogba next to the Ijaws with a number of common boundaries strengthens this point of view.

During the 18th century, the philanthropists in Britain and their friends propounded the theory that the best plan for striking at the root of the slave trade and its evils was to explore the hinterland, establish friendly relations with African Chiefs and thus lay the foundations which would permit the infiltration of Christianity, social progress, and beneficent trade. Mungo Park explored the Niger in 1775 and 1805 but discovery of its numerous estuaries had to await the efforts of the Lander Brothers who, having reached Aboh were taken from there to the mouth of one of the distributaries of the Niger. The tremendous influence exercised by Aboh on the lower Niger area can be gauged from this single incident. The successful use of quinine in the Baikie Expedition of 1854 opened the way to intensified hinterland exploitation. Macgregor Laird, the pioneer of British enterprise in this area, obtained in 1857 a subsidy from the

---

15 K.O. Dike *Op. cit* p. 26.
16 Perhaps the Umuezealis arrived Ali-Ogba in the 14th century and other Ogbas arrived later. Dr. Nzewunwah's excavations have shown that the Ogba area was occupied in 3000 B.C. apparently by non-Ogbas.

British Government to enable him maintain a steamer on the Niger. This new enterprise provoked the hostility of the coast British Merchants, the coast native middlemen and their native allies along the lower Niger.

During the decade after Laird's modest beginnings, the British Foreign office deliberately encouraged trade expansion on the Niger, even against the opposition of the local rulers. It enthusiastically accepted that:

> if we can open out the Niger to the trade of this country, it will be another and a considerable step in the right direction.

The possibilities of British trade in palm oil, cotton, groundnuts and ivory were therefore over-riding considerations naval power was, as on the coast, an essential ingredient of the policy of informal sway. At one time or another, Onitsha, Aboh and Idah were shelled and burnt to the ground. The aim of these operations was summarised by the leader of the expedition against Onitsha:

> Our proceedings at Onitsha will have a most salutary effect up and down the Niger[17]

In fact, the "proceedings" caused inevitable friction between British interests and the local middlemen.

The British Protectorate of Southern Nigeria was officially recognised as the territory between fifty degrees and ninety degrees East longitude and between the sea coast, known as the Bights of Benin and Biafra, and seventy degrees North latitude which was arbitrarily partitioned for the benefit of two sets of British controlling agencies - the Royal Niger Company[18] and the administration of the Oil Rivers Protectorate appointed by the Foreign Office[19]. The <u>"Boundary between the Royal Niger Company's sphere and the Oil Rivers had deliberately never been defined"</u>[20] (my underlining).

---

[17] J.C. Anene. *Op. cit.* p.41
[18] Anene *Op. cit.* p.4
[19] Anene *Op. cit.* p.115
[20] Anene *Op. cit.* p.110

In 1889, a conference was called in Brussels following a letter from Lord Salisabury, the Foreign Secretary, to the Belgian king urging for-

> effective means to combat the evils of slavery and liquor in tropical Africa... as to open to civilisation the only part of our globe where it has not yet penetrated, <u>(and) to pierce the darkness which envelopes whole populations</u>... (my underlining).

Major (later Sir) Claude Maxwell Macdonald[21] was appointed Commissioner to the Niger District (in 1889) to ascertain then best way to consolidate British rule in the Oil Rivers[22]. He visited Bonny, Opobo, New Calabar, Old Calabar and Brass... At New Calabar, the feeling against the Royal Niger Company was most marked ... The hinterland markets of New Calabar, <u>including the Oguta lake</u> (my underlining), had been effectively cut off by the Royal Niger Company[23] ...

Macdonald also found that in the region of the lower Niger, the Royal Niger Company had an impressive number of treaties[24] in which the indigenous rulers surrendered their sovereignty and territories in perpetuity". In the Aboh District alone, there were thirty-two treaties; in the *Oguta Distric*t, ten; in the Anambra, sixteen; and in the Igara area, forty-six ...Macdonald encountered the rulers of the strategically placed town-State of Onitsha. The king and his councillors emphatically denied ever signing a treaty with the Royal Niger Company. Macdonald observed that the Royal Niger Company had "a well equipped constabulary which was employed in punitive expeditions at least once a month." Onitsha, Obosi, Aboh, to mention but a few, had at one time or another been burnt down by the Niger Company's constabulary.

---

21 Born 1852. Educated at Uppingham and Sanhurst. Entered 74th Highlanders and took prominent part in Egyptian Compaign in 1882. Military attache to Sir Evelyn Baring in Cairo. Consul-General Zanzibar 1887/88.

22 Anene *Op. cit.* p. 121.

23 Consequently, Ali-Ogba which lies thirty miles south of Oguta Lake nearer the Atlantic Ocean was also effiectively cut off by the Royal Niger Company.

24 No evidence has been found of any treaty with Ali-Ogba kings, but they may be included in the "Oguta District" with only a handful of treaties.

On 29th July, 1891 the Foreign Office wrote (F.O. 84/2110) to Macdonald defining the boundary between the Royal Niger Company territory and the area comprising the Oil Rivers:

> (1) On the west of the Nun the line starts in the middle of the mouth o Forcados River and follows the river to the mouth of Warri Creek, anc thence follows the Creek leading to Oagbi and Ahiabo. From that place the line runs north-east for ten miles and then due north to fifty miles...
>
> (2) <u>On the east of the Niger the boundary is formed by a straight line from a point midway between Brass and Nun and terminating at Idu...</u>[25] <u>Idu itself is to be under joint administration.</u> (my underlining)

At this time, as Prof. K. Dike has stated. "The Itsekiri exploited the trade of the Urhobo country. The Ijaw organised trading expeditions on the Niger. <u>The Kalabari tapped the resources of the Oguta Lake Basin</u>"[26] (my underlining)

In the Ogba area proper, Kalabari traders established a trading settlement on the Western bank of the Orashi River opposite Idu,[27] just below Kreigani within the Usomini area of Ali-Ogba. They went further inland to establish posts on the banks of the Oguta Lake twenty-five to thirty miles beyond Ali-Ogba. At the Idu posts, they bought palm oil and kernel and sold to Ogbas various goods which they themselves obtained from European traders on the coast. In course of time, this trade grew in importance and more Kalabaris came to settle in Ali-Ogba leaving descendants some of whose members have become full members of the Ogba community today. The Don Pedros of *Ahia Orie* fame are one notable example. Others are the Dakorus of Obakata and the Benibos of Usomini.

---

25   There are two "Idus" in Ogba viz Idu Osoble and Idu Obosikwu. There is also an Idu-Ekpeye and another Idu in the Ijaw area. The indications are that the Idu nearest the Royal Niger Company factory in Kreigani (Idu Osoble) Ogba was most probably intended.

26   The Oguta Lake basin includes Ali-Ogba.

27   The name "Idu" taken by an Usomini village near Kreigani is reminiscent of the Igbo name for Benin which is "Ado-na-Idu". There are in fact two Idus in Ogba and one in the Ijaw area which may be somewhat confusing. However, the proximity of Idu (Osoble or Ogba) to Kreigani, which became a Royal Niger Company (and later United Africa Company) trading or administrative centre makes it (i.e. Idu Osoble or Idu Ogba) the most likely "Idu" under reference in the records.

Some indication of the fate awaiting the Ogbas was given by the fact that "Idu" an Ogba village on the eastern bank of the River (about three miles south of Omoku), was to be under "joint administration" between the consular authorities in the "Oil Rivers" Protectorate and the Royal Niger Company.

The Abohs And Ali-Ogba

Because of its location at a strategic point on the Niger, and especially in the light of the overriding British policy of penetration of the Niger, Aboh occupied a most crucial position in the trade and politics of the period. As Professor Dike has said,[28]

> A century ago the town of Aboh exercised what amounted to a monopoly of trade up and down the Niger valley. It occupied a strong strategic position 147 miles from Forcados - the most important mouth of the Niger - and was about the same distance from Bonny, Brass, New Calabar, and Akassa on the sea.

The entire trade of the Niger was held up at will by her war-canoes armed with brass and iron cannon. This explains why Aboh loomed so large in the narratives of the British Niger expeditions of the first half of the Nineteenth century, and why the Aboh Chief, Obi Ossai, who had no power beyond the banks of the Niger, was wrongly styled by them as the "King of the Ibos". All of these expeditions bear testimony to the commercial importance of Aboh. Laird notes its strategic position in 1832 as being "at the head of the three great outlets of the Niger- the Benin, the Bonny and the Nun". And following Laird, Captain Williams Allen and Dr. T. N. H. Thompson, members of the Niger Expedition of 1841, declared:

> Aboh is much the largest town in the (northern) Delta... Obi Ossai, king of Ibu (Ibos), is therefore one of the most powerful and influential rulers on the banks of the river, which is aided much by the position of this town, Aboh, at the upper part of the Delta enabling him to control very much the trade towards the sea.

While the commercial and political supremacy of Aboh in the 19th century is not at all in doubt, it appears indisputable that in so far as Ali-Ogba was concerned, Aboh influence began some

---

28 K.O Dike *Ibid.*, page 25.

centuries before 1800. Oral history indicates that emigrants from Benin arrived at Aboh (as they did at Ali-Ogba) in the early 14th century. Judging by Abo king lists which contained the names of eighteen kings as at 1971, the occupation of Aboh by Benin emigrants may be dated from C. 1330. This inference is confirmed by a news item which appeared in the *Sunday Observer* of 5th May, 1985 entitled "5 Century-Old Curse Revoked" describing how "Chief James Apongo the Ikonmo of Orogun and Chief Charles Ugbomah of Aboh (together with their numerous followers) carried out a revocation ceremony in respect of a mutual curse between Aboh and Orogun which occurred during the reign of Obi Ogwezi 1, the second king of Aboh, over five centuries ago".

The Onita Creek which joins the Niger and the Orashi Rivers at Aboh and Idia (between Omoku and Obrikom) respectively, provided easy access from Aboh to Ali-Ogba. Through the Onita creek, Aboh slave raiders visited Ali-Ogba periodically. They had to pass through Ndoni before gaining access into the Onita. This led to frequent battles between Aboh and Ndoni, although they belong to the same sub-tribe or clan and speak the same dialect. The earliest slave raids through *uhwo ka - obigwe* (then a wide and deep tributary of the Orashi river or in fact an older route of the Orashi river) gave rise to the dispersal of Ogbas from Obigwe (Diaspora) in C.1390-C1400. The incident involving Nweze the father of Agbda, the ancestor of Umuagbda, is another ancient instance. Nweze the father of Agbda, the ancestor of Umuagbda, fled Omoku and went to live near Ebogro "due to troubles from the Abohs". Later, he left that site and went further into Njita. Later still, he moved to the western bank of the Sombreiro and eventually crossed to Uju on the opposite bank. And yet the periodic raids of the Abohs continued to pursue him. Ultimately, the Abohs were killed by crocodiles in the Sombreiro River believed to have been set against them by Nweze and his extended family, hence the latter acquired its title of Umu-Omela-ekiri[29] which is still current today.

---

29   Sons of those whose strength lies in eddies.

As Abohs increased their wealth and power during the period of the slave trade and the palm oil and palm kernel trade that replaced it, they became more daring and persistent with these raids. During the reign of Obi Ossai, Aboh successes drove them to a level of arrogance and aggression which antagonised and alienated their closest neighbours, friends and relatives. From time to time, as has been demonstrated, some of the neighbours had their revenge, as in the "Aboh-Ogba War",involving heavy casualties against the Abohs.

And yet it must not be presumed that a perpetual state of hostility existed between Aboh and Ogba during this early period. As we have already seen[30] a few Ogba *Onuobdos* in fact came to Ali-Ogba through Aboh. Examples are Umunkaru, Umuoyro and Umuchi who came from Aboh villages of Adiawai and Utuochi respectively. Possibly because of their "relationship" with the Abohs, the Umunkarus allowed Abohs free access into Omoku, leading to the incident in which an Ogba traditional ruler was beheaded by the Abohs. This event earned the Umunkarus the title "Umuodilura Ke Ebo gahureri."[31]

This situation was of course eventually saved by the strategy of felling some trees at Onu Omoku which prevented Aboh exit and resulted in the complete destruction of the Aboh war engine. Perhaps, the Umunkarus were eventually provoked into action against their traditional associates by the enormity of Aboh cruelty in beheading Obi Okoya at Omoku.

The Umualinwas who came to Ali-Ogba through another Aboh village (Ogu Aniocha near Isala) had a similar experience. It is said that the Umualinwas bluntly refused to fight in the Aboh-Ogba war for some undisclosed "private reason". Apparently, the "private reason" is the "relationship"between the Abohs and Umualinwas. Even when a slave of the Umualinwas was deliberately captured in order to provoke the Umualinwas into action, they would not budge, thereby earning for themselves the title or nick-name *Umu aju aju ohu*.[32] As a result

---

30   See relevant traditional histories and legends.
31   Those asleep when the Ebos passed.
32   Those who would not enquire about a lost slave.

of their refusal to participate in the war, Umualinwas are not permitted to be members of the *Igbu* society. Also, the "procession" in *"Ogudu"* or "great mourning" does not extend to Obakata where the Umualinwas live.

Aboh aggression most probably reached its height in the early 1820s. As Elizabeth Isichei has stated in her *History of the Igbo People;*

> The most celebrated conflict -which Ossamari's local historian places in the 1820s - was when Aboh made an unsuccessful attempt to invade Ossamari, but lost both its general, the Odogun, and its man of war canoe,

She goes on to quote an account of a dialogue which took place between Obi Ossai of Aboh and one of the Commissioners on the Niger expedition of 1841:

Commissioner:	Does Obi sell slaves for (from) his own dominions?
Obi:	No, they come from far away.
Commissioner:	Does Obi make war (simply) to procure slaves?
Obi:	When other Chiefs quarrel with me and make war, I take all I can as slaves.

The Obi's replies do not appear to reflect the whole truth because it seems conclusive from the available evidence that Obi Ossai or his subordinate chiefs waged several wars consistently in order to capture slaves. The celebrated Aboh/Ogba conflict in which the Abohs beheaded Obi Okoya but had their war canoes destroyed by Ogbas occurred most probably in the early 1820s. That battle must have been the last episode in the centuries'-old Aboh slave raids into Ali-Ogba. The damaged Aboh war-canoes, which (it is said) still lie under the sombre waters of *ede ebu* bear evident witness to that calamity.

Colonial Activities in Ali-Ogba

Agha-Ka-Olowu nwa Amadi nwa Ekiodu

Now that the Aro Long juju had been demolished, and the Oba of Benin had been banished, and Aboh and Onitsha had been bombarded; it was left for such places as Ali-Ogba to be "pacified". It will be recalled that after receiving their charter, the

Royal Niger Company had established a "factory" and security post at Kreigani[33] on the Orashi Water Front half-way between Idu and Omoku. From this out-post, Royal Niger Company soldiers interrogated all travellers on the Orashi River. The paddlers of every important-looking canoe were ordered to stop for a search and if they disobeyed the order, they were held by force, interrogated and punished. Obviously, the intention was to stop Ogbas from trading with their old customers, the Kalabaris, either as a result of Niger Company/Oil Rivers rivalry, or in an effort to break the monopoly of the coastal middlemen and facilitate British penetration into the interior palm produce markets.

Now, Idu had become a very strategic out-post as a result of the imaginary boundary line drawn in 1892:

> To the east of the delta, the boundary (between the Oil Rivers under the Consulate and the area under the Royal Niger Company) was defined as a straight line from a point midway between Brass and the Nun and terminating at Idu.[34]

It will be recalled that in a dispatch to Macdonald, the Foreign office included the puzzling suggestion that Idu should be under the "joint administration" of the protectorate and the Royal Niger Company.

Like other Ogba "businessmen", Olowu nwa Amadi Nwa Ekiodu, a prominent member of Uriem *Onuobdo* in Obrikom, was being ferried to Idu in his canoe. As the canoe passed in front of the "factory" in Kreigani, a harsh order was shouted by the Company soldiers. On hearing the orders, Olowu whispered to his paddlers not to obey anyone but himself. As the canoe moved on stubbornly, the soldiers gave chase, and within minutes Olowu and his paddlers were apprehended, and conveyed to the "factory" premises, flogged mercilessly, and left

---

[33] "The Blue Book For 1900, Protectorate of Southern Nigeria gives the strength of the military forces at Gregianic (Kreigani) as 25" (Taken from *The British Occupation of Niger Territories, 1830-1914* by Dr. Nwanze Obi, p.92).

[34] F.O. 84/2110, F.O. to Macdonald, 29th July 1891.

Kreigani Residence of United Africa Company Agent (Successors to Lord Lugard's Royal Niger Company)

half-dead. Rumour spread that Olowu had in fact been killed by white men.[35]

The Burning of Ogu, Obloko and Obrikom

When the sad news of the "murder" of Olowu reached Obrikom, there was instant pandemonium. Every owner of a fire-arm (and there were many such "Warriors" in the land of *Enyike nde Ogu*) brought out his gun, loaded it with gun powder and missiles, and rushed to Obloko (Ogu)[36] to way-lay the Royal Niger Company boats which went up and down the Orashi river. In the absence of an organised army, the motley assembly of men armed with antiquated weapons, waited impatiently, having been provoked to the point of utter recklessness.

The "local militia" comprising hundreds of Obrikom warriors did not have to wait too long. Within hours, a boat arrived at night on its way to Oguta. The "waiting miltia" fired ineffectual shots at the passing boat. At once, the boat steered round briskly heading for the shore, with a dozen rifles at the ready. The local troops fled in disarray after a transient, unequal skirmish. The small "navy" disembarked on reaching the shore and gave chase to the local "troops".

Within a short time, the invaders had trekked a distance of about two miles and arrived at Obrikom. It was then early morning and they found that the whole town had been completely deserted, except for livestock and assorted personal effects. A dry breeze was blowing against the mud and wattle buildings. The leaves and grass all around were dry and crisp. Within minutes, a small fire would become a conflagration. The patrol members' imagination ran riot. They set Obrikom town ablaze. Everything - houses, artifacts, livestock - were burnt to ashes. The patrol-men seemed perfectly satisfied with the work of their own hands.

---

[35] Paraphrase of an authenticated account by Chief John Wokocha Ellah Eze Ogba Nwadei Ogbuchi, in his palace in Omoku on 26th September, 1979.
[36] The former flourishing village known as **Ogu is now** called Onosi ogu and marked by ruins only.

A similar incident which occurred at Asaba (Ase) on 18th November 1882 is recorded in a letter from Edward H. Hewett to Earl Granville

> Slave Trade No. 17
> My Lord
> ..... We left Ase about 5.30 p.m. the same afternoon and while returning by Asaba - the town at the entrance of the creek and close to where the Victoria Factory stood - we were fired upon from the bush..... After coming to an anchor, fire was immediately opened and the natives driven away..... Our guns were directed upon this town and the shell rockets etc soon did much damage ....A landing party was subsequently sent on shore and completed the destruction of the town by setting fire to the anchorage she had left in the morning... Later in the afternoon, fire was again opened on that town and having, as well as could be seen, driven the natives out, it was treated in the same manner as Abari, after this work had been done, canoes were noticed at Abari so Commander Hammick ordered a couple of shells to be fired on them..... I was unable to get hold of the principal offenders, namely Opali of Asaba (Ase) and Abudukama and Manimana of Abari, so I have offered a reward of three puncheons worth of cargo, valued a little under £30 (thirty pounds) for each of these men.

The breaking of weapons at Omoku

Having burnt down Obrikom, the "patrol men" waited in vain to deal with any townsfolk who might come prying about; but no one appeared. They combed all the nearby bushes for stragglers but all in vain. The *Eze Ogba Nwadei Ogbuehi* had moved to Obor when the Royal Niger Company first established themselves in Kreigani. He chose the comparative seclusion of Obor in preference to the glare of Obrikom immediately he saw the strange phenomenon of white men appearing on the economic and political scene of Ali-Ogba. When Obrikom was attacked, the townsfolk fled to *Ogboru*, to their second homes where they settled down to contemplate the unusual happenings. The "patrol men" searched in vain and were puzzled and confounded.

Eventually, the patrol decided to move to Omoku three miles to the south. Meanwhile, their terrible reputation had reached Omoku since the torture of Olowu nwa Amadi nwa Ekiodu and the whole town had been deserted. At first, the patrol men hoped to find a traditional ruler in Omoku, but none had merged since the beheading of Okoya by the Ebohs. They asked if no one at all was in charge of Omoku and Olowu nwa Ajie Nkwo of Umuezeali stepped forward. Olowu was actually the oldest member of the Umuezeali *Onuobdo*. It appears he was so old and feeble that he remained behind when everyone else had fled. In any case, in Ogba tradition,"gerontocracy shines brightly as a king until a king be by".

The soldiers interrogated, flogged, tortured and detained Olowu nwa Ajie Nkwo. He was warned that if he wished to remain alive he should get all Ogbas to surrender the guns with which they had fired at the passing boat, as well as any other fire arms they might have in their possession. Olowu knew he had no power to order Ogbas (other than Umuezealis) to do any act or refrain from any action. But he found an indirect solution to the problem: Bearing in mind the fact that shrines of all kinds were greatly feared and highly venerated by Ogbas, he publicly invoked a much dreaded *erisi* [37] asking it not to spare any owner of a gun or other similar weapon who failed to surrender it as the soldiers had ordered. In the twinkling of an eye, all guns and gun powder were surrendered to the soldiers.[38] Then, the soldiers made a great bonfire of the weapons. But when it was all over, and the soldiers departed and the dust settled, Ogbas came one by one and recovered the charred remains of their gun barrels. Ogbas have always applied a strict and technical interpretation to the demands of *erisi* when it suits them. Nwa Ajie Nkwo had not ordered through his *erisi* that guns should not be taken back after they had been surrendered.

It may be that the soldiers who burnt down Obrikom were different from those responsible for the breaking of guns in Omoku. For one thing, the latter operation must have taken fairly long to accomplish - enough time had to be allowed for the collection of a sufficient number of guns and for the making of a bonfire. It does not appear that a company vessel on a definite

---

[37] Shrine.
[38] This event most probably occurred around (1902) when the new Colonial Government (not the Niger Company) were destroying fire-arms in various parts of Southern Nigeria.

trading mission under military escort could easily divert its attention for so long. What most probably happened was that after the burning of Obrikom by the Royal Niger Company Constabulary, the company reported the incident to the Consulate in Degema which subsequently planned further reprisals or punitive expeditions. During the period in question (1880-1905), punitive expeditions were being carried out almost indiscriminately to subdue difficult areas. Besides, the policy of "Joint administration" which the Foreign Office advised Macdonald to adopt in the "Idu" area must have involved constant consultations between Royal Niger Company agents and Consulate Officials. We read in the "diary" of P. Amaury Talbot,[39]

> 1901-2... The Aro Expeditionary force, with bases at Akwete, Oguta and Unwana, subdued and brought under control Owerri, Aba and the Northern part of Degema District (my underlining).

Occupation of Ali-Ogba

When eventually the British "occupation troops" arrived in Ali-Ogba, they encountered little or no resistance at all. As Mr. Standfield said in his Intelligence Report (p.9), "British influence was first felt via Elele (in the Ikwerre Clan to the East). Such villages as Ikiri[40] on the Sombreiro put up fight, but Omoku displayed caution and welcomed the appearance of troops". Apparently, the prophecy of the leader of the expedition against Onitsha had been fulfilled-the "proceedings at Onitsha" had indeed had "a most salutary effect up and down the Niger". In fact further "proceedings" in Benin, Arochukwu and elsewhere had produced a most intimidatory effect. The local proceedings against Olowu nwa Ekiodu at Kreigani, the "battle of Onosi Ogu in which the Obrikom "aggressors" were put to flight, the torture of Olowu nwa Ajie Nkwo at Omoku and the

---

[39] "Anene, *Op. cit.* pp. 272-275. The Ogba area or Ali-Ogba was included in "the Northen part of Degema District". Joint action by the Consulate and the Royal Niger Company is most likely because of the "Joint Administration" clause in the 1892 Foreign Office despatch to Macdonald.

[40] Ikiri was the headquarters of the Umuebe kingship group.

breaking of weapons had made submission by Ogbas to colonialism inevitable and conclusive.

"Pacification" of Ali-Ogba

Establishment of "Native Courts"

After "conquest" came "pacification" of Ali-Ogba. As A.E. Afigbo has said, quoting the Resident of Calabar (F.P Lynch),[41]

> It was invariably the rule to open a Native Court in an area after a patrol

However, it appears that the opening of Omoku Native Court took place not merely because "a patrol" had been carried out but also as part of a comprehensive exercise which covered the whole protectorate for Prof. Anene has narrated[42] that

> Sir Ralph instructed a judge of the Supreme Court, M.R. Menendez, to undertake an extensive tour of investigation throughout the "protectorate" presumed to be under British control.
>
> The number of "native" councils visited by the judge amounted to sixty ..... The judge undertook to establish "Native" councils at Onitsha (with the Obi as vice-president), Abo, Agbari, <u>Omoku</u> (my underlining), Aguleri and Ida.'

The term "Native Council" used in place of Resident Lynch's "Native Court" appears significant as it indicates that what was established was not only a judicial but also a legislative and executive organ.

Warrant chiefs

The "Court members" or "judges" were known as "Warrant Chiefs", a description which has executive and legislative connotations. In practice, the chiefs were responsible for providing forced labour for public works (mainly road building and food for school children,) Warrant chiefs also heard cases in court where they were expected to administer traditional "law" provided that it was "not repugnant to natural justice". In principle the "native courts" were supposed to concentrate on the administration of "native law and custom" but the

---

[41] Ep 1138 vols.x, *Annual Report Calabar Province*, 1924, p.5 quoted at p. 2.50 of *The Warrant Chief* by Afigbo.
[42] J. C. Anene, *Op cit* pp. 263/264.

Native Court Building, Omoku.

"repugnance" proviso left much room for official discretion in setting aside native court decisions on "appeal" or "review". It is not suggested here that there were not many "laws and customs" in existence which were thoroughly obnoxious and reprehensible,such as slavery and abandonment of twins, which deserved to be set aside or overruled; but the way and manner in which "warrant Chiefs" were appointed in Ali-Ogba tended to ensure that some of the best customs and traditions did not survive the colonial onslaught. As Newington has noted (1930 para. 4):

> There is a long list of some 28 court members of whom one is Malam Agu the head of the Hausa community of Omoku, and of whom only two others Osakwe Ezeala of the Obekata section of Omoku and Eke Akabuta are heads of sections of extended kindreds (Newington 1930 para. 4).[43] At the moment there are 28 court members who with few exceptions mentioned in paragraph 4 and Appendix 1 appear to have been made regardless of their position in their kindred. Consequently, the powers of the Ezealas have waned through lack of support and through being over-shadowed by men appointed by Government. The court members were not evenly distributed amongst the kindreds, many of the kindreds not having one at all. (Newington 1930 para. 47 and 48).

In recognition of the tripartite structure of the Ogba people (Egi, Igbru and Usomini), two more courts (or councils) were established in Obigwe (for the Igbru) and at Akabuka (for the Egi). For years, the villages of Okprukpuali, Ebogro and Obo continued to petition against having to trek to Obigwe four (4) miles south of Omoku to attend the Igbru court. While confirming that they were Igbru by traditional classification, they argued that it did not make any sense for them to trek to Omoku and then go four (4) miles beyond it (that is a total of over seven to nine miles) to attend court when they had been attending the Omoku court for some years without any problems. Eventually, the petitions were favourably considered and the petitioner's representatives were appointed as members

---

43 The fact that Mallam Agu, a hausa could be accepted as a warrant chief in Ogba shows the extent to which 'Pax Britannica' affected "native law and custom". It also demonstrates the natural goodwill with which Ogbas are endowed as a people, other things being equal.

of the Omoku Native Court in Usomini instead of the Obigwe Native Court (Igbru).

By 1921, the number of warrant chiefs had increased to forty (vide appendix), thereby making their overshadowing of traditional native rulers (Ezealas), as observed by Newington, almost complete. We may here recall Anene's observation (on p.27) that after defeating the Aros, Sir, Ralph requested for substantial increase in the civil establishment because "he had to do away with practically all the systems of the natives" It would appear that in many instances,such as the case narrated by Mr. Newington which took place at Omoku, the colonial officials, in organising the native courts, knowingly or unknowingly, did away with practically all the systems of the natives.

In regard to the general position of a warrant chief, Prof Afigbo has written:[44]

> The supreme handicap or demerit of the warrant chief system is its lack of any real root in the political traditions of the people. The very idea of a man, no matter what he was called, who had power to "issue" order to his village and to its neighbours or to a whole clan was a political novelty... the very conferment of a judicial warrant on anybody in this area no matter how the appointee was selected or his traditional position among his people, meant the creation of a hitherto unheard of political prodigy. A warrant or even a headman's cap invested on the recipient more powers and prestige than any single individual enjoyed under the indigenous political order. The conferment of the warrant was a public proclamation that the recipient had behind him... the support of the protectorate police and army...In Ali-Ogba, as Newington observes (1930 paras 49-50), The court members consider themselves Government servants .... naturally the idea that a court member was a government servant gave him unlimited power (emphasis mine).

Forced Labour

All adult males in Ogba were made to participate in the communal work involved in building the Native Court. Citizens were also made to carry the district officer's touring baggage by force, in relays, from one Native court to the next. The baggages of other touring colonial officials - surveyors, judges, police officers, soldiers - were carried over even greater distances. And it was not only baggages that were carried. The owners of the

---

44 Afigbo,. *Op. cit.* p. 256.

baggages were also carried in hammocks by human porters over the longest distances. Some administrative devices adopted by colonial officials were often varied, ingenious and frequently dehumanizing. It did not matter whether the citizens "conscripted" to carry the human or material baggage had urgent personal commitments, or whether they were sick or tired or "leaders" in their family groups.In some cases, they did not have an opportunity to inform their kith and kin that they had been "conscripted". Any one caught shirking the "civic responsibility"of supplying his labour free of charge was summarily tried by the warrant Chiefs and imprisoned for two weeks. In some cases, stubborn "labourers" were mercilessly beaten up by court messengers.

Abuse of the powers given to the warrant chiefs under the Roads and Rivers Ordinance made the warrant chiefs very unpopular. In the absence of taxation, there were no votes for road works or for payment of official carriers. The colonial government had to devise some economic methods for running the public services. But the indignities of "forced labour" could only have been devised by a despotic, race-conscious, imperialistic officialdom.

Colonel Moorehouse, the Secretary Southern Provinces continued to seek for funds to run the "public service". In 1922/23, he managed to obtain a vote of £3,000 for road work; but forced labour continued, due perhaps to insufficiency of the vote. It was not until April 1927 that the Native Revenue Ordinance was passed (effective from 1st April, 1928) after some feeble opposition by some African members of the legislative council. It is to the credit of the colonial government that on the same date when the Native Revenue (i.e. taxation) Ordinance was passed, the Roads and Rivers (i.e. forced labour) Ordinance was immediately repealed.

Nevertheless, in course of time, warrant Chiefs became unpopular throughout the area south-east of the Niger. The last straw was an incident which occurred in Oloko (Bende Division) in 1929. Captain John Cork an enthusiastic District Officer had asked Warrant Chiefs to revise the nominal rolls in their families, but rumour went round that government was extending the newly introduced taxes to women. This rumour spread far and wide. At Oloko, Mark Emeruwa, a school teacher sent by Warrant Chief Okugo to revise the nominal roll for him was attacked by a band of women. Warrant chiefs and officials as well as government property were attacked in the neighbouring districts, Opobo, Abak, Utu Etim Ekpo, and elsewhere. The women appear to have relied on a false sense of security that whiteman's government would not deal seriously with the weaker sex. As Professor Afigbo says, they learnt -

> the tragic lesson that a colonial power would stop at nothing to maintain its position of authority in time of crisis.

Government fought back with all the forces at its cammand. In Calabar province alone, thirty-two persons were killed, two hundred and thirty-one were wounded in Opobo, eighteen were killed and nineteen wounded in Utu Etim Ekpo, and three were killed in Abak. Not much commotion took place in Ali-Ogba, except that *Ozegbe Nwa Ajie* of Umualinwa (an Ogba *Onuobdo*) was killed in Opobo where she lived and traded.

Prof. Afigbo concludes that:

> the unpopularity of the warrant chief system derived not only from its utter divergence from the indigenous political system but also from the fact that it was to many people a reign of terror. The enforcement of the Roads and Rivers Ordinance, the use of conscripted carriers as the main means of transportation, the depredations of the court messengers, the use of the court itself as an instrument for oppressing the weak, and the fact that owing to a number of factors the people had little effective redress against these ills, engendered in many a sense of oppression which alienated them from the warrant chief regime... Truly, some of the old Native Courts continued to linger on for many years after 1929 because the problems of staff shortage and the need to make thorough investigations the basis of the re-organisation caused delay. But in point of fact the policy and system of local rule through Warrant chiefs came to an end with the Women's Riot

Education:

Soon after the opening of the Omoku Native Court, a government school was established at Omoku in 1904 which served "pupils" from all Ogba, as well as those from neighouring groups such as Oguta and Ndoni.[45] Similar government schools were establishment at Bonny, Ahoada, Aba, Owerri, Abak and Ikot Ekpene. At first, the Omoku government school was located at "Ogbo Onosi" on the eastern bank of the Omoku River Water front where it shared the same premises with the Anglican Church. In 1906, the government school was moved to its present site, which is about two kilometres from the Omoku River.

In the early years of the life of the school, no fees at all were charged. Indeed youths were "arrested" by "Court Messengers"[46] and sent to "prison" in the school. Each of the warrant chiefs was made to pay the equivalent of £20.00 a year per *onuobdo* to government in respect of school fees. Whenever the occasion offered itself, a warrant chief would strive to "rescue" his "arrested" son by withdrawing him from the "prison school" through the back-door. Warrant chiefs recovered the fees they paid to government (and more) through a levy of fish and yams imposed twice a year on the members of their *onuobdos*.

The first teachers posted to Omoku government school were from Old Calabar (Teacher Eyo), New Calabar (Kalabari), and Ossamari (Teacher Obi). These teachers had attended schools in Calabar, Bonny and Onitsha where primary schools and Teacher Training Institutions (Hope Waddel Training Institute, Bonny Normal College) had previously been established. In due course Ogba sons led by Chief Victor O. Obowu (Umunkaru), Tom Odu (Akabuka-Egi) and Asawa Eke (Umuorodu) trained initially in Omoku Government school and later at Bonny became

---

[45] See schedule of government schools in the appendix. The government school was subsequently handed over to the missionaries (N.D.P.) in 1936 and taken over again by government after the Nigerian Civil War in 1970.

[46] The "Court Messengers" were the lowest grade of Native Court staff whose duty was to run errands in the Court. Apparently, they arrogated "police" powers to themselves and terrorised the citizens. But, as development occurred in the rural areas, they became generally despised and even derided by the common man. School children composed a "song while you work" - *Cotuma otulantu, elabra Kagi nma* or "Poverty stricken Court Messenger, the labourer's lot is better than yours."

Old Omoku Government School Building

government school Teachers and Headmasters. Two Sierra-Leone businessmen, Mr. Richards and Mr. "One-Third" (Nickname), who lived in Omoku at this time associated themselves very closely with the government school which was the only centre of learning and enlightenment in Ali-Ogba and the surrounding areas within a radius of about twenty miles.

Subsequently, the government school was handed over to the Niger Delta Pastorate Mission in 1936. Various missionary bodies (R.C.M., S.D.A., S.D.N.C., N.N.A) established other primary schools in Ali-Ogba, but no secondary school was established until 1961 when Sancta Maria High School was established by the Catholic Mission. Among its earliest students were Chukwumela Obi II (Umuebe), "Oba of Ogba" and Dr. Joseph O. Ellah (Umuenyike) . Before Sancta Maria was established in Ali-Ogba, a handful of Ogbas had attended secondary schools elsewhere. Among these were Amua Ekwere (Umuebe) Martin Ewo and Mrs. Clara Ajie (nee Ewo) (Uriem); Victor, Josephus and Christopher Chinwa (Umuogidi); Emmanuel Yoko (Umunkaru), Francis Ellah (Umuenyike), Israel Woko (Umuriem), Athenasius Ukwosa (Umunkaru), Sunday Ugoji (Umuebe) and Christopher Wokocha (Uriem, Okposi). Victor Chinwa of Obagi (Egi) was the first Ogba son to obtain a university degree in the early nineteen fifties, followed by his brother Josephus Chinwa and Francis Ellah of Umuenyike (Omoku).

Olu Oyibo [47]

With education came the quest for white collar jobs. It has already been narrated how Victor Obowu of Umunkaru and Asawa Eke of Ihiukwu and Tom Odu of Akabuka blazed the trail as Teachers and Headmasters in Government Schools. Dickson Ewo (alias Ogranya Nwegwogba) (Uriem) rose to become a District Clerk in the administrative service. George Chinwa of Obagi attained a high clerical grade in the secretariate in Lagos. Orekoma of Ihiukwu was also among the early Ogba Technicians in Lagos. Tom Eke of Akabuka entered the police

---

[47] Colonial Service.

force at an early stage. Daniel Ukwosa and Johnson Okara Yoko (both of Umunkaru), served various commercial companies. Lazarus Odu of Umuebe made his career in the Nursing service. John Woko of Umuebe started in the Posts and Telegraphs and rose to the post of Supervisor of Native Treasuries in Ikot Ekpene Native Administration Service.

Other notable workers in the Native Administration included Zacheus Woko (Umuorodu) and Samade Omoku (Umueke) (clerks of Omoku Native Court); J. Oburu Ahuo (Umuezeali) (Sanitary Inspector); Oburu Ugoji of Umuebe (Dispensary Attendant); and Theo Ekuku of Uriem, the Champion Wrestler (Court Messenger). John Ajie (Ihiukwu), Isreal Woko (Umuorodu), and Samuel Ogbowu (Umunkaru), joined the Army and fought in international campaigns in World War II. J. Ajie later made his career in hospital administration as Almoner.

Akidu (of Ogbogu?), Elemele (of Ede), and Samuel Masi (Uriem) embarked on modern retail commerce. Samuel Masi later entered politics in the First Republic, rising to the post of Parliamentary Secretary and Provincial Commissioner. Victor Chinwa and Josephus Chinwa made their mark in the Education service. Francis Ellah of Umuenyike became the first Ogba to attain a Senior Service position as Adminstrative Officer (District Officer) in the colonial service. Joel Ahiakwo of Umuenyike and Ekeukwu Wokocha of Umuorodu also achieved Senior Service positions in the Administrative service at an early date.

Christianization

Within three decades after the establishment of the Native Court and the Government school, no less than ten Christian denominations were established in Ali-Ogba, all of them vying for converts among the people. The first denomination was the Anglican Pastorate which was used by the colonial authorities on official occasions. It is significant that the first Anglican Church shared the same premises with the Government school at *Ogbo Onosi* before it was transferred to its present site.

The first church was built by communal labour and became in due course an object of contention between the Anglican Church and the supporters of the United African Church. The former won the day apparently due to the sympathy it received from

Niger Delta Pastorate Church Building Omoku

colonial officials. Nevertheless, it is to the credit of the British Colonialist that they allowed other religions and denominations to flourish together in Ali-Ogba and other areas in Southern Nigeria. This was obviously due to the bitter experience which their own country had had during the crusades and religious wars of earlier centuries.

However, in Northern Nigeria, the position was quite different as a result of the prior entrenchment of the moslem religion. In that part of the country, colonial administration adopted an ambivalent attitude which culminated in what may be termed "ethnic apartheid", which has, at least in part, prevented the north and the south from becoming co-culturalists, which is a crucial element in the emergence of a nation-state. Much of the tragedy of post-independence Nigeria can be traced to the separatism and dichotomy between Northern Nigeria and Southern Nigeria, or between a dominant ethnic group in the north and the other ethnic groups in the country, which originated from colonial times.

Oso Chochi

The "Garrick Movement" reached Omoku about 1916. The evangelist, Garrick (a Kalabari) sent two of his "disciples" to Omoku and they were accommodated upstairs in Ada nwa Osia's storeyed building (the first building of its kind in Ogba). When the disciples took their bath upstairs, the believers congregated downstairs below them so that the bath water leaking through the wooden floor boards may wash, purify and sanctify them. In course of time, the number of believers grew so large that no private building could accommodate them; so they held their prayer meetings in the town square at *Ahia-Orie*.

Eventually, they dismantled and destroyed the terrible *Iwu Ahia-Orie* shrine in a feat of pious iconoclasm. The people as a whole were completely dumb-founded by what was happening and they looked upon it with stony amazement. But after the initial shock, the "leaders" awakened to their responsibilities and decided to take prompt action. Warrant Chiefs who had not been converted to Christianity, such as Ako and others, ordered that, on the following Sunday, Christians must clear several miles of road in every direction. This order was given under the obnoxious Roads and Rivers Ordinance whereby anyone could be ordered by a warrant chief to give his labour free. However, this particular order appeared patently discriminatory and vindictive in that only Christians had been asked to work on a Sunday, which is sacred to Christians as *Eke* day is sacred to "pagan", The intended message was clear - a deliberate and premeditated attack on the Christian religion. Christians resolved to obey God rather than man, and ignored the warrant chief's order completely.

In a swift reaction, the warrant chiefs sent their court messengers against the Christians and they arrested and imprisoned a number of very eminent women Christians. Immediately, word was passed round and all Christians rose together as one body, attacked the "prison", and released all the inmates. Thereafter, they turned against the warrant chiefs and beat up the brother of Eke nwa Orekugbola of Umunkaru (Chief Isiodu nwa Orekugbola) mercilessly. Eke raised an alarm that his brother had been killed and, fearing terrible consequences from the colonial government, all Christians great and small fled to *Ogboru*. Warrant Chief Ada nwa Osia of Umunkaru who was a Christian, fled to *Onita ederi*, close to the junction of the Orashi and the Onita creek, but Obi nwa Chukuma of Umuebe, another (christain) fled far away to Arumka (i.e. near Ellah's *Ogboru)* close to the Abohs of Ndoni. This great flight is known to Ogba history as *OSO CHOCHI* i.e. "flight on account of christainity"

Salvation Army

In 1918, Dickson Ewo (alias Ogranya nwegwuogba) established a Christ Army Church and school. The church, with its band music and military airs, appealed very much to the Ogba love of song, worship and discipline. Many converts were made in Ali-Ogba in the early years of the new church; but fortunately or unfortunately, Ogaranya obtained civil service employment as a clerk in the provincial administration service. Immediately he left Omoku to assume duty in his new post, his followers(churchmen, school children and all) went back to the Anglican church and the Government school respectively. Thus the first attempt to establish a Salvation Army Sect in Ogba was complete fiasco.

Seventh Day Native Church of God.

In 1921, Akwokwu Dickay (SIC) of Umuebe, the first Ogba court clerk originally posted to Okwuzi on first appointment, resigned or retired from Native court service. At his last post in Azumini, he had been converted to the "Seventh Day" faith. Upon leaving Native administration service, he returned to Omoku and established a new sect known as Seventh Day Native Church of God (SDNCG) with headquarters in Omoku. When the SDNCG was first established, Akwokwu Dickay was installed as a pastor and Head of the church. In due course, he became a *Bishop* with Supreme powers. The new church attracted many adherents as it had much in common with the traditional religion of the people-polygamy, complete abstention from exertion on Sabbath Day (like traditional abstention from work on *Eke* Day), abstention from strangled animals (as in traditional divination), and prayer-healing with oil.

Eventually, Akwokwu Dickay of Umuebe *Onuobdo* (the Bishop of SDNCG) was installed as the "Oba" of Ogba by the Umuebe *Onuobdo* in July 1928. That was the first occasion on which the title "Oba" was used to refer to a traditional ruler in Ali-Ogba or indeed anywhere within the Old South Eastern" Benin Empire". The concentration of temporal and spiritual powers in the hands of Oba Akwokwu was the first attempt ever made to introduce theocracy into Ali-Ogba. However, Akwokwu's influence did not appear to have extended beyond the Umuebe *Onuobdo* and the Seventh Day Church of God.

Catholicism

In 1924, Catholicism started in the form of rotational prayer meetings on Sunday led by teachers Ikem and Akpuaka of the Government school and John Wokocha Ellah who returned that year from Onitsha where he had been attending Holy Trinity Catholic School. He had gone to Onitsha from Arumka Ogboru which is only one mile from Ndoni and the River Niger. The three pioneers (Ikem, Akpuaka and Ellah) invited others- court

Seventh Day Native Church of God *(Akwokwu Dickay's Church)*

African Church Omoku

Catholic Church and School

messengers and other Catholics and they began the Sunday prayer meetings together on rotational basis from the residence of one member to the other.

In 1925, a temporary Catholic Church was built at the site of the present state school.[48] Father O' Connor paid periodic visits to the church from Emekuku. Later, Fr. Timon visited the church from Oguta.

In 1961 Omoku became a separate parish with a resident parish priest, a mission hospital and a secondary school (the Sancta Maria secondary school). That was the first effort ever made by any church or government to establish a secondary school and a full-fledged hospital in Ogba. Due to the pioneering efforts of John Wokocha Ellah, a high proportion of Ogba Catholics belong to the Umuenyike (Nwadei) *Onuobdo*.

African Church

D.B. Vincent (later known as Mojola Agbebi) who was among those who broke away from the American Baptist Mission, had in 1889 written a pamphlet entitled *Africa and the Gospel* calling for the creation of African churches in which he stated:

> To render Christianity indigenous to Africa, it must be watered by native hands, pruned with the native hatchet, and tended with native earth... It is a curse if we intend for ever to hold at the apron strings of foreign teachers, doing the baby for aye. As for the United Native African Church, which came into existence in 1891, it is now known, that William Emmanuel Cole, the retired post master who was the architect of the church, remained until his death a monogamist.[49]

However, by the time the Native African church reached Omoku in 1927, it had adopted polygamy and allowed considerable latitude on questions affecting traditional religious beliefs and practices. This liberal attitude made the church very popular in Omoku. The leader of the church in Ogba was Pastor (later Bishop) E. Wokocha of Uriem (Okposi).

---

[48] The Catholic School built on the same site was taken over by the state Government after the Civil War 1967-1970.
[49] *Ibid* p. 201.

Seventh Day Adventist

In 1930, Edwin Oburu and his wife broke away from the Seventh Day Native Church of God. Conflicts appears to have arisen in connection with prophesies and visions which reflected certain individuals in bad light. Before then, a branch of the Seventh Day Adventist Church had been established in Elele.

Edwin Oburu and his wife, extended the new branch to Omoku in 1930. All the members of the Seventh Day Native Church who sided with the Oburus became members of the new church. It seemed a very thriving affair from its inception, but it appears to have made greater progress in Egi than in other parts of Ogba.

Jehovah's Witnesses

In 1936, Dickson Ewo (alias Ogranya Nwegwogba) the founder of the abortive Christ Army Church and School spear-headed the establishment of the Jehovah's Witnesses Sect (owners of the famous Watchtower Bible Society with headquarters in the United States of America). Leading members were Daniel Ukwosah of Umunkaru and Douglas Igwe of Obrikom Umuenyike. The new church made considerable progress in Ogba, although their apparent lack of a recognised place of worship has adversely affected their development and their impact on Ogba society.

Ultimate Battle Line

Eventually, the battle line was drawn in Ali-Ogba, not between the different christian denominations, but between the latter on the one hand and their fellow Ogbas who retained their traditional worship and practices especially the performance of *Okrosu*. Frequent disputes and clashes occurred between the Christians and the "pagans" as they were styled, which were adjudicated upon in the Native Courts. Judging from the numerous petitions sent to the District Officer and the Native Court proceedings, the latter tended to favour the "pagans" but the District Officer's fiat protected the Christians. Polarisation of the society on grounds of religion appeared inevitable, with disastrous consequences for social, political and economic development.

Observations

Colonialism first reached Ali-Ogba in the form of "travellers tales" through Benin, Aboh, Aro Chukwu, and coastal sources. In due course, an Ogba village (Obrikom) was burnt down and weapons were broken in Omoku. Then the colonialists marched into Ali-Ogba through Ikiri where they met a feeble resistance. Thereafter, Ogbas co-operated fully with the "Pacification" strategy of the colonialists, viz introduction of Native Courts, Native Councils, schools and churches. "pacification" was so successful in Ali-Ogba that the small Hausa community in Omoku was represented in the Native Court by an Hausa "Warrant Chief", Mallam "Agu".[50] Native cultural standards and mores received a rude shock as a result of collision with foreign standards. As much as possible, the native traditional rulers were avoided, while at the same time, what was termed "indirect rule" which implied retention of native traditions was ostensibly practised. The ensuing contradictions led to the "women's riots" of 1929. Although a few Ogbas who happened to have been living elsewhere lost their lives during the riots, Ali-Ogba was not a prominent theatre of the riots.

However, Ali-Ogba was fully involved in the re-assessment and revision of colonial policy which the riots brought about. Eventually this led to the introduction of "Local government" in Ali-Ogba, but apparently, the "contradictions" have continued under different forms (e.g. splitting of Egbema ethnic group between Oguta Local Government and Ogba Local Government and between Imo State and Rivers State) as will be shown later. Similar problems and "contradictions" exists in various groups in Nigeria, which are most likely to prolong national instability and underdevelopment.

---

[50] This Mallam probably 'borrowed' the apparently Igbo nickname (Agu i.e. Leopard) from the hinterland during the course of his travel from the North.

Chapter 6

Change And Continuity

Undoubtedly, colonialism and its aftermath have had the most profound effect on the lives and standards of Ogbas. In many respects, the history of Ali-Ogba, like that of other similar communities, is characterised by change and continuity.

From the nature of Ogba emigrations, it cannot be said that those who migrated were cowards or nonentities. Most of the cowards and nonentities remained behind carrying on with old traditions and doing exactly as they were told.Many got sold into slavery. Many an over-bold "strong man" without tact or understanding got killed in battle.Citizens who were able to get away amidst the grave dangers at home and abroad were apparently men and women of consequence who were brave and determined enough to venture into the unknown, in an effort to change what appeared to be their man-made lot in life. Most probably, the emigrants were led by courageous members of the nobility, accompanied by their traditional supporters and closest kinsmen. Small numbers of traditional "fighters", or dare-devils and "undesirables" may have joined the departing band, chiefly in pursuit of spoils of "war"; but, on the whole, the emigrants were solid bands of rulers, soldiers and commoners "marching" out together in search of freedom and safety.

Zig-Zag Movements

The earliest group led by "Aklaka", the ancestor of Ekpeye and Ogba, went far south in their effort to escape the "long arm of the Oba of Benin" until they encountered the Ijaws, before turning round and going north. Some emigrants (e.g. Umuigro) reached Igala before going south through Ossamari. Others *Umu-Obosi, Umu-Oba* and *Umu-Ogidi* may somehow be connected with the ancestors of the neighbouring contiguous towns of Oba, Obosi and Ogidi near Onitsha. Umuenyike (Umudei) crossed the Niger at Oko, went to Oguta and from there to Obrikom, to other Usomini villages and to Omoku. Umunkaru and Umualinwa crossed the Niger at Adiawai and Utuochi (respectively) in Abo territory before reaching Ali-Ogba. Umuagbda reached Omoku from the South, then went east to Uju before returning again to Omoku.

In these zig-zag movements, Ogbas encountered new sites, new languages and dialects, new customs and traditions. When they first reached Ali-Ogba, they found, to their joy or sorrow, that some thriving groups, with their own language, customs and traditions, who were already working in iron, had settled there for over four thousand years; but the latter probably lived in scattered communities and were encountered only occasionally by the new arrivals, hence the silence of the oral accounts on the question of predecessors in Ali-Ogba.

Armed with a more systematic political system, better organised fighting techniques, and higher diplomacy inherited from their original homeland and acquired enroute their long and risky journeys, Ogbas were able to establish themselves in three geographical areas to which they assigned the descriptive names of Egi, Igburu and Usomini.

Political System

In course of time, the new immigrants were able to super-impose their political system on that of the host communities, hence Stanfield was able to say that:

> the Eze-Ogba system is alleged to be super-imposed on the basic "ezeala" system.. (as in Aboh), the councillors (there are scores of them) have recognised titles some of which definitely derive from Benin.

One of the titles is *Iyasra* or "prime minister" which is common to practically all the groups with a legend or history of Benin origin (e.g. Onitsha, Aboh, Oguta) and must have been derived from the *Iyase* of Benin.

Following the introduction of the slave trade, Ali-Ogba became a veritable halfway house between buyers and sellers, between the Arochukwu oracle and its clients, between *Oru* and *Igmo* compatriots. The profits of the slave trade helped to bolster up the position, dignity and importance of the Eze-Ogbas, particularly the Nwadei group. Consequently,when colonisation occurred and the slave trade was abolished, it was the ruling *onuobdos* that suffered most. Besides, the way and manner in which colonial officials chose and appointed Warrant Chiefs in Ali-Ogba, as in some other parts of Eastern Nigeria, reduced the importance of traditional rulers, and sent them temporarily into political limbo. Eventually, the womens' riot spelled doom for "Warrant" chieftancy. Just before independence, traditional rulers began to attract attention again but up till now, Nigerian governments appear quite uncertain how to integrate the Nigerian brand of traditional or "constitutional monarchism" with "republican" or "military democracy".

When Ogbas arrived in their new home and began to impose their peculiar "kingship" system on the existing communities, those communities themselves exerted tremendous influence on Ogba life and culture: Ogba speech changed beyond recognition into a combination of tongues, "into something rich and strange". As Prof.Njaka has stated in his *Igbo Political Culture* (p.23),

> A completely different Igbo dialect is spoken among the Ikpaye (i.e. Ekpeye) and Omoku or Oba (i.e Ogba) peoples.

It has been observed that the dialect of the Ogbas closest to the Ekpeye (the Egis) is very close to the Ekpeye language and that the latter still retains much of the Benin or Edo accent and a little of the vocabulary. Similarly, the Ogbas closest to Ikwerre, Oguta, Egbema, Ndoni, Utuochi, Aboh, Ohaji have much in common with their respective nieghbours.But despite the variations in Egi, Igburu and Usomini dialects, a typical "Ogba" tongue, marked by a unique nasalization, intonation and construction, has survived to this day.

Thus, it is clear that Ogbas as a people have the combined attributes and qualities of many ethnic groups in Nigeria. Similarly, other small ethnic groups in Nigeria have acquired the attributes,cultures and qualities of other neighbouring and distant groups through migrations, and economic and cultural contacts over the centuries. In a discussion with the writer, the Eze *Ekpeye Logbo*, Eze Robinson O. Robinson, narrated that many Ikwerre towns and villages are of Ekpeye origin, notably, Rumuekpe (i.e. Umu-Ekpeye or children of Ekpeye), Ibaa, Ndele, Ogbakiri, Okporowo, Udoha, Emohua, Rumuji, Elele Alimini etc. He also quoted the Eze Umudioga (an Ikwerre village east of Ali-Ogba) as saying that Umudiogas came from Ogba. There is in fact one Ikwerre group known as Rumuogba (or sons of Ogba) and another group known as Rumuoprikom (or sons of Obrikom the ancient capital of Usomini Ogba). Curiously enough a family in Rumuoprikom of the Ikwerres produces famous traditional "bone doctors" just as the Ogbaji family in Obrikom (Ogba) is noted for its "bone doctors". I have myself seen fantastic cures performed by these "doctors" through the use of herbs and traditional "massage" usually described in local parlance as "laying of hands".

Reference has been made to the relationships between the post-*Ogiso* dynasty in Benin and the legendary Oduduwa/Oranmiyan of the Yorubas. The case of Ossamara has also been mentioned. Here the local masqeurade still speaks Igala, from where Ossamaras originated. We may recall the evidence from glottochronology which shows that most of the members of the *Kwa* language sub-family (e.g. Edo, Igbo, Ijo Idoma) began to diverge from their roots only between five thousand and six thousand years ago. *In other words, most ethnic groups in Nigeria are related in one way or another. So, infact, there is a strong underlying homogeneity among Nigerian ethnic groups. Consequently, much of the fuss made by cynics about Nigeria being a mere "geographical expression" which cannot become a viable nation appears to be largely hocus-pocus. In a way, practically all nations of the world were "mere geographical expressions" at one point in time or the other. What we require is the ability to establish a fair and equitable system of government, based on a true perspective of the ethnic situation as it really is, in which there will be mutual respect and equal opportunity for all groups and persons, which will tend towards greater homogeneity in course of time.*

Language

Commercial contact with their neighbours (especially Kalabaris and Abohs) enabled many Ogbas to become bi-lingual or multi-lingual. Older generation Ogbas from Umuenyike, Umunkaru and Umualinwa can still speak faultless Aboh dialect as well as impeccable Ogba. Ogbas near the Ekpeyes also speak good Ekpeye dialect. Ogbas who visited the Ijaw and Kalabari areas frequently in the interest of trade, spoke Kalabari and Ijaw. Ogba culture has been so much affected by Kalabari and Ijaw cultures that Ogba age grades still beat their drums in Kalabari dance rhythm. Until recently, *asawa* songs were sung in Kalabari language. Today, only the Kalabari *tunes* remain, the words having been fully "Ogbanised". *Okrosu* still speaks in the "Nkaba" tongue through the nose like a ghost from Hades. *Okrosu* now finds it difficult to distinguish between *Opokisi* and the initiated members because of the growing cosmopolitan nature of Omoku. So, in order to sustain the traditional belief that *Okrosu* "chases *Opokisi* about", some semi-professional groups have arisen in modern times which make it their business to operate on agreed terms whenever *Okrosu* is about to appear. These groups comprise substantial numbers of able bodied youths who engage themselves in enticing *Okrosu* to pursue them through the length and breadth of the town. When the chase begins, the fleeing youths jump every hurdle and smash all obstacles, as if there was a real danger to life and limb. The youths are usually paid with food and drinks for helping to make *Okrosu* display look as traditional as possible.

Colonialism has affected Ogba culture tremendously especially Ogba speech. The youths of every succeeding generation tend to study and speak more and more English, and less and less Ogba, because the former is essential for passing examinations and for social and economic success in the new Nigerian society. On the other hand, the Ogba language as it stands, appears ill-equipped as a vehicle for the conveyance of modern social, economic, political and scientific thought. Some effort is now being made to teach the Ogba language in primary schools in Ali-Ogba, thanks to the tireless energy and devotion of Prof. Kay Williamson of the University of Port Harcourt and her professional colleagues. Ogbas born during the colonial period bear English or Christian first names; but this trend has begun to change slightly due to a change in modern Christain doctrine and the new nationalism.

Dress

Let us now consider Ogba dress which was affected by every new fashion seen during the course of Ogba trading activities. The Benin cloth of the earliest period has practically disappeared from Ali-Ogba. The cumbersome elephant tusk anklets previously worn by women of distinction has also disappeared. But Ogba women still adore beads and bangles of all descriptions. Indeed Nigerian women as a whole love to adorn their dressing with an array of decorative metal, glass, coral or even wooden objects worn around the neck or fingers or in artificial holes in the ears. In addition, some northern Nigerian women wear decorative metals in artificial holes in their *noses*. This has not yet been copied by Ogba women. Traditional dress fashions seem to have become standardised for Nigerian women as follows: Most Eastern women (including Ogbas) wear a small blouse (or *buba*) and a long wrapper(or skirt) reaching to the ankles and some modest headgear. Western women (especially Yorubas) wear more elaborate headgear *(onile gogoro)*, a short wrapper (or skirt) and a loose blouse *(buba)*. Northern women's fashion is largely influenced by moslem morality which enjoins the concealment of almost every part of the body. A good number of women in parts of Nigeria adopt European fashions of dressing (skirt and blouse, hat and hand bag to match) from time to time as occasion may demand. However, in Ali-Ogba, the wearing of European styles by women is not very common.

The commercial association of Ogbas with the Kalabari Ijaws led to the introduction of Kalabari dress styles in Ali-Ogba. Instead of the long *arigidi* cloth, younger Ogbas began to wear the customary one fathom "george" round their waists. Over this, they have long shirts that reach the knee and are buttoned up to the neck. The sleeves may be long or short, depending on taste. Instead of such shirts, older Ogba folks wear a heavy, long gown known as "don" which is also buttoned up to the neck. These Kalabari fashions were exaggerated versions of contemporary European styles. To this day, no Ogba would dream of attending an age-grade meeting dressed in any way other than the "george" or "don". Ogba men and boys have clung religiously to these styles at least for all traditional celebrations (Nchaka, age-grade dances etc.). From time to time an Ogba male person may be seen wearing the *Osiba* (a long wrapper reaching the ankles) more or less in the Abo fashion. In working situations, Ogba men and boys now appear in all manner of foreign clothes - french suits, coats and trousers, jeans and pullovers of all descriptions.

Food

Ogba food has also been affected by the new developments. As has already been narrated, the earliest staple food appears to have been yam which was roasted, or boiled or pounded. By the late 17th century, cassava which was pounded or made into *iwu* became the staple food for all, except the "aristocracy". In modern times, particularly after the windfall oil boom, Ogbas like other Nigerians, developed a strange taste for imported rice and imported iced fish. With the present economic difficulties in the country, these "exotic" tastes are once more receding into the background, and yam and garri (the new form of cassava food) are once more becoming the staple foods. Ogbas still drink palm wine and "kaikai"[1] in season and out of season, but the most modern drink now appears to be beer. Although no brewery exists in Ali-Ogba at present, there are a number of breweries (Nigeria's favourite and most thriving industry!) in areas adjoining Ali-Ogba.

---

[1] *Kaikai* or "illicit" gin is made from fermented palm wine. *Kaikai* is probably derived from the Hausa word of abuse ('Kai) which may have become popular among intoxicated people in the northern parts of the country.

Housing

The sudden increase in incomes helped Ogbas build more substantial homes. Practically every house in Omoku now has a corrugated iron roof and cement plasterd walls; but many mud and wattle structures can still be seen in the surrounding villages. Most of the villages and Omoku, the Ogba "Capital", still have "open spaces in the middle about the size of a small parade ground", but the "parade ground" is growing smaller and smaller due to indiscreet encroachment. Besides, the open spaces are not so clean nowadays. As a result of much dirt and squalor in Nigerian towns and villages (especially the large urban centres)the military authorities have declared environmental sanitation as a "phase" of the new "War Against Indiscipline (WAI)" which is still raging in the country. But the undeclared war against economic depression is the greatest challenge facing Nigeria today.

Dancing

As the open spaces in Ali-Ogba diminish in size and elegance, the purposes for which they were originally established tend to diminish in importance for lack of patronage. The age-grade dances*(egwu asawa)* are still in vogue but only half of the age-grade members take part in them. The other half now work "abroad" as employees in industry, commerce, the public services; or study as full-time students in distant educational institutions. Older Ogba dances such as *ekworu, Oruorie, orabrochi, egwu elende, egwu ayamba, egwu oregbu, obiemeni, egwu alikiri, egwu abana, egwu awudi,* are now regarded as objects of curiosity heard and seen periodically when there is an event to celebrate or some celebrity to entertain.

Wrestling

The most regular performances in the "open spaces" used to be wrestling matches between the three major quarters of Omoku (Obakata, Obieti, Usomini) or between one of them and some Ogba villages. These matches now rarely occur, and when they occur, the performances now involve only very young age grades *(Okprukpuako aja)*.[2] In recent times, the Rivers State Government has done much to encourage wrestling and there are such trophies as the "Opigo Cup" to be won; but as Ogba wrestling is so peculiar to Ali-Ogba, Ogbas have not featured prominently in these wrestling competitions. Because of their different approach to wrestling, Ogbas seem to look upon what is going on now with an air of superior detachment and contempt.

Another reason for the present attitude of Ogbas towards wrestling may be due to the fact that it has lost its charm as a local evidence of "power". In the past, champion wrestlers such as Theo Nwekuku were regarded with awe and respect. Such people went around showing their "power" in the market place and at age grade meetings, depriving people of their rights by force. When the powerful colonial police and "court messengers" invaded the remotest rural areas, "wrestling power" waned and eventually disappeared. The inglorious manner in which Theo Nwekuku, one of the greatest Ogba wrestlers, died in Ahoada prison, did not at all enhance the position of wrestling as a reputable traditional pre-occupation in Ali-Ogba.[3]

Religion

Simultaneously, "juju power" disappeared rapidly as the devotees of traditional religion got converted to christainity. Leading Ogbas (e.g. the Warrant Chiefs) were ready to accept christainity partly because of its association with the powerful colonial administration. Those who would have been deterred by the new culture of monogamy found solace in the liberal doctrines of the United Native African Church and the Seventh Day Native Church of God. The traditional Ogba worshipper always invokes *Chukwu Abiama* (i.e. God Almighty, God of Love), but he throws morsels of food or pours drinks away on the ground for ancestors to "come and eat or drink" or he may invite *Ndeze,* or *Egbamini* or *Odu-ka-Ogidi,* or *Orji Aligu* or

---

[2] Youths who are frequently "thrown down" at wrestling
[3] **Theo Nwekuku** was imprisoned after an encounter with an Urhobo itinerant labourer whom he had intimidated and manhandled . He died in prison.

Odu-Ocha, which are inanimate objects to come to his aid. Some healing or mystical powers which might have been possessed by the "juju doctor" or "herbalist" (who was priest, doctor, prophet and occultist combined) may be lost to posterity due to the mystery, secrecy and abracadabra with which the whole traditional process is surrounded. Nigerian governments are today striving to salvage whatever is possible from "traditional medicine"; but it will not be easy to overcome the superstitious conservatism of the ubiquitous "juju doctor".

The development of education in Ali-Ogba helped to convert people from worship of natural phenomena to christianity. Up to eight different religious denominations vied with one another for Ogba members in the early colonial days; but the Seventh Day Native Church of God and the United Native Africa Church appear to have been particularly attractive to Ogbas because of their practice of polygamy and "divination". Today, up to twenty-six different christian organisations have been established in Ali-Ogba, especially those known as "spiritual churches" viz "Celestial Church of God", "Brotherhood of Cross and Star", "Cherubim and Seraphim" etc.

These latter groups have certain characteristics in common which some Ogbas find attractive (e.g. they use traditional drumming and vigorous dancing in their worship and they have "prophets" and "apostles" who see visions" and "heal" the sick). But many Ogbas (say fifty percent) still practise the traditional religion. Many Ogba christians still abstain from mushroom or cocoyam or some types of fish or whatever may be the traditional taboo of their extended families chiefly because of dread of ostracism by their family members who still believe in these taboos.

Today, in Ali-Ogba, no one (Christian or traditional worshipper) dares raise an *"Okrosu* cry" *(mkpu Okrosu)* out of season, especially if he is not entitled as a member to raise it. *Okrosu* adherents still worship "echina". A bitch is still not welcome in Omoku. Libation is still poured to the god of the land. *Nchakas* (small wooden idols) are still "fed" on *Nchaka* festive occasions. Some traditional rulers still believe strongly in unadulterated fetish - all in the name of culture and tradition. It would appear the time has come when greater effort should be made to distinguish what is fetish from what is cultural, what is obscene from what is uplifting and religious in Ogba traditions, so that coming generations are not entirely deprived of an indigenous cultural background on which our identity as a distinct people ultimately depends. *Nchaka, Okrosu* and other traditions can be preserved and improved in such a way that all Ogbas of all generations and creeds can participate in them without scruples. Similar actions have been taken in some of our neighbouring communities with entirely satisfactory and beneficial results. All our traditional rulership positions must be modified and suitably adapted (as has been done in at least one notable instance) to fit in with modern political and religious changes. Claims to extra-sensuous capabilities (as in transmigration and some aspects of traditional medicine) must be vigorously and critically investigated in the interest of educational advancement.

Education

Education, the accepted vehicle of human enlightenment, was introduced into Ali-Ogba ,mainly by the missionaries.It brought considerable improvement which helped "to pierce the darkness which eneveloped whole populations" in Ali-Ogba. Although the colonial authorities had established only one government primary school in Omoku which served the whole Ali-Ogba and beyond, its standards and reputation were high. As late as 1961 only one secondary school (Sancta Maria) was in existence in Ali-Ogba, and Ogbas went to other parts of Nigeria to attend secondary school. Now there are seven post-primary institutions and one post- secondary institution (the new College of Technology) in Ali-Ogba. However, there are Ogba university graduates and professionals in practically all modern fields of endeavor. How does one feel as the first university graduate in Omoku and the first Ogba Senior Civil Servant? Naturally, there is some feeling of satisfaction that something has been achieved in spite of fearful odds. But there is a deeper feeling of dissatisfaction in view of the vast outstanding work that still has to be done to improve the lot of Ogba society as a whole.

Economics

And yet; despite historic strains and stresses, Ogbas have achieved substantial economic success today compared with their standard of living in the earliest colonial times. An outstanding example is the improvement of houses in Omoku where practically all buildings now have corrugated iron sheet roofs with concrete floors and cement plastered walls, instead of the former mud and wattle structures. There are now roughly fifty kilometres of macadamised roads in Ali-Ogba, in place of the former earth roads lined with oil bean trees which sheltered officials on hammocks borne by human porters. A handful of Ogbas now own their own motor cars. Omoku now has electricity and pipe-borne water supply. What is left now is more systematic organisation of the society and improvement of the general standard of living through more imaginative industrialiazation.

The development and improvement of Ogba towns and villages has systematically impoverished Ogba *Ogborus*. Most of the distant *Ogborus* which used to teem with life for half of the year have now been virtually deserted. A good number of Ogbas have paid employment and reside at state or local government headquarters. Many have adopted trading in Nigerian cities or long distance trade involving long absences from Ali-Ogba. On the whole, the general standard of living has not been stagnant. Indeed, it seems to be improving slowly, but it appears there has not been comparable political development.

Political Development

Political developments, or political fortunes, in Ali-Ogba, as in many parts of Nigeria, have been precarious, and hazardous since colonial times. The effect of the women's riot of 1929 which ended the "Warrant Chief" system was not greatly felt in Ali-Ogba either because the iniquities complained about were less pronounced in Ali-Ogba or perhaps because Ogba women were not as forward as their counterparts in Aba and Owerri. As in other aspects of our lives, Ogbas trod the middle path.

As a result of the women's riot, the colonial government took "urgent" measures to redress the situation. Greater effort was made to understand the social and traditional background of the various communities. It was at this period that the famous "Intelligence Reports" were commissioned by the government. These reports have now become one of the most authoritative documents on the areas they cover. Although their authors faced severe linguistic and cultural handicaps, they were energetic, impartial and diligent enquirers at a time when their informants had as yet limited ulterior motivation and little or no sophistication in political manipulation.

The colonial authorities spent an unduly long period before any significant changes were introduced into the local administrative structure. This was, no doubt, due to the larger issues confronting colonialism at this period, such as the great depression from 1929, the development of nationalist activities, the effects of the Second World War (1939-45), and enlightened world opinion.

It was not until 1954/55 that "Local Government" was introduced by that name in Ali-Ogba and Eastern Nigeria to replace the old "Native Councils" or Native Courts. The intention was to make people more independent and free from the District Officer's control so as bring the system nearer to democratic standards. As an Assistant District Officer myself during the period, I had the opportunity of participating in the changes that took place in Local Governments in various parts of the Eastern Region of Nigeria. Besides, the colonial government gave Nigerian Officers good opportunities for improving their competence.[4] Although the new Councillors had the privilege to debate all issues at length and take their own decisions, District Officers continued to play a vital role as "Local Government

---

[4] I had the opportunity of attending a special Post-Graduate Local Government Course in Oxford University and Abingdon County Council in the United Kingdom through arrangements made by the colonial office. I was also given an opportunity to undergo Diplomatic Services training in America under the auspicses of the British Embassy. Similar arrangements were made for a number of other Administrative and Diplomatic officers during the period.

Advisers" and representatives of the Regional Government on the spot. This arrangement saved the Local Government Council from disaster despite the inefficiency and ignorance of many Councillors.

One recalls vividly one's experience as a District Officer in the dying days of colonialism. During the last decade before independence,"Nigerianisation" had been pursued as a policy with redoubled vigour and enthusiasm in all branches of the public service, thanks to the sustained efforts of the leading nationalists (notably Azikiwe and Awolowo). It was in "field administration" (i.e. the administration of the rural areas with which District Officers were concerned) that the most dramatic changes occurred. The Nigerian population has been predominantly rural. It was therefore to the District Officer that the bulk of the people referred whenever they thought or spoke about "government". Consequently, a majority of Nigerians only knew and believed that colonialism was coming to an end when they saw Nigerians serving as District Officers.

Colonialism was essentially a government by officialdom, devoted and loyal to a distant imperial power. Before the British handed over political power in the historic ceremony of 1st October 1960, the policy of "Nigerianisation" or the training of, and handing over to, indigenous officials had been in operation, on a substantial scale, for roughly one decade. In practice, training one's relief or replacement was by no means an easy task. Colonial officials who could not stand the mental or psychological strain claimed their "lump sum compensation"[5] and sailed home to England. Those who remained behind, by and large, acquitted themselves and their nation creditably.

In retrospect, one finds it hard to say whether one derived greater job satisfaction from one's initial position as a District Officer under colonialism or from one's later exalted positions as Permanent Secretary, Ambassador, University Registrar, Head of the Rivers State Civil Service and Secretary to the State

---

5 One of the decisions reached during the course of the independence negotiations was that British colonial officials should be paid compensations which averaged £7,000.00 each for loss of career.

Government,[6] not to speak of one's short-lived adventure into the Nigerian Senate in the Second Republic or one's recent appointment as Federal Minister of Labour in Babangida's Transition Government. The outstanding difference between the two situations (colonial and post-colonial) appears to have been that under the bondage of colonialism, there was principle, reason, law, order, stability, except where these high ideals conflicted with the overriding colonial ambition of dominating subject peoples; whereas subsequently, under self-government, the whole country became engulfed in countinuous trouble, inter-tribal acrimony, mutual suspicion, political and economic manipulation by ethnic groups and individuals, mediocrity, insecurity, crisis, civil war, and chronic instability. Under colonialism, we were "free" slaves. After independence, we became "enslaved" free men. Colonialism was inhuman. African independence has by and large, proved to be characteristically inhumane. It has been a great privilege to have had the opportunity to serve one's country in various high positions at a momentous period in the unique history of decolonisation and nation building in Africa.

It is relevant to observe here that the problems of instability in Nigeria and other newly independent African countries today can be traced mainly to colonial "heritage". Those who blame post-independence "Nigerians" alone for our tragedy are uncharitable and unfair to their predecessors. A craftily "divided" people will always be in trouble as individuals and as groups, until the dividing lines are obliterated. But the overriding question is why has it taken so long to remedy the situation? Before we can answer that crucial question, we must understand precisely what happened, not only in regard to great national issues, but also in regard to the affairs of the local ethnic groups such as Ali-Ogba, which make up the nation.

When the local government system was introduced half a decade before independence, Ali-Ogba was included in what was

---

[6] Thanks to the maturity and understanding of the Military Governor, General (Then Lt.Colonel) Zamani Lekwot, which made that career appointment possible, amidst typical strife and jockeying.

described as "Western Ahoada County Council". There were a number of "District" and "Local" Councils within that County Council. Due purely to political agitation, three out of the sixteen villages of Egbema were grouped with Ali-Ogba (after a scandalous, rigged, "plebiscite") in what became known as "Ogba/Egbema" Council.

In course of time, the two sections of Egbema (within and outside Ogba/Egbema) found themselves under two different state governments (viz Rivers and Imo), an anomalous situation which has been allowed to continue to this day. Recently, some Ndoni villages which belong to the larger Aboh sub-tribe have been included in a new Ogba/Egbema/Ndoni (One Local Government Area) Local Government leaving the Aboh capital and other Aboh villages in Delta State. Surely, if we deliberately divide and dismember our ethnic groups at the lowest, most intimate, traditional level, it is difficult to see how the country can be unified or integrated at the highest national level. This strange, puzzling feature, which is evident at every level of our political structure, is obviously one of the most fundamental causes of our national tragedies. I have always believed that the structure of a nation is like that of a building - the local and state governments are the blocks and walls of that building. Poor quality blocks and crooked walls have never made a solid building.

Initially, no constitutional provision was made for the chieftaincy institution in the "independence" local government structure of Eastern Nigeria, apparently as a result of the *Igbo enwe eze* [7] conception or misconception, although appropriate provision was made for a House of Chiefs in each of the other two regions (North and West). This imbalance was subsequently adjusted after an enquiry by Mr. G.I. Jones, a former District Officer, and a House of Chiefs was established in Eastern Nigeria. As membership of the House was very limited, Silk Obi of Umuebe in Ali-Ogba was the only Ogba traditional ruler appointed to the Eastern Nigeria House of Chiefs at Enugu. He

---

[7] "Igbos make no Kings".

was graded second class. The next highest chieftaincy position in Ali-Ogba was occupied by John Wokocha Ellah of Usomuenyike (Nwadei Ogbuehi) who was Chairman of the Ogba Council of Chiefs from 1959 to 1967 when the civil war broke out. Provision was made under the earliest local government system for a formal relationship between the chiefs or traditional rulers and the local government councils in recognition of the fact that Nigeria is mainly a traditional, ethnic, society. Traditional rulers were made ceremonial presidents of various local government councils.

In 1959, "Customary Courts" were established to replace the former "Native Courts". The structure, buildings and staff of the Native Courts remained practically unchanged, but the District Officer's jurisdiction was eliminated. Before then, the District Officer was both a judicial and administrative Officer, who eventually became a Resident in charge of a province and then a Governor in charge of a Region.

When customary courts were introduced into Eastern Nigeria in 1959, a separate Ministry of Chieftaincy and Customary Courts Affairs was established at Enugu and a legal officer entitled "Customary Courts Adviser" was appointed to supervise the customary courts. This had the salutary effect of separating the administration (as represented by the District Officer, Resident and Governor) from the judiciary in consonance with the separation of powers doctrine; but a single customary courts Adviser and his limited staff at Enugu could hardly cope with the work previously entrusted to more than one hundred field administrative officers of various grades. Besides, no allowance at all was made for continuity or dove-tailing of the old with the new structure to ensure a smooth transition. The Customary Courts Adviser and his staff, although learned in British Law and Jurisprudence, had very scanty idea of native law and custom or the traditions of the various local areas. Consequently, the administration of justice under the customary courts deteriorated progressively along with some other failings of the First Republic. The First Republic was brought to an end by *coup d'etat* and civil war in 1966/70.

As the civil war hostilities approached Ali-Ogba, Ogbas not in active service or the civil service fled *aliulo en masse* in their *ugbakiris* and went to their respective inaccessible second homes in *Ogboru*. This had the effect of reducing the number of casualties among unemployed Ogbas during the war. Most of the Ogbas in government service throughout the federation returned to the Eastern Region and joined the Biafran military or civil service.

When the war ended, Ogbas found themselves in the Rivers State, one of the twelve states created by Gowon on 27th May 1967. At the end of the war, there was no real local government in the state. As far as I can recall, as the first permanent Secretary in the Ministry of Local Government and Information, we ran the Local Governments from headquarters, through a new breed of "district officers" who had not had the benefit of training on the job like their pre-war predecessors.

There were sad incidents in various parts of the state (including Ali-Ogba) where "Igbos" were chased away from places where they had lived for generations before the civil war due to inter-tribal animosity arising from the civil war. In many cases, Igbos were accused of serious war crimes against the indigenous population. The incidents which occurred in some parts of Omoku were inspired by a leading traditional ruler. Perhaps it is time we asked and answered the question who are the Ibos?

G.T. Basden says in the introduction to his *Niger Ibos,*

> All my attempts to trace the origin of the name "Ibo" have been unsuccessful. My most reliable informants have been able to offer no other alternative than that it is most probably an abbreviation of a longer name connected with an ancestor long since forgotten.

The Rev. S.A. Crowther, writing in 1854, states that he inquired of Odiri, the son of King Akazua of Onitsha, who replied that the people of Idah, and higher up the river (Niger), not knowing the difference, call them all Igbo, which is the name of a small town called "Igbo Inam".

(Compare Samuel Johnson's comment in the introduction to his *History of the Yorubas* that "the early history of the Yoruba territory is almost exclusively that of Oyo Division"). Today all

Yorubas (it is believed) recognise their common identity as Yorubas. Till today, some Onitsha people still use the expression "*nwa onye Igbo*" (son of an Igbo) as a derogatory term referring to hinterland Igbos but not to Onitsha people. A similar pathetic attitude is also prevalent in Ogba (no thanks to the itinerant labour relationship).

Ogbas must realise quickly that the days of living between *Oru* and *Igmo* are over. A person's tribe is a scientific fact which cannot be wished away. It is like the family to which one belongs. There is no question of choice or brainwashing in the matter. Not to know or recognise one's family is simply an absurdity. We may recall Afigbo's comment that Igbo, Ijo, Edo and Idoma started diverging from their ancestral root between five hundred and six hundred years ago, and the fact that Edo and Yoruba, and Ossamara and Igara are historically related. Ultimately, we would be on the verge of realising that all groups in Southern Nigeria are, somehow, inter-related. Nothern Nigeria is related to Southern Nigeria through such connections as the relationship between the Igara and the Ossamaras of Anambra State and the Umuigros of Ogba in Rivers State. It is comforting that after the disasters and disorganisation of the Civil War, "Ibos", "Hausa" and other Nigerians returned to Ali-Ogba (where Mallam Agu, a Hausa, was one of the early "Warrant Chiefs") and other parts of Rivers State and are living and carrying on their businesses and professions without let or hindrance. The Civil War "wounds" have now healed, but, as the saying goes, "the scar still remains" as a warning to future generations.

In 1973, the state government appointed a small committee, headed by Professor Tekena Tamuno to enquire into the chieftaincy (Rulership) position in Rivers State. After submitting its report, the Chairman (Professor Tamuno) was appointed Vice Chancellor of the prestigious Ibadan University, a great and well deserved honour. Later, a new administration in Rivers State appointed Professor E.J. Alagoa, a member of Professor Tamuno's team to chair an expanded committee with expanded terms of reference to enquire into new issues arising from the Report of the earlier committee.

Based on the report submitted by the Alagoa and Tamuno Committees (after touring all areas and studying their oral and written representations), the Rivers State Government recognised three traditional rulers in Ali-Ogba, viz; (i) "Oba of Ogbaland", Chukwumela Obi II (ii) *Eze Ogba Nwadei Ogbuehi*, John Wokocha Ellah(iii) *Eze Ohali*, Moses Igwe. These recognitions appear to agree generally with the three broad divisions in Ali-Ogba - Egi, Igbru and Usomini and the traditional story of Ali-Ogba.. Traditionally, each of the three "natural" rulers has his own cabinet in which the different *onuobdos* in Ogba towns and villages within his jurisdiction are duly represented, each *onuobdo* in its own right and in accordance with its traditional title (See the Table of *Onuobdo* in Chapter III).

In March 1978, the then Military Government promulgated a Land Use Decree whereby all lands (including Ali-Ogba) are held in trust for the community by the State Governor and the Council of States. Nevertheless, Ogbas have continued to observe the *whekeja* of Umuezeali as well as other Ogba traditions affecting the land. The attitude of the average Ogba to the current land law is one of complete puzzlement or lack of comprehension even though it affects the very roots of Ogba culture and tradition.

In 1979, when Nigeria returned to civilian rule, new local governments which were created in 1976 were all entrenched in a brand new constitution. Soon after coming to power, the new Rivers State Government, quite out of the blue, created thirty or forty more local government units. "Omoku Urban" was separated from Ogba/Egbema and the latter's headquarters shifted to Obite in Egi, contrary to precedence and tradition. The State Government also created other parallel organisations known as "functional committees" which exceeded even the local government units in number and conflicted with them in responsibility and functions. The sole aim, it would appear, was to create numerous political posts in order to win political support. (The mushroom local government councils and "functional committees" were all dismantled in 1983 on the fall of the Second Republic.) Subsequently, the Federal government created new local governments (five hundred and eighty-nine (?) of them) all over the country. Just now, there are rumours that the number will be increased to one thousand. A new Federal

Ministry of States and Local Government has been created which is an anomaly in a federal structure and a contradiction in terms.

The introduction of pseudo-democratic practices into the chieftaincy tradition (e.g. popular elections and new-fangled chieftaincy titles) can only hasten the demise of traditional rulership, as the two concepts are clearly antithetical. If the Ogba traditional institution fails, Ali-Ogba would thereby lose a vital traditional link with the past which would adversely affect its prospects of survival as a distinct group in Nigeria.

Today, Ogba society, like other Nigerian societies, is still recognisable as a distinct entity, in that it has a distinct dialect and certain recognisable traditional features; but many of these are in a state of flux and change -the dialect is changing, customs are changing, occupations are changing, traditional religion is changing, man's attitude to life and the world is changing. There is a state of stress and uncertainty caused by the changing times and the changing, uncertain environment in which Ogbas and other Nigerian ethnic groups find themselves.

Most Ogbas today (like the members of other Nigerian groups and clans) are evidently groping about in search of new bearings - a new political and social culture and a new way of life, to replace what was affected by the colonial experience. This may create temporary chaos and confusion. But, in the long run, the ultimate result is bound to be good because the old parochial order must disintegrate, in order that a new and truly national order can emerge - just as nature rises to new life through suffering and death. We can minimise the pain and anguish by careful, sympathetic and sensible nursing but we cannot eliminate it altogether. Present problems will pass away in due course when the larger political order becomes more stable, perhaps after many generations of trial and error. But whatever happens, the stability of the larger environment will depend, to a large extent, on the responsibility and simple decency displayed by leaders of all grades and by the ordinary man and woman in Ali-Ogba and other ethnic communities in Nigeria.

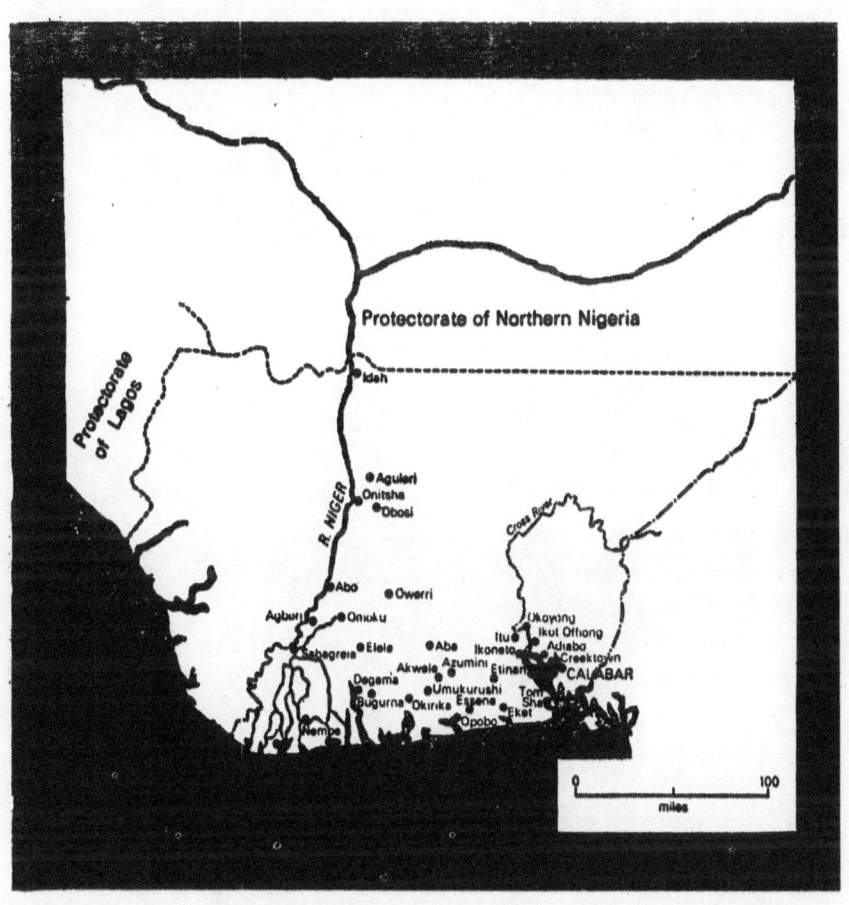

THE DISTRIBUTION OF NATIVE COURTS IN THE PORTION OF THE SOUTHERN PROTECTORATE EAST OF THE NIGER IN JANUARY 1903

Appendix

A • Names of the Onuobdos in Omoku compared with those of Egi, Igburu and Ekpeye

S/No.	Omoku	Igburu	Egi	Ekpeye
1	Umuebe	Umuebe	Ede-Ihuru	Edihuru
2	Umueyinke	Eyinke	Umu-Ngwu	Isi-Okoloko
3	Ihikwu	Ihikwu	Umuakpa	Umuakpa
4	Umuohali			Umuzi
5	Umunkaru	Umuodu	Obeye	Umu-chi
6	Umu-chi	"	"	"
7	Umu-oyoro	"	"	"
8	Umuoba		"	"
9	Umuezeali	Umuezeali	Ezeali	
10	Umuagburu	"	"	
11	Umuokparame	"	"	
12	Umungah	"	"	
13	Umualinwa	Umualinwa	Odogu	Odogu
14	Umuiyesara	Iyesara	Imeaji	Imeaji
15	Umuogidi	"	"	"
16	Umuchikere	"	"	"
17	Umuagbda	"	"	"
18	Uriem	Uriem	Uriem	
19	Umuokirie	"	"	
20	Umuimegi	"	"	
21	Umueriechi	Umueriechi	Eriehi	
22	Umuodogu	"		
23	Umuokorocha			
24	Umuakocha			
25	Umuorodu	Agwolo	Agwolo	Agwolo

B. List of Age Grades in Omoku including the Ages of Members

S/No.	Names of Age Groups	Years of Birth of Members
1	Imere Ogbo	1866-1867
2	Osukwu-Ogbo	1868-1869
3	Okpurukpu	1870-1871
4	Awarawa	1872-1873
5	Owigba	1874-1875
6	Ijii	1876-1877
7	Ibagwa	1878-1879
8	Nnunu	1880-1881
9	Agba-Eka	1882-1883
10	Ebulogwe	1884-1885
11	Ogbulor	1886-1887
12	Ogbomdi	1888-1889
13	Abaam	1890-1891
14	Abraah	1892-1893
15	Ogboshoe	1894-1895
16	German	1896-1897
17	Okpamma	1898-1899
18	Awusa	1900-1901
19	Wire	1902-1903
20	Iyer	1904-1905
21	Akpuruka	1906-1907
22	Afunenya	1908-1909
23	Abrass	1910-1911
24	Owajiri Ogbo	1912-1913
25	America	1914-1916
26	Government	1917-1919
27	Lagos	1920-1922
28	Soldier	1922-1924
29	Ibrogwu	1924-1926
30	India	1926-1928
31	Eluoyibo	1928-1930
32	European	1930-1932
33	Nigeria	1932-1934

34	Ibadan	1934-1936
35	Full power	1936-1938
36	London	1938-1940
37	Omoku	1940-1942
38	Zik	1942-1944
39	Freedom	1944-1946
40	Ekwela	1946-1948
41	Ghana	1948-1950
42	Niger	1950-1952
43	West Africa	1952-1954
44	Rivers State	1954-1955
45	Africa	1956-1957
46	Naira	1958-1959
47	China	1959-1960
48	Fighter	1960-1961
49	Danger	1961-1962
50	Congo	1963-1964

C. List of Warrant Chiefs in Omoku showing year of appointment.

S/No.	Name	Town	Year	Remarks
1	Chief Akoh	Omoku	1905	
2	Chief Akpe	Omoku	1905	
3	Chief Ebreka	Obede	1906	
4	Chief Oku	Akabuka	1906	
5	Chief Ono-Otu	Omoku	1907	
6	Chief Okani (Okeanyi)	Obogu	1907	
7	Chief Wagi (OGI)	Kreigani	1907	
8	Chief Asakwe	Omoku	1907	
9	Chief Wodu (Odo)	Omoku	1908	
10	Chief Adamya (Edemaya)	Idu-Obichuku	1909	
11	Chief Abara	Oboboru	1909	

12	Chief Diko (Dike)	Ama	1909	
13	Chief Eke	Akabuka	1909	
14	Chief Orisa	Okposi	1909	
15	Chief Atu	Obibo	1909	
16	Chief Oduo	Okporukpoani	1911	
17	Chief Ikweke (Nkweke)	Obogoro	1911	
18	Chief Chilekwe	Agita	1911	
19	Chief Okiribo	Obio	1911	
20	Chief Eyiche (Oyiche)	Iju	1911	
21	Chief Owere	Idu Osobele	1911	
22	Chief Chibo	Okasu	1911	
23	Chief Osiah	Odigwe	1911	
24	Chief Okiridu	Abada	1911	
25	Chief Uke	Erema	1911	
26	Chief Wabali	Oboboru	1911	
27	Chief Omoku	Omoku	1911	
28	Chief Eleberi	Ohani	1912	
29	Chief Agu	Omoku	1915	
30	Chief Okirta	Ohali-Mini	1916	
31	Chief Ada	Omoku	1916	
32	Chief Amakiri	Obakaji	1916	
33	Chief Ajie	Alieta	1919	
34	Chief Orukwuwu	Obidi	1920	
35	Chief Eke	Erema	1920	
36	Chief Owu	Osiakpu	1920	
37	Chief Iwaya	Erema	1920	
38	Chief Nkweke	Obirikom	1920	
39	Chief Obowu	Oboh	1920	
40	Chief Obara	Ogbogu	1921	

Appendix 215

D. Population of Ogbaland as compiled by the District Officer, Mr. Stanfield in his "Intelligence Report" (1935)

3. The clan is divided into three sections, IBURU, EGI and OSOMINI. Fifteen villages compose the first section and the parent village is Obigwe, which is also acknowledged to be the parent village of the whole clan. One of the new Group Courts is at Obigwe. In the Egi section there are sixteen villages, the parent being Akabuta (not to be confused with Akabuka). The Group Court of this section has been located at Akabuka since this village is on the main motor road which runs throughout the length of the clan, north and south.This has met with the approval of the whole section including the parent village. The Osomini section consists of the town of Omoku and seven villages. Omoku town is divided into three quarters (sometimes called compounds) called Obietiti, Obakata and Osomini. The latter must not be confused with the section of the same name, to which Omoku and the seven villages belong.

4. Some of the villages are very small. Details are tabulated below:-

Section	Village or Quarter	Population	Number of Families	Composition of Village Council	Succession to the Title of Ezeala
IBURU	Obigwe	130	4	4 family heads	To the oldest man in the senior family
	Obidi	210	3	3 family heads plus 1 junior elected man	-ditto-
	Okposi	740	6	6 family heads plus a junior from each family	?
	Ama	300	3	3 family head plus a junior man from each family	? ?
IBURU	Eleita	200	4	4 family heads	To the oldest man in the senior family
	Ohiugha	160	4	4 family heads	From father to son in senior family. Also succession to family head is from father to son.
	Elehia	170	2	2 family heads	To the oldest man in the senior family.
	Ikri	330	3	3 elected elders	Most suitable man in senior family.
	Oshiakpo	250	1	Family head and 3 elders	To the senior man in the family

	Abada	420	6	6 family heads	From father to son in senior family
	Uju	150	4	4 family heads plus 1 elder	To the oldest man in the senior family
	Okasu	280	3	?	?
	Okpurupuali	180	5	5 family heads	?
	Abogoro	70	2	2 family heads	To the oldest man in senior family
	Obor	370	4	4 family heads	?
EGI	Akabuta	180	1	Family head plus 1 elder	To senior member of the family
	Erema	1240	9	9 Family heads	To the oldest man in senior family
	Akabuka	1000	6	6 family heads plus an elder from each family	To the oldest man in the senior family. Title distinct from "Okparuku"
	Obiebi	220	4	4 family heads	?
	Obakagi	300	4	4 family heads	To each family head in rotation
	Ibewa	130	6	6 Family heads	?
	Obiesimini	100	2	2 family heads plus 4 elected members.	To senior member of senior family
	Oboburu	1300	8	8 family heads plus 8 elected members	To senior member of senior section of senior family
EGI	Obagi	400	3	3 family heads plus 3 elders	?
	Ede	370	5	5 family heads plus 2 elected elders	From father to son
	Obogu	1000	10	10 family heads plus 1 elected member from each family	To the oldest man in the senior family.
	Agita	240	2	2 family heads.	ditto
	Itu	70	1	?	?
	Obite	420	5	?	?
	Obibor	200	2	?	?
	Ohalelu	200	2	?	?
OSOMINI	Obietiti (Omoku)		6	?	?
	Obakata (Omoku)	6200	6	?	?
	Osomini (Omoku)		6	?	?

Obrikom	1600	7	7 family head plus 2 elders from each family	?
Alenzoh	170	1	Family head plus several elders	To the oldest man in the family
Kreigani	320	3	3 family heads	To senior member of senior family
Idu Obisobele	520	6	6 family heads	ditto
Idu Obisuku	400	6	6 family heads	ditto
Ohalimini	140	1	?	?
Obie	250	3	3 family heads plus the Ezeala	From father to son.

E. **Extract from Intelligence Reports by Newington, 1930**

55. Regarding the election of these councillors there is a divergence of opinion, some say that EZE OBA elected his own councillors and some say that they were elected by their own villages. The latter method appears to be the opinion of the majority and it would certainly appear to be the safest method of election. The Egi group stated that in olden days every one of the sixteen villages of the groups elected two men to represent them at a group council which met at AKABUKA These representatives were known as OBAUKU, but the EGIS do not admit attending a council at OMOKU, in former times, though individuals have stated that their group attended the election of the present EZE-OBA.

56. The following is a list of the titles and the families to which they belong:

1. Eze-Oba   Umu Ebe
2. 1st Iyasara   Umu Iyasara
3. 2nd Iyasra   Umu Ogidi
4. Akogu   Umu Karu
5. Isoma   Umu Ihuuku
6. Igbazu   Umu Orodu
7. 1st Ewor   Umu Ohali
8. 1st Ajie   Umu Uriom
9. 2nd Ajie   Umu Ekede
10. 1st Owere   Umu Eke
11. 2nd Owere   Umu Oba
13. Ojoka   Umu Obosi
14. 2nd Ewor   Umu Aliwa
15. Ubuehin (Ogbuehi) Umu Ekhin (Umuenyike)
16. "   Umu Ebe

F. **Intelligence Report Showing that OBA Clan Originally Lived around Omoku then under Aboh/Ndoni**

Letter from District Officer Ahoada to District Officer Kwale Division (Aboh Headquarter now in Delta State)

M.P.Tour/31.
District Office. Ahoada.
7/8/31.

From: D.O. Ahoada Division.
To: D.O. Kwale Division.

ABOH-Ndoni

In compiling an intelligence report on the OBA clan, who live around OMOKU to the East of the Orashi River, information came to light suggesting that the clan originally lived in a village called ABUKU, under ABOH/NDONI, and that they left there on account of the extortions of the Eze-ABUKU.

They also claim that for years prior to arrival of Government they lived in a state of war with ABOH.

It would be of interest to know if you have heard any confirmation of this story.

Appendix 219

G. Approval for the Creation of Native Courts in Ogba in 1933

M.P. No. OW:1396/2/
15 June, 1933.

MEMORANDUM

From,
The Resident Owerri Province
Port Harcourt

To,
The District Officer
AHOADA

Okogba Clan

With reference to your memorandum <u>No. 93/68 of the 25th May, 1933</u>, I have to inform you that I approve of the three Group Courts proposed and consider that the question of the appeal court can wait for the completion of the Intelligence Report.

Senior Resident
OWERRI PROVINCE.

Bibliography

Achebe, Chinua	*Things Fall Apart*. London, Heinemann, 1958.
Afigbo, Adiele,	*Ropes of Sand; Studies in Igbo History and Culture*, University Press Ltd. 1981.
————————	*The Warrant Chiefs, Indirect Rule in South-Eastern Nigeria 1891-1929*, Longman, London, 1972.
Alagoa, E.J.,	*A Chronicle of Grand Bonny*, Ibadan University Press,1972.
Amadi, Elechi,	*Ethics in Nigerian Culture*, Heinemann Educational Books (Nigeria) Ltd., Ibadan,1982.
Amucheazi, E C.,	*Church and Politics in Eastern Nigeria 1945-1966: A Study in Pressure Group Politics,* Macmillan Nigeria, 1986.
Anene, J.C	*Southern Nigeria in Transition 1885-1906*, Cambridge University Press, 1966.
Akpan, N.U.,	*Public Administration in Nigeria*, Longman, Nigeria, 1982.
Ayandele, E. A.,	*The Missionary Impact on Modern Nigeria 1842-1914, A Political and Social Analysis*, Longman, UK, 1966.
Boahen, Adu,	*Topics in West African History*, Longman, London, 1966.
Booth, Newell, S.,	*African Religions, A Symposium*, N O K Publishers Ltd., London,1977.
Boseman, Adda B.,	*Conflict in Africa, Concepts and Realities*, Princeton University Press, New Jersey, USA, 1976.
Burns, Alan,	*History of Nigeria*, George Allen and Unwin Ltd., London, 1929.
Clough, Raymund Gore	*Oil Rivers Trader, Memories of Iboland*, C. Hurst and Co., London, 1972.

Bibliography

Cohen, David William	*Womunafu's Bunafu : A Study of Authority in a Nineteenth Century African Community*, Princeton University Press, New Jersey,1977.
Davidson, Basil,	*The Growth of African Civilisation: A History of West Africa 1000-1800*, Longman London,1965.
Dike, K. Onwuka,	*Trade and Politics in the Niger Delta 1830-1885, An Introduction to the Economic and Political History of Nigeria*, Oxford, Clarendon Press, New Jersey,1956.
Edeh, Emmanuel M.P.	*Towards an Igbo Metaphysics*, Loyola University Press, Chicago, 1985.
Ellah Francis J,	*Nigerian Society and Governance*, Chief J.W. Ellah, Sons & Co., Ltd., Port Harcourt, 1987.
Fashole-Luke *et.al*,	*Christianity in Independent Africa*, Ibadan University Press, 1978.
Hargreaves John D.	*Prelude to the Partition of West Africa*, Macmillan, London, 1966.
Harlech Lord,	*Lord Hailey's African Survey*, Macmillan, London, 1939.
Hastings, Adrain,	*A History of African Christianity 1950-1975*, Cambridge University Press, London, 1979.
Hopkins, A.G.,	*An Economic History of West Africa*, Longman, London,1973.
Iwe, N.S.S.,	*Christianity, Culture and Colonialism in Africa*, RSNC Port Harcourt, 1979.
Kinsnorth, G.W.,	*Africa South of the Sahara*, Cambridge University Press,1966.
Makozi, .A.G.,	*The History of the Catholic Church in Nigeria*, Macmillan, Nigeria,1982.
McCall, Daniel F.,	*Africa in Time-Perspective: A Discussion of Historical Reconstruction from Unwritten Sources*, Oxford University Press, New York, 1969.
McEwan, P.J.M.,	*Nineteenth Century Africa*, Oxford University Press, London, 1968.

McIntyre, W., David, *The Imperial Frontier in the Tropics 1965-1975*, Macmillan & Co., Ltd., London, 1967.

Murray, D.J., *Studies in Nigerian Administration*, Hutchinson University Library for Africa, London, 1970.

Njaka, E.N., *Igbo Political Culture*, North-Western University Press, Evanston, 1974.

Nwankwo, A.A *The African Possibility in Global Power Struggle*, Fourth Dimension Publishing Co., Ltd., 1995.

Nzula, A.T.I.I. Potekhin and A.Z.Zusmanovich, *Forced Labour in Colonial Africa*, Zed Press, London, 1979.

Obichere, Boniface I., *Studies in Southern Nigerian History*, Frank Cass and Co., Ltd.,1982.

Oliver, Roland and Atmore Anthony, *Africa Since 1800*, Cambridge University Press, London, 1967.

Parrinder,Geoffrey, *West African Religion*, Epworth Press, London, 1969.

Preiswerk, Roy and Dominique, Perrot, *Ethnocentricism and History*, NOK Publishers International, USA, 1978.

Rogers, Everett M., *Social Change in Rural Societies*, Prentice-Hall, Inc. Englewood Cliffs, New. Jersey.

Selby, John, *Shaka's Heirs*, London, George Allen & Unwin Ltd., 1971.

Steinhart, Edward I., *Conflict and Collaboration: The Kingdoms of Western Uganda, 1890-1907*, Princeton University Press, New Jersey, 1977.

Tienabeso, W.E., *The Prisoner of Ihitenansa*, Ibadan University Press, 1975.

Wason,P.C.and Johnson-Lair P.N., *Psychology of Reasoning:Structure and Content*, B.T. Batsford Ltd., London, 1972.

Webster, J.B. *The Growth of African Civilisation: The Revolutionary Years of West Africa Since 1800*, Longman, London, 1967.

Index

Aba, 58
Aboh, 7, 19, 33, 35, 36, 42, 44, 46, 47, 52, 54
Aboh-Ndoni, 6
Aboh-Ogba War, 80, 90, 163
Abohs, 42, 45, 49-54, 62-64, 73, 79, 84-86, 89, 105, 109, 129, 161-164, 183, 194
Abonnema, 6, 20
Afigbo, Adiele, 20, 57, 95-97, 171, 174
Age-grades, 16, 95-97, 135
Ahoada, 97, 177, 198, 204
Aklaka, 14-16, 21-27, 53
Akwokwu Dickay (SIC), 184
Ali-Ogba, 1, 2, 13-36, 46, 48, 53-64, 71-80, 82, 85, 87, 89-91, 95-100, 108-112, 117, 121-130, 134-139, 143, 147, 149, 151-157, 160-164, 168, 170-176, 179-184, 189-210
Aliulo, 7, 8, 12
Alpha and Omega, 14
America, 119, 124, 140
Ancestor, 14, 24, 25, 29, 33, 35, 40, 41, 71, 72, 79, 80-83, 89, 92
Arochukwu, 74, 94, 95, 103, 112, 128, 136, 147, 152-155, 170, 192
Asawa dances, 5
Asia, 109, 124
Atlantic Ocean, 6
Awara, 6, 52
Awka, 103, 128, 131
Azikiwe, Nnamdi (Dr.), 136

Benin, 12-25, 30-39, 53, 56, 57, 64-66, 79, 92, 97, 100, 101, 123, 128, 130, 138-140, 147-149, 155-158, 161-164, 170, 184, 190-195
Benue, 20
Biafran War, 83
Bida, 20
Births, 92, 133
Bride price, 11, 92, 93
British, 72, 97, 170

Cameroon, 136
Cannibalism, 105
Capital, 3, 4, 18, 36, 37, 54, 73, 75, 77, 79, 93, 137, 139, 193, 205
Casto, Diogo, 147
Catholicism, 184
Christ Army Church, 183, 189
Civil Service, 183, 203, 206, 207
Civilization, 55, 78, 123
Colonial activities, 2, 78, 79, 87, 97, 99, 107, 111, 123, 135, 136, 145, 147, 154, 164, 173-176, 180-183, 190, 192, 195, 198-204, 210
Colonies, 150
Consul-General, 148, 149
Consulate, 165, 170
Councillors, 66, 159, 191, 202
Court Clerk, 64, 66, 184
Court of Appeal, 94, 155
Cowries, 74, 111, 130-133, 152
Crowther, S.A. (Rev.), 73, 207
Crude oil, 4
Cult of witchcraft, 10

Dancing, 7, 92, 117, 138-140, 144, 197, 199
Death and Burial Ceremonies, 143
Deaths, 9, 92, 107
Degema, 20, 170
Delphic Oracle, 150
Dialect, 14, 41, 100, 140, 141, 162, 192, 194, 210
Dibias, 133, 134
District, 65, 66, 102, 159, 170, 174, 175, 179, 180, 189, 202-206
Divorce, 92

Eastern Nigeria, 11, 16, 150, 192, 202, 205, 206
Ebiam Creek, 71
Economic Organisation (Ali-Ogba), 53, 55, 59, 73, 95, 97, 120-123, 131, 149, 150, 152, 168, 175, 189, 193-197, 200, 204
Edo, 16, 19, 20, 21, 192, 193, 208

Education, 176, 179, 180, 199, 200
Egbema, 6, 32, 100, 129, 130, 190, 192, 204, 205
Egharevba, Jacob, 20, 21
Egi, 2, 3, 14, 16, 25
Egis, 3, 21, 65, 67, 72, 121, 126, 129, 192
Egypt and Egyptians, 20, 101
Eke, 20, 24, 25, 29, 38-42, 47, 77, 82, 83, 86, 105, 113, 115, 116, 121, 129, 173
Ekpeye, 2, 3, 5, 14, 16, 17, 21-27, 38, 53, 129, 139, 194
Ellah Oriogu, 79
Ellah, Francis, 179, 180
Ellah, John Wokocha 78, 184, 188, 208
Employment, 183, 201
Engeni, 5
Erisi Omoku, 115
Euphrates and Tigris, 3
Ewo, Dickson, 179
Executive, 91, 95, 96, 97, 171
Exogamous group, 1
Expedition, 32, 36, 41, 42, 44, 154-158, 161, 164, 170
Extended family, 22, 30, 162
Ezegbrika, T., 82

Forcados River, 101, 160
Foreign Office, 158, 160, 165, 170
Foreign Secretary, 159
Fr. Timon, 188

Ganges, 3
Garrick Movement, 75, 182
Gerontocracy, 169
Ghana, 136
Glottochronology, 193
Government Schools, 177, 179, 180, 183, 184
Government, 4, 67, 71, 79, 87, 89, 102, 121, 154, 158, 173-177, 183, 188, 193, 198, 200-209
Governor-General, 136
Greek mythology, 108
Greeks, 150
Guinea, 147, 156

Hausa, 99, 136, 173, 190, 208
Hawaian Islands, 139
High priest, 104, 113, 116
Himalayas, 156
Hinduism, 109
Honolulu, 139
Hope Waddel Training Institute, 177

Ibibio, 131, 151
Ibo, 141, 150, 157
Ida, 24
Idah, 158, 207
Idia, 7
Idols, 199
Idoma, 20, 193, 208
Idu, 3, 6, 45, 47
Igara, 24
Igbo, 13, 19, 20, 56, 57, 91, 107, 117, 118, 130, 131, 150, 151, 157, 164, 192, 193, 205-208
Igbru, 2, 3
Igmo, 52, 53, 125, 192, 208
Igwe, Douglas, 189
Ihiala, 33
Ijaw (Ijo), 5, 20, 129, 130, 136, 141, 156, 160, 193, 194, 208
Ijaws, 56, 129, 156, 157, 190, 195
Ikot Ekpene, 177, 180
Ikwerre, 100, 140, 150, 170, 192, 193
Ile-Ife, 20, 64
Imo River, 152, 153
Imo State, 143, 190
Independent Nigeria., 136
Indian Ocean, 130
Indus, 3
Inheritance, 44, 92, 93
Intelligence Report, 3, 44, 56, 57, 60, 64, 66, 71, 79, 170
  Newington, W.H.F., 3, 14, 65-67
  Stanfield, D.P, 66 67
Isiali ceremony (praise names), 12, 44, 56, 57, 60, 64, 71, 79, 83, 96, 127
Isichei, Elizabeth, 56, 107, 123, 130, 164
Isiokloko, 2, 16, 30, 71

Isu person, 6
Iyase, 23, 79, 191

Jehovah's Witnesses, 189
Joa d'Aveiro, 147, 148
John II of Portugal, 147, 175
Jones, G.I., 130, 205

Kalabari, 87, 130, 136, 141, 160, 177, 182, 194-196
Kalabaris, 129, 160, 165, 194
Kelly, (Mr.), 67
King, Prester John, 147
Kingsley, Mary, 156
Kwa language, 20, 193
Kwale, 6

Lagos, 179
Laird, Macgregor, 157
Lander Brothers, 157
Local government, 190, 201-209
Long Juju (Arochukwu), 74, 95, 96, 97, 135, 136, 147, 151-155, 164
Lord Lugard, 102, 136
Lord Salisbury, 148

Manillas, 130, 131
Marriage, 77, 92, 132
Meek, C.K, 102
Menendez, M.R., 171
Migration, 19-21, 35, 55, 56, 156
Monarchical hierarchy, 56
Morality, 93, 195
Murder, 10, 23, 47, 77, 92, 93, 114
Music, 139, 140, 183

Ndoni, 7
New Calabar, 154, 159, 161, 177
Newington, W.F.H., 14, 65-67, 72, 97, 110, 173, 174
Niger Delta, 179
Niger River, 3, 5, 6, 19, 20, 22, 24, 30, 35, 40, 41, 57, 63, 73, 76, 77, 97, 127, 147, 150, 155-162, 164, 165, 170, 175, 185, 191, 207
Niger-Congo family, 20
Nile, 3
Nkaba, 5
Nkwerres, 129
Nkwo market, 6
Northern Nigeria, 136, 182
Nzewunwah, Nwanna (Dr.), 128, 156

Oba of Ogba, 179
Obi, Chukwumela (II), 179, 208
Obigwe, 3, 25, 27-29, 32, 36-39, 41, 42, 44, 46-50, 54, 59, 60, 80, 83, 85, 90, 125, 162, 173, 174
Obiosimini, 3
Obo, 6
Obosi, 21, 22, 24, 25, 33, 38-40, 45, 58, 83, 159, 191
Obowu, Victor O. (Chief), 177
Obrikom, 3, 6, 7, 13, 30, 32, 33, 36, 62, 65, 66, 71-73, 75,-80, 99, 131, 133, 153, 156, 162, 165-170, 189-191, 193
Odu, Tom, 177, 179
Oduduwa, 20, 193
Ogba and Ogbas, 1-22, 25, 27-30, 36-57, 60, 61, 63-67, 70-75, 77, 79, 81, 82, 87, 91, 92, 95, 97-102, 106, 108, 109, 111-113, 117, 118, 120-141, 143, 145-150, 152, 155, 157, 160-165, 169, 171, 173, 174, 176, 177, 179, 180, 182-184, 188-201, 206-210
Ogba Law and Custom, 91-95, 171, 174, 206
Ogba *onuobdos*, 16, 17, 21, 22, 29, 33, 36, 39, 53, 55, 56, 60, 74, 76, 79, 83, 89, 96, 97, 102, 108, 109, 111, 112, 113, 127, 132, 134, 155, 163, 169, 176, 184, 188, 192, 209
Ogba Political Organisation, 56-59, 191-193
Titles, 1, 8, 12, 57-89, 191, 201
Ogboru, 7, 8, 12
Ogidi, 24, 29, 35, 45, 46, 50, 79, 191
Oguta, 6, 16, 19, 33, 53, 71, 79, 100, 130, 150, 154, 159, 167, 170, 177, 188, 190-192
Ohafias, 128
Ohaji, 129, 143, 192
Oil Rivers, 158, 159, 160, 161, 165
Okposi, 3, 46, 47, 49, 58, 179, 188
Okroma, S., 49, 82
Okrosu, 5, 12
Old Calabar, 150, 159, 177
Omoku Creek, 38-41, 72
Omoku, 3-7, 13, 18, 33-54, 58-90, 97, 99, 113, 115, 125, 129-131, 137, 142, 154, 161-163, 165, 168-184, 188-201, 207, 209
Onita Creek, 38-41, 72, 84, 85, 162

Onitsha, 6, 16, 19, 24, 71, 73, 79, 130, 154, 156-159, 164, 170, 171, 177, 184, 191, 207
Opobo, 154, 159, 176
Orashi River, 32, 33, 35, 36, 39, 41, 47, 72, 73, 77, 84, 160, 165
Orupata, 14
Osi, V., 82
Ossamara, 24, 29
Ossiah,Adah (Chief), 87
Ostracism, 96, 199
Owerre (Guard Commander), 81, 82
Owerri, 67, 170, 177, 201
Owu masquerade, 5

Pacification (Ali-Ogba), 171-189
Parliamentary Secretary, 180
Philips, J.R., 148
Polygamy, 92, 184, 188, 199
Portugal, 101, 123, 124, 139, 147, 148, 155, 156
Posts and Telegraphs, 180
Praise names, 1, 8, 12, 53
Prime Minister (Iyasra), 53, 58, 59, 78, 79, 191
Probyn,Leslie, 154
Provincial Commissioner, 180

Re-incarnation (Ogba belief), 10, 17, 18, 114, 118, 133, 134, 135, 145
Religion, 101, 117, 138, 198
Rituals, 91, 143, 144
River Nun, 127
Rivers State, 79, 136, 190, 197, 203, 207-209
Romans, 109
Royal Niger Company, 158-161, 165, 167, 168, 170
Ruy de Pina, 148

Sancta Maria High School, 179
Sao Tome, 147
Shrines, 1, 113, 115, 116, 169
Slave trade, 11, 44
Southern Nigeria, 136
Stanfield, D.P., 65, 67, 90
Stanford, 110
Sub-family, 20, 193
Sudan, 20
Sunday Observer, 162
Supreme Court, 171

Taboos, 12, 113, 120, 125, 133, 199
Talbot, P. A., 101, 170
Taxation, 87, 175
Territory, 17, 21, 24, 62, 71, 73, 78, 130, 136, 150, 154, 158, 160, 191, 207
The Trading States of the Oil Rivers, 130
Totems (Ogba Onuobdos), 1, 4, 12, 58, 102-112, 146
Trade, 14, 56, 57, 73, 78, 93, 101, 117, 122, 129, 130, 135, 147-163, 168, 191-194, 201
Transmigration (Ogba belief), 9, 102-106, 108
Tributary, 162

Ugbakiri, 7, 8, 12
Ugbomah, Charles (Chief), 162
Uguta, 2, 30, 32
Umuagbda *onuobdo*, 35, 53, 79, 80, 106, 109, 128, 131, 162, 191
Umuahia, 119, 152
Umuebe, 2, 16, 21, 25, 49, 59-65, 70, 72, 77, 85, 89, 110, 179, 180, 183, 184, 205
Umuekedi, 21, 24, 25, 29, 41, 42, 58, 84
United Native African Church, 188, 198
United States of America, 119, 189
University of Port Harcourt, 195
Uriems, 58, 85, 104, 105, 108, 112, 113, 116
Usomini group, 2, 3, 4, 7, 35, 49, 60, 62, 66, 71-75, 79, 100, 121, 125, 126, 129, 130, 131, 137, 145, 160, 173, 174, 191-197, 209

Vincent, D.B., 188

Warri Creek, 160
Watchtower Bible Society, 189
West Africa, 122, 148
Western Sudan, 147
Witchcraft beliefs, 109
Withford, John, 73
Wokocha, Bishop E. 188
World War II, 109, 180
Wrestling, 137-139, 141, 146, 197, 198

Yorubaland, 20, 138

www.ingramcontent.com/pod-product-compliance
Lightning Source LLC
Chambersburg PA
CBHW031549300426
44111CB00006BA/232